CUSTOMARY INTERNATIONAL LAW IN TIMES OF FUNDAMENTAL CHANGE

This is the first book to explore the concept of "Grotian Moments." Named for Hugo Grotius, whose masterpiece *De Jure Belli ac Pacis* helped marshal in the modern system of international law, Grotian Moments are transformative developments that generate the unique conditions for accelerated formation of customary international law. In periods of fundamental change, whether by technological advances, the commission of new forms of crimes against humanity, or the development of new means of warfare or terrorism, customary international law may form much more rapidly and with less state practice than is normally the case to keep up with the pace of developments. The book examines the historic underpinnings of the Grotian Moment concept, provides a theoretical framework for testing its existence and application, and analyzes six case studies of potential Grotian Moments: Nuremberg, the continental shelf, space law, the Yugoslavia Tribunal's *Tadic* decision, the 1999 NATO intervention in Serbia, and the 9/11 terrorist attacks.

Michael P. Scharf is the John Deaver Drinko-Baker & Hostetler Professor of Law and Associate Dean for Global Legal Studies at Case Western Reserve University School of Law.

"Seize the Grotian moment!

Michael P. Scharf

Other Books by Michael P. Scharf

International Criminal Justice: Legitimacy and Coherence (Edward Elgar, 2012) (with G. Boas and W. Schabas)

Henry T. King, Jr.: A Life Dedicated to International Justice (Carolina Academic Press, 2011) (editor)

Shaping Foreign Policy in Times of Crisis: The Role of International Law and the State Department Legal Adviser (Cambridge University Press, 2010) (with P. Williams)

Criminal Jurisdiction 100 Years After the 1907 Hague Peace Conference (T.M.C. Asser Press/Cambridge University Press, 2009) (with W. M. van Genugten)

Enemy of the State: The Trial and Execution of Saddam Hussein (St. Martin's Press, 2008) (with M. Newton)

The Theory and Practice of International Criminal Law: Essays in Honor of M. Cherif Bassiouni (Martinis Nijhoff Publishers, 2008) (with L. Sadat)

Saddam on Trial: Understanding and Debating the Iraqi High Tribunal (Carolina Academic Press, 2006) (with G. McNeal)

Peace with Justice? War Crimes and Accountability in the Former Yugoslavia (Rowman & Littlefield, 2002) (with P. Williams)

Slobodan Milosevic on Trial: A Companion (Continuum Press, 2002) (with W. Schabas)

The Law of International Organizations: Problems and Materials (Carolina Academic Press, 2001; 2nd ed. 2007, 3rd ed. 2013)

The International Criminal Tribunal for Rwanda (Transnational Publishers, 1998) (2 vols.) (with Virginia Morris)

Making Justice Work (Century Foundation Press, 1998) (with Paul Williams and Diane Orentlicher)

Balkan Justice: The Story behind the First International War Crimes Trial since Nuremberg (Carolina Academic Press, 1997)

International Criminal Law: Cases and Materials (Carolina Academic Press, 1996; 2nd ed. 2000, 3rd ed. 2007, 4th ed. 2013) (with Jordan Paust et al.)

An Insider's Guide to the International Criminal Tribunal for the Former Yugoslavia (Transnational Publishers, 1995) (2 vols.) (with Virginia Morris)

Customary International Law in Times of Fundamental Change

RECOGNIZING GROTIAN MOMENTS

Michael P. Scharf

Case Western Reserve University School of Law

CAMBRIDGE
UNIVERSITY PRESS

CAMBRIDGE UNIVERSITY PRESS
Cambridge, New York, Melbourne, Madrid, Cape Town,
Singapore, São Paulo, Delhi, Mexico City

Cambridge University Press
32 Avenue of the Americas, New York, NY 10013-2473, USA

www.cambridge.org
Information on this title: www.cambridge.org/9781107610323

First published 2013

Printed in the United States of America

A catalog record for this publication is available from the British Library.

Library of Congress Cataloging in Publication data
Scharf, Michael P., 1963–
    Customary international law in times of fundamental change : recognizing Grotian
    moments / Michael P. Scharf.
        pages   cm
    Includes index.
    ISBN 978-1-107-03523-2 (hardback) – ISBN 978-1-107-61032-3 (pbk.)
    1. Customary law, International.   I. Title.
    KZ1277.S33   2013
    340.5–dc23   2013001455

ISBN 978-1-107-03523-2 Hardback
ISBN 978-1-107-61032-3 Paperback

For Trina, on our 25th Anniversary

Contents

Author's Biography

Michael P. Scharf is the John Deaver Drinko-Baker & Hostetler Professor of Law and Associate Dean for Global Legal Studies at Case Western Reserve University School of Law. Scharf is the author of fifteen books, including BALKAN JUSTICE, which was nominated for a Pulitzer Prize in Letters in 1997; THE INTERNATIONAL CRIMINAL TRIBUNAL FOR RWANDA, which was awarded the American Society of International Law's Certificate of Merit for outstanding book in 1999; PEACE WITH JUSTICE and ENEMY OF THE STATE, which won the International Association of Penal Law's Book of the Year awards for 2003 and 2009, respectively; and SHAPING FOREIGN POLICY IN TIMES OF CRISIS, which was published by Cambridge University Press in 2010.

During the elder Bush and the Clinton administrations, Scharf served in the Office of the Legal Adviser of the U.S. Department of State, where he held the positions of Attorney-Adviser for Law Enforcement and Intelligence, Attorney-Adviser for United Nations Affairs, and delegate to the United Nations Human Rights Commission. In February 2005, Scharf and the Public International Law and Policy Group, a nongovernmental organization he cofounded and directs, were nominated for the Nobel Peace Prize by six governments and the prosecutor of an international criminal tribunal for the work they have done to help in the prosecution of major war criminals, such as Slobodan Milosevic, Charles Taylor, and Saddam Hussein. During a sabbatical in 2008, Scharf served as Special Assistant to the Chief Prosecutor of the Cambodia Genocide Tribunal.

A graduate of Duke University School of Law (Order of the Coif and High Honors) and judicial clerk to Judge Gerald Bard Tjoflat on the Eleventh Circuit Federal Court of Appeals, Scharf is an internationally recognized expert who has testified before the Senate Foreign Relations Committee and the House Armed Services Committee and hosts the radio program *Talking Foreign Policy* on WCPN 90.3 FM ideastream (law.case.edu/TalkingForeignPolicy).

Acknowledgments

Several people and entities deserve special recognition for their invaluable contributions to this book. In particular, my thanks go to John Berger and his team at Cambridge University Press for encouraging me to write this book and helping me refine the text. I am also grateful to my old friend Chris Greenwood of the International Court of Justice, who helped me come up with the case studies of potential Grotian Moments that are the subject of this text. I also thank the editors of the Harvard and Cornell International Law Journals, noting that portions of this work were originally published in Michael P. Scharf, *Universal Jurisdiction and the Crime of Aggression*, 53 HARVARD INTERNATIONAL LAW JOURNAL 358–389 (2012), and Michael P. Scharf, *Seizing the "Grotian Moment": Accelerated Formation of Customary International Law in Times of Fundamental Change*, 43 CORNELL INTERNATIONAL LAW JOURNAL 440–469 (2010). My appreciation also goes to Dean Lawrence Mitchell of Case Western Reserve University School of Law, who provided me a generous grant to support this project, to Cindy Hill-Graham who helped prepare the index, and to the following law students who assisted with the research: Matthew Carlton, Rachel Heckelman, Malea Hetrick, Richard Hilbrich, Allison Mahan, Roxana Malene, Pooja Patel, Jennifer Spencer, and Danyella Tonelli. Finally, I express my utmost gratitude to my wife, Trina, and son, Garrett, who support my writing and fieldwork even when they complicate their lives in immeasurable ways.

1 Introduction

THIS BOOK EXAMINES THE CONCEPT OF "GROTIAN Moments," a term that denotes radical developments in which new rules and doctrines of customary international law emerge with unusual rapidity and acceptance. Though I am an academician, my interest in this concept did not begin as purely academic. During a sabbatical in the fall of 2008, I had the unique experience of serving as Special Assistant to the International Prosecutor of the Extraordinary Chambers in the Courts of Cambodia (ECCC), the tribunal created by the United Nations and government of Cambodia to prosecute the former leaders of the Khmer Rouge for the atrocities committed during their reign of terror (1975–9).[1] While in Phnom Penh, my most important assignment was to draft the Prosecutor's brief[2] in reply to the Defense Motion to Exclude "Joint Criminal Enterprise" (JCE)

---

[1] For background on the creation of the ECCC, see Michael P. Scharf, *Tainted Provenance: When, If Ever, Should Torture Evidence Be Admissible?* 65 WASHINGTON & LEE LAW REVIEW 129 (2008).

[2] Co-Prosecutors' Supplementary Observations on Joint Criminal Enterprise, Case of Ieng Sary, No. 002/19–09–2007-ECCC/OCIJ, 31 December 2009. A year later, the Co-Investigating Judges ruled in favor of the Prosecution that the ECCC could employ JCE liability for the international crimes within its jurisdiction. See Order on the Application at the ECCC of the Form of Liability Known as Joint Criminal Enterprise, December 8, 2009, Case No. 002/19–09–2007-ECCC-OCIJ, December 8, 2009.

liability as a mode of liability from the trial of the five surviving leaders of the Khmer Rouge.[3]

JCE is a form of liability somewhat similar to the Anglo-American "felony murder rule,"[4] in which a person who willingly participates in a criminal enterprise can be held criminally responsible for the reasonably foreseeable acts of other members of the criminal enterprise even if those acts were not part of the plan. Although few countries around the world apply principles of coperpetration similar to the felony murder rule or JCE, since the decision of the Appeals Chamber of the International Criminal Tribunal for the Former Yugoslavia in the 1998 *Tadic* case,[5] it has been accepted that JCE is a mode of liability applicable to international criminal trials. Dozens of cases before the Yugoslavia Tribunal, the International Criminal Tribunal for Rwanda, the Special Court for Sierra Leone, the Special Panels for the Trial of Serious Crimes in East Timor, and the Special Tribunal for Lebanon have recognized and applied JCE liability during the last ten years.

These modern precedents, however, were not directly relevant to the Cambodia Tribunal because the crimes under its jurisdiction had occurred some twenty years earlier. Under the international law principle of *nulem crimin sine lege* (the equivalent to the U.S. Constitution's *ex post facto* law prohibition), the Cambodia Tribunal could only apply

---

[3] Pursuant to the Co-Investigating Judges' Order of 16 September 2008, the Co-Prosecutors filed the brief to detail why the extended form of JCE liability, "JCE III," is applicable before the ECCC. The Defense Motion argued in part that JCE III as applied by the *Tadic* decision of the International Criminal Tribunal for the former Yugoslavia (ICTY) Appeals Chamber is a judicial construct that does not exist in customary international law or, alternatively, did not exist in 1975–9. *Case of Ieng Sary*, Ieng Sary's Motion against the Application at the ECCC of the Form of Responsibility Known as Joint Criminal Enterprise, Case No. 002/19–09–2007-ECCC/OCIJ, July 28, 2008, ERN 00208225–00208240, D97.

[4] For background about, and cases applying, the felony murder rule, see David Crump & Susan Waite Crump, *In Defense of the Felony Murder Doctrine*, 8 HARVARD JOURNAL OF LAW & PUBLIC POLICY 359 (1985).

[5] *Prosecutor v. Tadic*, Judgment, Case No. IT-94–1-A, ICTY Appeals Chamber, July 15, 1999.

the substantive law and associated modes of liability that existed as part of customary international law in 1975–9. Therefore the question at the heart of the brief that I drafted was whether the Nuremberg Tribunal precedent and the United Nations adoption of the "Nuremberg Principles" were sufficient to establish JCE liability as part of customary international law following World War II.

The attorneys for the Khmer Rouge Defendants argued that Nuremberg and its progeny provided too scant a sampling to constitute the widespread state practice and *opinio juris* required to establish JCE as a customary norm as of 1975.[6] In response, the Prosecution brief I drafted maintained that Nuremberg constituted "a Grotian Moment" – an instance in which there is such a fundamental change to the international system that a new principle of customary international law can arise with exceptional velocity. This was the first time in history that the term was used in a proceeding before an international court. Despite the dearth of State practice, the Cambodia Tribunal ultimately found JCE applicable to its trials on the basis of the Nuremberg precedent and UN General Assembly endorsement of the Nuremberg Principles.[7]

* * *

Dutch scholar and diplomat Hugo Grotius (1583–1645) is widely considered to be the "father" of modern international law as the law of nations and has been recognized for having "recorded the creation of order out of chaos in the great sphere of international relations."[8] In the mid-1600s,

---

[6] For the definition of customary international law, see *North Sea Continental Shelf (Federal Republic of Germany v. Denmark; Federal Republic of Germany v. Netherlands)*, Merits, February 20, 1969, ICJ Rep. 3, para. 77.

[7] In Case 002, the ECCC Trial Chamber later confirmed that JCE I and JCE II reflected customary international law as of 1975 but questioned whether JCE III was actually applied at Nuremberg and therefore was not applicable to the ECCC trial. Decision on the Appeals against the Co-Investigative Judges' Order on Joint Criminal Enterprise (JCE), Ieng et al. (002/10–09–2007-ECCC/TC), Trial Chamber, June 17, 2011.

[8] *See* CHARLES S. EDWARDS, HUGO GROTIUS, THE MIRACLE OF HOLLAND (1981).

at the time that the nation-state was crystallizing into the fundamental political unit of Europe, Grotius "offered a new concept of international law designed to reflect that new reality."[9] In his masterpiece, *De Jure Belli ac Pacis* (The Law of War and Peace), Grotius addresses questions bearing on international legal personality, interstate legal obligations, when resorting to war is lawful, and when the conduct of war becomes a crime.[10]

Although scholars such as New York University professor Benedict Kingsbury have argued that Grotius's actual contribution has been distorted through the ages, the prevailing view today is that his treatise had an extraordinary impact as the first formulation of a comprehensive legal order of interstate relations based on mutual respect and equality of sovereign states.[11] In "semiotic" terms,[12] the "Grotian tradition" has come to symbolize the advent of the modern international legal regime, characterized by a community of states operating under binding rules, which arose from the 1648 Peace of Westphalia.[13]

The term "Grotian Moment," on the other hand, is a relatively recent creation, coined by Princeton professor Richard Falk in 1985.[14] Since

---

[9] John W. Head, *Throwing Eggs at Windows: Legal and Institutional Globalization in the 21st Century Economy*, 50 KAN. L. REV. 731, 771 (2002).

[10] HUGO GROTIUS, DE JURE BELLI AC PACIS (n.p. 1625). *See also* HUGO GROTIUS: ON THE LAW OF WAR AND PEACE (Stephen C. Neft., ed., Cambridge University Press, 2012).

[11] Benedict Kingsbury, *A Grotian Tradition of Theory and Practice? Grotius, Law, and Moral Skepticism in the Thought of Hedley Bull*, 17 QUINNIPIAC L. REV. 3, 10 (1997).

[12] Semiotics is the study of how meaning of signs, symbols, and language is constructed and understood. Michael P. Scharf, *International Law in Crisis: A Qualitative Empirical Contribution to the Compliance Debate*, 31 CARDOZO L. REV. 45, 50 (2009) (citing CHARLES SANDERS PEIRCE, COLLECTED PAPERS OF CHARLES SANDERS PIERCE: PRAGMATISM AND PRAGMATICISM [Charles Hartshorne and Paul Weiss, eds., 1935]).

[13] Michael P. Scharf, *Earned Sovereignty: Juridical Underpinnings*, 31 DENVER J. INT'L L. 373, 373 n. 20.

[14] THE GROTIAN MOMENT IN INTERNATIONAL LAW: A CONTEMPORARY PERSPECTIVE 7 (Richard Falk et al., eds., 1985), excerpt reprinted in BURNS H. WESTON ET AL, INTERNATIONAL LAW AND WORLD ORDER 1087–92 (Thomson/West, 2d ed., 1990).

then, scholars and even the UN secretary-general have employed the term in a variety of ways,[15] but here the author is using it to denote a transformative development in which new rules and doctrines of customary international law emerge with unusual rapidity and acceptance.[16] Usually this happens during a period of great change in world history, analogous in magnitude to the end of European feudalism in Grotius's times, "when new norms, procedures, and institutions had to be devised to cope with the then decline of the Church and the emergence of the secular state."[17]

Drawing from the writings of Professor Bruce Ackerman, who used the phrase "constitutional moment" to describe the New Deal transformation in American constitutional law,[18] some international law scholars have used the phrase "international constitutional moment" to convey the "Grotian Moment" concept. Stanford Law professor Jenny Martinez, for example, has written that the drafting of the UN Charter was a "Constitutional moment" in the history of international law.[19] Washington University Law professor Leila Sadat has similarly

---

See also INTERNATIONAL LAW AND WORLD ORDER 1265–86 (Burns H. Weston, Richard A. Falk, Hilary Charlesworth & Andrew K. Strauss, eds., Thomson/West 4th ed. 2006). For the early seeds of this concept of a changing paradigm in Falk's work, see Richard A. Falk, *The Interplay of Westphalia and Charter Conceptions of International Legal Order*, in 1 THE FUTURE OF THE INTERNATIONAL LEGAL ORDER 32 (R. Falk & C. Black, eds. 1969).

[15] Boutros Boutros-Ghali, *The Role of International Law in the Twenty-First Century: A Grotian Moment*, 18 FORDHAM INT'L L. J. 1609, 1613 (1995) (referring to the establishment of the International Tribunal for the Former Yugoslavia as part of the process of building a new international system for the twenty-first century).

[16] Saul Mendlovitz & Marv Datan, *Judge Weeramantry's Grotian Quest*, 7 TRANSNATIONAL L. & CONTEMPORARY PROBLEMS 401, 402 (defining the term "Grotian moment").

[17] BURNS H. WESTON, INTERNATIONAL LAW AND WORLD ORDER, 1369 (3d ed., 1997); B. S. Chimni, *The Eighth Annual Grotius Lecture: A Just World under Law: A View from the South*, 22 AM. U. INT'L L. REV. 199, 202 (2007).

[18] BRUCE ACKERMAN, RECONSTRUCTING AMERICAN LAW (1984).

[19] Bardo Fassbender, *The United Nations Charter as Constitution of the International Community*, 36 COLUM. J. TRANSNAT'L L. 529 (1998); Jenny S. Martinez, *Towards an International Judicial System*, 56 STAN. L. REV. 429, 463 (2003).

described Nuremberg as a "constitutional moment for international law."[20] Dean Anne Marie Slaughter (Princeton's Woodrow Wilson School) and Professor William Burke-White (University of Pennsylvania Law School) have used the term "constitutional moment" in making the case that the September 11 attacks on the United States evidence a change in the nature of the threats confronting the international community, thereby paving the way for rapid development of new rules of customary international law.[21] While the phrase "international constitutional moment" might be quite useful with respect to paradigm-shifting developments[22] within a particular international organization with a constitutive instrument that acts like a constitution, the term "Grotian Moment" makes more sense when speaking of a development in customary international law.

* * *

Normally, customary international law, which is just as binding on states as treaty law,[23] arises out of the slow accretion of widespread state

---

[20] Leila Nadya Sadat, *Enemy Combatants after Hamdan v. Rumsfeld: Extraordinary Rendition, Torture, and Other Nightmares from the War on Terror*, 75 GEO. WASH. L. REV. 1200, 1206–07 (2007).

[21] Anne-Marie Slaughter & William Burke-White, *An International Constitutional Moment*, 43 HARV. INT'L L. J. 1, 2 (2002). See also Ian Johnstone, *The Plea of "Necessity" in International Legal Discourse: Humanitarian Intervention and Counter-Terrorism*, 43 COLUM. J. TRANSNAT'L L. 337, 370 (2005) (arguing that 9/11 constituted a "constitutional moment" leading to recognition of a newly emergent right to use force in self-defense argued against nonstate actors operating with the support of third states).

[22] As defined by Thomas Kuhn in his influential book THE STRUCTURE OF SCIENTIFIC REVOLUTIONS 150 (1970), a paradigm shift is a change in the basic assumptions within the ruling theory of science. While Kuhn opined that the term should be confined to the context of pure science, it has since been widely used in numerous nonscientific contexts to describe a profound change in a fundamental model or perception of events. One such example is the Keynesian revolution in macroeconomic theory.

[23] While customary international law is binding on states internationally, not all states accord customary international law equal domestic effect. A growing number of states' constitutions automatically incorporate customary law as part of the law of the land and even accord it a ranking higher than domestic statutes. BRUNO

practice evincing a sense of legal obligation (*opinio juris*).[24] Consistent with the traditional approach, the U.S. Supreme Court has recognized that the process of establishing customary international law can take several decades or even centuries.[25] Not so long ago France took the position that thirty years is the minimum amount required, while the United Kingdom has said nothing less than forty years would be sufficient.[26] The International Law Commission, at the beginning of its work, demanded state practice "over a considerable period of time" for a customary norm to emerge.[27] In the 1969 *North Sea Continental Shelf* cases, however, the International Court of Justice observed that customary norms can sometimes ripen quite rapidly, and that a short period is not a bar to finding the existence of a new rule of customary international law, binding on all the countries of the world, save those that persistently objected during its formation.[28]

SIMMA, INTERNATIONAL HUMAN RIGHTS AND GENERAL INTERNATIONAL LAW: A COMPARATIVE ANALYSIS 165, 213 (1995). In the United States, customary international law is deemed incorporated into the federal common law of the United States. Some courts, however, consider it controlling only where there is no contradictory treaty, statute, or executive act. See *Garcia-Mir v. Meese*, 788 F.2d 1446 (11th Circ. 1986) (holding that attorney general's decision to detain Mariel Cuban refugees indefinitely without a hearing trumped any contrary rules of customary international law).

[24] For the definition of customary international law, see *North Sea Continental Shelf* (*Federal Republic of Germany v. Denmark*; *Federal Republic of Germany v. Netherlands*), Merits, 20 February 1969, ICJ Rep. 3, para. 77.

[25] *The Paquete Habana*, 175 U.S. 677, 700 (1900).

[26] Franscesco Parisi, *The Formation of Customary Law*, Paper Presented at the 96th Annual Conference of the American Political Science Association, August 31, 2000, at 5.

[27] *See Working Paper by Special Rapporteur Manley O. Hudson on Article 24 of the Statute of the International Law Commission*, [1950] 2 Y.B. International Law Commission 24, 26, U.N. Doc. A/CN.4/16.

[28] *North Sea Continental Shelf* (*Federal Republic of Germany v. Denmark*; *Federal Republic of Germany v. Netherlands*), Merits, 20 February 1969, ICJ Rep. 3, paras. 71, 73, 74. The Court stated: Although the passage of only a short period of time is not necessarily ... a bar to the formation of a new rule of customary international law, ... an indispensable requirement would be that within the period in question, short though it might be, State practice, including that of States whose interests are specially affected, should have been both extensive and virtually uniform in the sense of

By positing that there is a third factor (a context of fundamental change) that can be as important to the creation of new rules of customary international law as the traditional ingredients of state practice and *opinio juris*, the Grotian Moment concept illuminates how and why customary international law can sometimes develop with surprising rapidity and limited state practice. The concept reflects the reality that in periods of fundamental change, whether by technological advances, the commission of new forms of crimes against humanity, or the development of new means of warfare or terrorism, rapidly developing customary international law may be necessary to keep up with the pace of developments.

While the Grotian Moment concept may account for accelerated formation of customary international law, it should be contrasted with the view that there can be such a thing as "instant customary international law," as suggested, for example, in an oft-cited 1965 article by University College London professor Bin Cheng.[29] Professor Cheng opined that not only was it unnecessary that state practice should be prolonged, but there need be no state practice at all provided that the *opinio juris* of the states concerned can be clearly established by, for example, their votes on UN General Assembly resolutions.[30] Legal scholars have been largely

the provision invoked; – and should moreover have occurred in such a way as to show a general recognition that a rule of law or legal obligation is involved.

Id. at para. 74. While recognizing that some norms can quickly become customary international law, the ICJ held that the equidistance principle contained in Article 6 of the 1958 Convention on the Continental Shelf had not done so as of 1969 because so few states recognized and applied the principle. At the same time, the Court did find that Articles 1 and 3 of the convention (concerning the regime of the continental shelf) did have the status of established customary law. *Id.* at pp. 24–7, paras. 25–33.

[29] B. Cheng, *United Nations Resolutions on Outer Space: "Instant" International Customary Law?* 5 INDIAN J. INT'L L. 23 (1965). In contrast to Cheng's conception, the "Grotian Moment" concept contemplates accelerated formation of customary international law through widespread acquiescence or endorsement in response to state acts, rather than instant custom based solely on General Assembly resolutions.

[30] *Id.* at 36. Other scholars and commentators who have asserted the possibility of "instant customary international law" include PETER MALANCZUK, AKEHURST'S MODERN INTRODUCTION TO INTERNATIONAL LAW 45–46 (7th ed. 1997); Jeremy Levitt, *Humanitarian Intervention by Regional Actors in Internal Conflicts: The*

critical of Cheng's "instant custom" theory, at least to the extent that it does away with the need to demonstrate any state practice other than a country's vote in the UN General Assembly.[31]

The Grotian Moment concept, in contrast, requires a foundation of state practice, but it also recognizes that in times of fundamental change UN General Assembly Resolutions can take on heightened significance in terms of declaring existing customary law or crystallizing emerging customary law, despite a relatively small amount and short duration of state practice.[32]

* * *

Little has previously been written about the Grotian Moment concept. Indeed, an exhaustive search of law review databases revealed only sixty-one previous references to the term "Grotian Moment," and few that use the term in the way it is being employed here. This book develops and explores the concept of "Grotian Moment" in international law. This book does not, however, constitute uncritical advocacy of a new paradigm that supports assertions of speedy formation of customary international law that are not backed up by state practice. Rather, it seeks to present a balanced exploration, including an examination of cases in which commentators and NGOs have been too quick to claim the existence of a new rule of customary international law.

To set the stage, Chapter 2 provides a discussion of the historic underpinnings of the Grotian Moment concept, focusing on the impact of Hugo Grotius's scholarship during the advent of the modern international system. Chapter 3, in turn, provides a theoretical framework for

---

Cases of ECOWAS in Liberia and Sierra Leone, 12 Temp. Int'l & Comp. L. J. 333, 351 (1998); Benjamin Lengille, *It's "Instant Custom": How the Bush Doctrine Became Law after the Terrorist Attacks of September 11, 2001*, 26 B.C. Int'l & Comp. L. Rev. 145 (2003).

[31] *See* G. J. H. Van Hoof, Rethinking the Sources of International Law 86 (1983).

[32] Anthea Elizabeth Roberts, *Traditional and Modern Approaches to Customary International Law: Reconciliation*, 95 Am. J. Int'l L. 757, 758 (2001).

investigating and testing the existence and application of the Grotian Moment concept. The remaining chapters examine six case studies of potential Grotian Moments. ICJ judge Christopher Greenwood helped me identify these Grotian Moment candidates during a memorable birthday lunch at the Peace Palace in April 2012. Chapter 4 examines whether the Nuremberg precedent fits within the profile of a legitimate Grotian Moment, and the consequences of such a conclusion for modern war crimes trials. Moving along in chronological order, Chapter 5 examines how the post–World War II need for oil and technological advances in deep sea drilling brought about a rapid change in the law of the sea marked by the extension of sovereignty over the continental shelf. Chapter 6 then explores whether the advent of space rocket technology in the 1960s constituted a Grotian Moment, marked by rapid development of customary international rules concerning space flight. Chapter 7 examines how the return of genocide to Europe for the first time since the Second World War and the creation of the first international criminal tribunal since Nuremberg sowed the seeds for rapid recognition of individual criminal responsibility for war crimes in the context of internal armed conflict. Chapter 8 scrutinizes the development of the Responsibility to Protect Doctrine in the aftermath of the 1999 NATO Kosovo intervention as a possible Grotian Moment. Finally, Chapter 9 examines the rapid changes in customary international law that have arisen out of the international community's response to the attacks of September 11, 2001. The concluding chapter summarizes the findings of the previous chapters and examines the practical applications and potential consequences of recognition of the Grotian Moment concept.

While exploring the usefulness of the Grotian Moment concept through the lens of these six case studies, the author recognizes that "it is always easy, at times of great international turmoil, to spot a turning point that is not there."[33] With this admonition in mind, the book takes

---

[33] Ibrahim J. Gassama, *International Law at a Grotian Moment: The Invasion of Iraq in Context*, 18 EMORY L. REV. 1, 30 (2004).

a hard and balanced look at each scenario, focusing on three lines of inquiry: First, was the particular change in question of a sufficiently fundamental nature? Second, to qualify as a legitimate Grotian Moment, the case must be one in which the extent and duration of State practice are much less than is traditionally required for customary international law. Third, there must nevertheless be recognition that the rule did in fact acquire customary law status despite the dearth and short period of State practice. Together, these factors provide a prism for assessing whether the case studies examined in the book and other situations constitute legitimate Grotian Moments in international law. It is hoped that this approach will help scholars, courts, and government officials recognize and utilize Grotian Moments as they occur in the future.

2   Historical Context

THIS CHAPTER DESCRIBES THE HISTORIC UNDERPINNINGS of the Grotian Moment concept. In the mid-1600s, at the time that the nation-state was emerging as the fundamental political unit of Europe, Hugo Grotius – theologian, poet, historian, jurist, statesman, diplomat, and international lawyer – offered a new concept of international law designed to reflect and progressively develop that new reality. The chapter explains why Grotius is often characterized as "the father of international law"; the role played by his great work, *De Jure Belli ac Pacis* ("The Law of War and Peace"), in transforming international law; and why it is appropriate to characterize fundamental changes that spark rapid formation of customary international law as "Grotian Moments."

The Life and Times of Hugo Grotius

To comprehend the Grotian legacy, one must know something about the turbulent times in which Grotius lived and wrote.[1] Hugo de Groot

---

[1] Background facts in this section derived from W.S.M. KNIGHT, THE LIFE AND WORKS OF HUGO GROTIUS (Sweet and Maxwell, 1925); EDWARD DUMBAULD, THE LIFE AND LEGAL WRITINGS OF HUGO GROTIUS (University of Oklahoma Press, 1969); CHARLES S. EDWARDS, HUGO GROTIUS, THE MIRACLE OF HOLLAND: A STUDY IN POLITICAL AND LEGAL THOUGHT (Burnham, 1981); C. G. Roelofsen, *Grotius and the International Politics of the Seventeenth Century*, in HUGO GROTIUS AND INTERNATIONAL RELATIONS

(young Hugo would subsequently adopt the Latinized "Grotius") was born to one of the leading Protestant families of the Dutch city of Delft on April 10, 1583. He grew up during the Eighty Years' War (1558–1648) between the Dutch Provinces and the Spanish Empire, and as an adult Grotius witnessed the horrors of the Thirty Years' War (1618–48), which engulfed the whole of Europe.

Arising out of the Reformation, the Eighty Years' War began as a revolt of the Seventeen Dutch Provinces, which had embraced Protestantism, against Philip II of Spain, the sovereign of the Habsburg Netherlands. The revolt was a response to King Philip's heavy-handed efforts to enforce a policy of strict Catholic religious uniformity through-out the Spanish Empire, which at that time included the territory of Spain and its ally, Portugal, as well as Germany, the Netherlands, Belgium, most of Italy, various other principalities of Europe, Mexico, and Peru. Over the years, the fortunes of war whipsawed back and forth. After the initial Dutch revolt, Philip II's armies regained control over most of the rebelling provinces. Then the northern provinces, under the leadership of William of Orange, managed to oust the Habsburg armies and estab-lish the Republic of the Seven United Netherlands.

There was a temporary truce between Spain and the Dutch provinces from 1607 to 1619, followed by a resumption of conflict, which was accom-panied by the launch of the Thirty Years' War, involving most of the countries in Europe. Like the Eighty Years' War, the Thirty Years' War began as religious hostilities between Protestant- and Catholic-controlled regions of the Holy Roman Empire. It gradually developed into a more general conflict reflecting the Bourbon France–Habsburg Spain rivalry for European political preeminence. Both wars were marked by exten-sive destruction of entire regions, denuded by the foraging armies. The resulting ruin, famine, and disease reduced the populace of the German states, the Low Countries, and Italy by nearly 40 percent, while

98–9 (Hedley Bull, Benedict Kingsbury, and Adam Roberts, eds., Oxford University Press, 1990).

bankrupting most of the combatant powers. Armies were expected to be largely self-funding from loot taken or tribute extorted from the populations where they operated. This encouraged a form of lawlessness that imposed often severe hardship on inhabitants of the occupied territory. In the words of one historian, during the conflict "human beings, turned by misery into wild beasts, rivaled the beasts in ferocity and foulness."[2]

Despite the omnipresent war,[3] Grotius thrived as an exceptionally gifted and well-connected child prodigy. When Grotius was eight, he began writing skillful elegies in Latin; by eleven, he was a student in the Faculty of Letters at the University of Leiden, where his father served as curator. A year later, he published the first of his sixty books.[4] At age fifteen, he accompanied a friend of his father's, the leading Dutch politician of the day, Johan van Oldenbarnevelt, on a diplomatic trip to France, where Grotius received a doctorate from the University of Orleans. The French reaction to the accomplished young Grotius was similar to the reception Wolfgang Amadeus Mozart would receive a hundred years later. Thus, when the French monarch, Henry IV, met Grotius during the young man's visit to the royal court, the king of France publicly hailed Grotius as "the miracle of Holland."[5]

Upon his return to the Netherlands, Grotius was admitted to the bar of Holland at the age of sixteen. He established a law practice in the Hague, with clientele that included the Dutch East India Company, Oldenbarnevelt (then prime minister of the United Netherlands), and Maurice of Nassau (the prince of Orange). Meanwhile, at age eighteen,

---

[2] John W. Foster, *The Evolution of International Law*, 18 THE YALE L. J. 149, 151 (1909).

[3] Notable combat during Grotius's early years included the siege of Antwerp (1585) and the battles of Breda (1590), Zutphen, Deventer, Defzijl Nijmegen (1591), Steenwijk, Coevorden (1592), Geertruidenberg (1593), Groningen (1594), Grol, Enschede, Ootmarsum, Oldenzaal (1597), Dunkirk, Nieuwpoort (1600), and Grave (1602).

[4] Hedley Bull, *The Importance of Grotius in the Study of International Relations*, in HUGO GROTIUS AND INTERNATIONAL RELATIONS (Bull, Kingsbury, and Roberts, eds., 1990), at 67.

[5] *Hugo Grotius*, Stanford Encyclopedia of Philosophy (2011), available at: //Leibniz. standford.edu/previews/Grotius.png.

Grotius was retained by the United Dutch Provinces to write the official chronicle of their history. In 1607 (when he was twenty-four), Grotius was appointed attorney general of Holland, and in 1613 (at age thirty) he was appointed governor of Rotterdam. One of Grotius's contemporaries, French scholar and Advocate-General Jerome Bignon, declared that Grotius was "the most learned man the world had known since Aristotle."[6]

Grotius's string of successes were interrupted in 1619, when a Dutch Calvinist faction staged a coup d'état, and Grotius and other leading reformers (known as "Remonstrants") were charged with treason and imprisoned in Louvestein Castle. During his confinement, Grotius had access to a large collection of books and spent his time at Louvestein deep in study. Two years later, with the help of his wife, Maria van Reigersberg, Grotius was smuggled out of Louvestein in a large trunk and made his way to Paris. There, supported by a pension from the French government, Grotius spent the next few years writing his opus, *De Jure Belli ac Pacis*, which was published by a Parisian Press in 1625.

De Jure Belli ac Pacis was written in a unique style for the day, with voluminous references to ancient, medieval, and early modern works. Grotius relies, in his words, on "the testimony of philosophers, historians, poets, finally also of orators" to refute skepticism about international law and bolster his case for an international society governed by a system of norms.[7] He did not write "a dry textbook for law students but employed the ornaments of eloquence and wit ... wishing his work to be useful to practical men of affairs."[8] His style has been described as "penned by a sanguine spirit confident in the triumph of great principles even in a time of darkness, turmoil and confusion, with a moral glow

---

[6] Hamilton Vreeland, HUGO GROTIUS: THE FATHER OF THE MODERN SCIENCE OF INTERNATIONAL LAW 238 (1917).

[7] Hugo Grotius, *De Jure Belli ac Pacis*, PROLEGOMENA, section 40. Jon Miller, *Hugo Grotius*, Stanford Encyclopedia of Philosophy (2011).

[8] EDWARD DUMBAULD, THE LIFE AND LEGAL WRITINGS OF HUGO GROTIUS 76 (1969).

warming the ponderous masses of erudition with which the author over-laid his thoughts."[9] The book's content and style hit a chord with politi-cal leaders and elites across the continent and made Grotius a household name almost overnight.

Over the next twenty years, Grotius authored five dozen other books, but *De Jure Belli ac Pacis* was his masterpiece. The proliferation of printing presses during the time rendered Grotius's book one of the earliest worldwide "best sellers." During his lifetime and in the years that followed, nearly a hundred editions and translations of the book were published in Latin, Dutch, English, German, Italian, Russian, and French.[10] British author and statesman John Morley wrote that "along with Adam Smith's *The Wealth of Nations* it [*De Jure Belli ac Pacis*] 'is one of the cardinal books of European history.'"[11] American diplomat John Foster stated in 1909 that "it has been well said that it [*De Jure Belli ac Pacis*] is one of the few books that have changed the history of the world."[12]

Grotius tried to return to the Netherlands in 1631, but the Dutch authorities refused to issue him a pardon and placed a bounty on his head. He then lived briefly in Hamburg, Germany. In 1634, Grotius accepted an appointment by Sweden (one of the superpowers of mid-seventeenth-century Europe allied against Spain) to be ambas-sador to France – a position he held until just before his death eleven years later. His principal diplomatic accomplishment was helping to negotiate a treaty that drew France fully into the Thirty Years' War

---

[9] John MacDonell, *The Influence of Grotius, Transactions of the Grotius Society*, Vol. 5, Problems of Peace and War, Papers Read before the Society in the Year 1919 (published by Cambridge University Press), at xxi.

[10] Richard Tuck, *Introduction*, in HUGO GROTIUS, THE RIGHTS OF WAR AND PEACE (Richard Tuck, ed., 2005), at x.

[11] Hedley Bull, *The Importance of Grotius in the Study of International Relations*, in HUGO GROTIUS AND INTERNATIONAL RELATIONS (Bull, Kingsbury, and Roberts, eds., 1990), at 71.

[12] John W. Foster, *The Evolution of International Law* 18 YALE LAW JOURNAL 149, 153 (1909).

on the side of Sweden and the Protestant German princes, leading to the defeat of the Habsburg cause and the Peace of Westphalia thirteen years later. Grotius would die of illness following a shipwreck on the way from Stockholm to Germany in 1645, while the Peace of Westphalia was under negotiation.[13]

De Jure Belli ac Pacis

In the American Society of International Law's inaugural Grotius Lecture, Judge Christopher Weeramantry of the International Court of Justice observed that "it was an unprecedented situation that faced the newly emerging States of Grotius' time."[14] The medieval era, which the Thirty Years' War brought to a bloody end, had been characterized by "criss-crossing political, legal, religious and moral allegiances" to feudal rulers, to the Holy Roman Empire, and to the Catholic Church.[15] Thus, according to Judge Weeramantry, "detached from their traditional moorings to church, empire, and a higher law, [these new states] were groping for new principles of conduct and interrelationship to provide a compass for the tempestuous waters that lay ahead."[16]

Grotius sought to provide the nations of Europe with what they badly needed in the closing years of the Thirty Years' War – "a rational theory of international relations emancipated from theology and the authority of churches."[17] He was among the first to suggest how the binding force of the law of nations could be preserved and made vital in the kind

---

[13] Hedley Bull, *The Importance of Grotius in the Study of International Relations*, in HUGO GROTIUS AND INTERNATIONAL RELATIONS (Bull, Kingsbury, and Roberts, eds., 1990), at 69.

[14] Christopher Weeramantry, *The Grotius Lecture*, 14 AMERICAN UNIVERSITY INTERNATIONAL LAW REVIEW 1525, 1516 (1999).

[15] Mark W. Janis, *Sovereignty and International Law: Hobbes and Grotius*, in ESSAYS IN HONOR OF WANG TIEYA (Ronald St. John MacDonald, ed., Springer, 1994), at 392.

[16] Christopher Weeramantry, *The Grotius Lecture*, 14 AMERICAN UNIVERSITY INTERNATIONAL LAW REVIEW 1525, 1516 (1999).

[17] R. W. LEE, HUGO GROTIUS 57 (1930).

of anarchic and pluralistic environment that would emerge two decades later from the Peace of Westphalia.[18]

In explaining the motivation for writing *De Jure Belli ac Pacis*, Grotius writes in the book's prolegomena:

> Fully convinced ... that there is a common law among nations, which is valid alike for war and in war, I have had many and weighty reasons for undertaking to write upon this subject. Throughout the Christian world I observed a lack of restraint in relation to war, such as even barbarous races should be ashamed of; I observed that men rush to arms for slight causes, or no cause at all, and that when arms have once been taken up there is no longer any respect for law, divine or human; it is as if, in accordance with a general decree, frenzy had openly been let loose for the committing of all crimes.[19]

Grotius further explains that his book is meant as a response to "those who regard international law with contempt, as having no reality except an empty name."[20]

At the time that Grotius wrote *De Jure Belli ac Pacis*, Machiavellianism had for a century been the prevailing philosophical approach to interstate relations. In *The Prince*, Niccolo Machiavelli justified the state as a self-sufficient, nonmoral entity and advocated a worldview where international agreements are viewed as no more than temporary arrangements of mutual convenience.[21] During Grotius's time, "the empire was decaying, the church was corrupted and intolerant, and ... the Pope encouraged international faithlessness by absolving treaty makers from their oaths."[22]

Seeing the devastation of the Eighty Years' War and Thirty Years' War as confirmation of the folly of the Machiavellian method, Grotius

---

[18] Edward Keene, Beyond the Anarchical Society: Grotius, Colonialism, and Order in World Politics 2 (2002).

[19] Grotius, *De Jure Belli ac Pacis*, Prolegomena.

[20] Grotius, *De Jure Belli ac Pacis*, Prolegomena, Section 22.

[21] N. Machiavelli, The Prince and the Discourses 64 (Lerner, ed., 1950).

[22] Hamilton Vreeland, *Hugo Grotius*, 67 University of Pennsylvania Law Review and American Law Register 203, 204 (1919).

sought to replace it with a notion that states could exist in an international community governed by treaties, which natural law obligated them
to honor.[23] Grotius's book stresses mutual interdependence of states,
asserting that there is no state so powerful that it may not at some time
require the help of others outside itself, either for trade or for mutual
defense.[24] This principle that agreements should be carried out – *pacta
sunt servanda* – that Grotius advocated has been described as the *grund
norm* of modern international law.[25]

De Jure Belli ac Pacis does not contain any direct reference to
Machiavelli; rather Grotius uses the Roman philosopher Carneades
as his foil. Nevertheless, "it is principally against Machiavelli that
Grotius directs his argument."[26] And while others – in particular the
sixteenth-century Spanish theologians Vitoria and Suarez – had laid the
foundations for this approach, Grotius's unique contribution was that he
"secularized" international law, fashioning a system that would appeal to
Catholics, Protestants, and those outside the Christian tradition alike.[27]
It was partly for this reason that the Catholic Church banned Grotius's
book for 180 years.[28]

---

[23] Grotius, *De Jure Belli ac Pacis*, Book II, Chapters 11, 12; Mark W. Janis, *Sovereignty
and International Law: Hobbes and Grotius*, in Essays in Honor of Wang Tieya
(1993), at 396.

[24] Grotius, *De Jure Belli ac Pacis*, Prolegomena, Section 22.

[25] Maurice H. Mendelson, The Formation of Customary International Law 183
(1998).

[26] W. J. Korab-Karpowiez, *In Defense of International Order: Grotius's Critique of
Machiavellism*, 60 The Review of Metaphysics 55, 57 (2006).

[27] Hersch Lauterpacht, *The Grotian Tradition in International Law*, 23 Brit. Y.B. Int'l
L. 1, 24 (1946). Grotius writes: "In considering treaties, it is frequently asked, whether
it be lawful to make them with nations, who are strangers to the Christian religion; a
question, which, according to the law of nature admits not of a doubt. For the rights,
which it establishes, are common to all men without distinction of religion." Grotius,
De Jure Belli ac Pacis, Book II, Chapter 15, Section 8.

[28] Pope Urban VIII placed *De Jure Belli ac Pacis* on the Papal Index on February 4,
1627, and it was forbidden to all Catholics until the ban was lifted in 1901 by Pope
Leo XIII after the papal delegation's exclusion from the Hague Peace Conference
of 1899 in response to the ban of a book that contained the foundational principles

Although Grotius's observations and arguments were not completely original, *De Jure Belli ac Pacis* is said to have "commended itself to the conscience of the age. It restated the wisdom of the ancients and applied it to the unprecedented circumstances of the world of the Renaissance and Reformation."[29] Yet Grotius, the experienced diplomat and politician, was no mere idealist. He acknowledged that war was a natural feature of interstate relations. At the same time he advocated the application of law to initiating war and to waging it once commenced.

Grotius organized *De Jure Belli ac Pacis* as three books, totaling nine hundred pages. Following the prolegomena, in which Grotius articulates and defends his philosophical approach, book I advances his conception of war and natural justice, arguing that there are some circumstances in which war is justifiable. Book II identifies three just causes for war: self-defense, reparation of injury, and punishment. And book III takes up the question of what rules govern the conduct of war once it has begun; Grotius argued that all parties to war are bound by such rules, whether their cause is just or not.

One can easily connect the dots from book III of *De Jure Belli ac Pacis* to President Lincoln's 1863 "Lieber Code" – the first codified laws for the conduct of war[30]; to the "Marten's Clause" in the Hague Convention of 1899 – the natural law–inspired provision of the first multinational convention codifying the laws of war[31]; and ultimately to

---

of international law. HAMILTON VREELAND, HUGO GROTIUS: THE FATHER OF THE MODERN SCIENCE OF INTERNATIONAL LAW 167 (1917).

[29] Cornelius F. Murphy, Jr., *The Grotian Vision of World Order*, 76 AM. J. INT'L. L. 477, 482 (1982).

[30] See Andrew D. White, *Debt Due to Hugo Grotius, The Advocate of Peace (1894–1920)*, Vol. 61, No. 8 (September 1899), at 186–90 (address delivered July 4, 1899, in Delft, Holland, at the celebration given by the American Commission in honor of Grotius). The Lieber Code can be found in U.S. War Department, THE WAR OF THE REBELLION: A COMPILATION OF THE OFFICIAL RECORDS OF THE UNION AND CONFEDERATE ARMIES (Washington, DC: Government Printing Office, 1899), Series III, Volume 3, pp 148–64.

[31] The Martin's Clause is a catch-all provision of the Hague Regulations (repeated in the 1907 Hague Convention) that provides, "Until a more complete code of the laws of war is issued, the High Contracting Parties think it right to declare that in

the four Geneva Conventions of 1949 – the comprehensive set of modern rules for warfare. At a commemoration of Grotius during the 1899 Hague Peace Conference, the American representative, Andrew White, stated: "Of all works not claiming divine inspiration, that book [*De Jure Belli ac Pacis*], by a man proscribed and hated both for his politics and his religion, has proved the greatest blessing to humanity. More than any other it has prevented unmerited suffering, misery and sorrow; more than any other it has promoted the blessings of peace and diminished the horrors of war."[32]

The Grotian Legacy

Yet, *De Jure Belli ac Pacis* is celebrated for much more than providing the scholarly underpinning for the development of the laws of war. Indeed, many scholars contend that Grotius's famous book laid the intellectual foundation for the general approach embodied in the Peace of Westphalia, which ended the Eighty Years' War and Thirty Years' War in 1648 and inaugurated the modern international legal system. As James Bryce writes:

> When by the Peace of Westphalia a crowd of petty principalities were recognized as practically independent states, the need of a body of rules to regulate their relations and intercourse became pressing. Such a code (if one may call it by that name) Grotius and his successors compiled out of the principles which they found in the Roman law, then the private law of Germanic countries, thus laying the foundation whereon the system of international jurisprudence has been built up during the last three centuries.[33]

---

cases not included in the Regulations adopted by them, populations and belligerents remain under the protection and empire of the principles of international law, as they result from the usages established between civilized nations, from the laws of humanity and the requirements of the public conscience."

[32] Andrew D. White, *Dept Due to Hugo Grotius*, *The Advocate of Peace*, SEPTEMBER 1899, at 186–90.

[33] JAMES BRYCE, THE HOLY ROMAN EMPIRE 436 (1907).

The Peace of Westphalia was history's first general peace settlement, resulting from a six-year diplomatic conference with 109 participating delegations, including those of the Holy Roman Emperor, the House of Habsburg, the Kingdom of Spain, the Kingdom of France, the Swedish Empire, the Dutch Republic, the princes of the Holy Roman Empire, and sovereigns of the free imperial cities. The agreement was embodied in two separate accords: the Treaty of Osnabruck, concluded between the Protestant queen of Sweden and her allies on the one side, and the Habsburg Holy Roman Emperor and the German princes on the other; and the Treaty of Munster concluded between the Catholic king of France and his allies on the one side, and the Habsburg Holy Roman emperor and the German princes on the other.[34]

Aside from establishing fixed territorial boundaries for many of the countries involved in the conflict, the important provisions of these treaties were the recognition of the independent sovereignty of the states of Europe, their right to exercise exclusive jurisdiction within their own territory, the establishment of religious toleration, the right of each state to negotiate its own treaties, and the recognition that such treaties were binding. The Peace of Westphalia changed the relationship of subjects to their rulers. In earlier times, people had tended to have overlapping political and religious loyalties. Through Westphalia, it was agreed that the citizenry of a respective nation were to be subjected first and foremost to the laws and whims of their own respective government rather than to those of neighboring powers, be they religious or secular. This allowed the rulers of the imperial states to decide their religious worship independently, and it reaffirmed the authority of the state over the church. Protestants and Catholics were redefined as equal before the law, Calvinism was given legal recognition, and neither pope nor Holy Roman Emperor was permitted to interfere with the administration of the independent states.[35]

---

[34] For the full text of the Osnabruck and Muster Treaties, in both their Latin and English versions, see C. PARRY (ed.), CONSOLIDATED TREATY SERIES, Vol. 1 (Dobbs Ferry, NY: Oceana, 1969), at 119 and 270.

[35] Cornelius F. Murphy, Jr., *The Grotian Vision of World Order*, 76 AM. J. INT'L. L. 477, 479 (1982).

The conventional view is that by recognizing the German princes as sovereign, with the right to negotiate their own treaties, which would be binding upon them, the Peace of Westphalia signaled the beginning of a new era reflecting the Grotian conception of international community regulated by universal principles. Thus, one of the primary authors of the United States Constitution, James Madison, declared that Grotius "is not unjustly considered ... the father of the modern code of nations."[36] Stephen Field, one of the most eminent of nineteenth-century U.S. Supreme Court justices, similarly proclaimed Grotius to be the "father" of modern international law, a moniker that has been repeated by other high court judges.[37] More recently, Professor David Bederman of Emory University School of Law wrote that Grotius certainly "earned" the title "father of international law," and major international statesmen and stateswomen of the twenty-first century – UN High Commissioner for Human Rights Mary Robinson and former UN Secretary-General Boutros Boutros-Ghali to name two – have made similar pronouncements.[38]

To those who accept this view of history, the year 1648 marked a fundamental turning point for international law and relations. In light of the intellectual foundations Grotius provided for this historic development, we could call it the first "Grotian Moment" in international law.

This view of the Peace of Westphalia as a sudden paradigm-shifting[39] event inspired by the writings of Grotius is not entirely accurate, however. While coexisting with empire, the state system had emerged a hundred

---

[36] James Madison, *Examination of the British Doctrine, a Neutral Trade Not Open in Time of Peace*, in 2 LETTERS AND OTHER WRITINGS OF JAMES MADISON 1794–1815 at 230, 234.

[37] Charles J. Reid, *Hugo Grotius – a Case of Dubious Paternity*, UNIVERSITY OF ST. THOMAS SCHOOL OF LAW LEGAL STUDIES RESEARCH PAPER NO. 07–13 (2009).

[38] Mary Robinson, *Remarks*, 19 AM. U. INT'L L. REV. 1, 2 (2003); Boutros Boutros-Ghali, *The Role of International Law in the Twenty-First Century: A Grotian Moment*, FORDHAM INT'L L. J. 1609, 1609 (1995).

[39] THOMAS KUHN, THE STRUCTURE OF SCIENTIFIC REVOLUTIONS 150 (1970) (coining the phrase "paradigm shift").

years before Westphalia. Moreover, the power to conclude alliances formally recognized at Westphalia was not unqualified and was in fact a power that the German princes had already possessed for almost half a century. Furthermore, although the treaties eroded some of the authority of the Habsburg emperor, the empire remained a key actor according to the terms of the treaties. For example, the Imperial Diet retained the powers of legislation, warfare, and taxation, and it was through imperial bodies, such as the diet and the courts, that religious safeguards mandated by the treaty were imposed on the German princes.[40]

These nuances are perhaps beside the point. While the results of Westphalia may have been simplified by the lens of history, and Grotius's role may have been exaggerated,[41] Westphalia has unquestionably emerged as a symbolic marker and Grotius as an emblematic figure of changing historical thought. To understand how and why that perception has grown to be more important than reality, one can turn to the theory of semiotics. Derived from the Greek word *semeion*, meaning sign, semiotics was developed by Charles Peirce in the nineteenth century as the study of how meaning of signs, symbols, and language is constructed and understood. Semiotics begins with the assumption that phrases, such as "the Peace of Westphalia" or "the Grotian tradition," are not historic artifacts whose meanings remain static over time. Rather, semiotics posits that the meanings of such terms change over the years along with the interpretive community or communities.[42] Thus, the legend and mystique that surround Grotius and the Peace of Westphalia have attained their own significance, by which Grotius is now widely viewed as "the

---

[40] Michael P. Scharf, *Earned Sovereignty: Juridical Underpinnings*, 31 DENVER J. INT'L L. 373, 375 n. 20; Stephane Beaulac, *The Westphalian Legal Orthodoxy – Myth or Reality?* 2 JOURNAL OF THE HISTORY OF INTERNATIONAL LAW 148 (2001).

[41] EDWARD KEENE, BEYOND THE ANARCHICAL SOCIETY: GROTIUS, COLONIALISM, AND ORDER IN WORLD POLITICS 45–52 (Cambridge University Press, 2002); 45–52 (2002).

[42] CHARLES SANDERS PEIRCE, COLLECTED PAPERS OF CHARLES SANDERS PEIRCE: PRAGMATISM AND PRAGMATICISM 5 (Charles Hartshorne & Paul Weiss eds., 1935); Umberto Eco, A Theory of Semiotics (1976).

patron saint of the modern states-system."[43] That the legend suffers from historical inaccuracy does not diminish its usefulness as a metaphor for critical turning points in international law and relations.

Ultimately, the Grotian tradition,[44] while widely acclaimed, proved incapable of conferring order and stability on the destructive rivalries inherent in the nation-state system.[45] And in the centuries after the publication of his celebrated book, Grotius's reputation experienced great decline during the rise of positivism, and later of anticolonialism, in international law.[46] Yet, there has been renewed interest in the salience of Grotius's political thought to the world of today. Although Grotius did not foresee the advent of an international organization like the United Nations, he did envision a community of nations, and his just war approach is reflected in Chapter VII of the UN Charter. His concept that international law might properly be enforced through punishment by third states[47] anticipated the collective sanctions schemes of the League of Nations and UN Charter. His natural law approach presaged the modern concept of *jus cogens* – peremptory norms as to which states cannot by treaty derogate.[48] Grotius's justification for humanitarian

---

[43] MARTINE JULIA VAN ITTERSUM, PROFIT AND PRINCIPLE: HUGO GROTIUS, NATURAL RIGHTS THEORIES AND THE RISE OF DUTCH POWER IN THE EAST INDIES 1595–1615 (2006), at xxxviii.

[44] Hersch Lauterpacht, *The Grotian Tradition in International Law*, 23 BRIT. Y.B. INT'L L. 1, 5 (1946); MARY ELLEN O'CONNELL, THE POWER AND PURPOSE OF INTERNATIONAL LAW 3–9 (Oxford University Press, 2008).

[45] Cornelius F. Murphy, Jr., *The Grotian Vision of World Order*, 76 AM. J. INT'L. L. 477, 492 (1982).

[46] Edward Keene, *The Reception of Hugo Grotius in International Relations Theory*, 20/21 GROTIANA 135, 154 (1999/2000); EDWARD KEENE, BEYOND THE ANARCHICAL SOCIETY: GROTIUS, COLONIALISM, AND ORDER IN WORLD POLITICS 29–39 (Cambridge University Press, 2002); A. Claire Cutler, *The Grotian Tradition in International Relations*, 17 REV. INT'L STUD. 41 (1991).

[47] Grotius, *De Jure Belli ac Pacis*, Book II, Chapter 20, Sections 20, 40.

[48] See 1969 Vienna Convention on the Law of Treaties, Art. 53 (defining *jus cogens* norms as laws such as the prohibitions on the use of force and genocide "accepted and recognized by the international community as a whole … from which no derogation is permitted and which can be modified only by a subsequent norm of general international law having the same character").

intervention (he argues that the state that is oppressive and egregiously violates basic human rights forfeits its moral claim to full sovereignty)[49] is at the heart of the modern Responsibility to Protect doctrine – the subject of Chapter 8. His notion that individuals and nonstate actors could be subjects of international law[50] is relevant to modern human rights law and international criminal law, as well as notions of self-defense against terrorist groups – explored further in Chapters 4 and 9. And his defense of the force of international law is used today to dispute neorealist claims that international law is not binding.[51]

---

[49] Grotius, *De Jure Belli ac Pacis*, Book II, Chapter 2, Section 19.

[50] Grotius, De Jure Belli ac Pacis, Book I, Chapter 1, Section 1; Book 3, Chapter 23; 2.2.19.

[51] Mary Ellen O'Connell, THE POWER AND PURPOSE OF INTERNATIONAL LAW 3 (Oxford University Press, 2008).

3 Theoretical Underpinnings

To PROVIDE THEORETICAL INFRASTRUCTURE FOR THE
exploration of the Grotian Moment concept, this chapter
examines the scholarly debate about the nature and formation of customary international law. Then, building on the literature
examining rapid formation of customary international law, the chapter
explores the role played by context and fundamental technological and
tactical change as an accelerating agent.

The Importance of Customary International Law

To paraphrase Mark Twain, reports of the death of customary international law are greatly exaggerated.[1] Despite its widespread codification
in treaties during the last century, the unwritten norms, rules, and principles of customary law continue to play a crucial role in international
relations.[2] There are three primary reasons for customary international
law's continuing vitality.

---

[1] Mark Twain (Samuel Longhorne Clemens), Cable from London to the Associated
Press (1897), BARTLETT'S FAMILIAR QUOTATIONS 625 (15th ed., 1980); David
Bederman, *Acquiescence, Objection and the Death of Customary International Law*,
21 DUKE JOURNAL OF COMPARATIVE AND INTERNATIONAL LAW 31, 43 (2010).

[2] Their definitions vary, but in ordinary usage the terms "norms," "principles," and
"rules of customary international law" are often used interchangeably, as they are
here.

First, in some ways, customary international law possesses more jurisprudential power than does treaty law. Unlike treaties, which bind only the parties thereto, once a norm is established as customary international law, it is binding on all states, even those new to a type of activity, so long as they did not persistently object during its formation.[3] Since some international law rules coexist in treaties and custom, customary international law expands the reach of the rules to those states that have not yet ratified the treaty. In addition, the customary international law status of the rules can apply to actions of the treaty parties that predated the entry into force of the treaty. Moreover, states that were not even in existence at the time the norm evolved, such as colonies or former parts of a larger state, and therefore never had an opportunity to express their positions as a particular rule emerged, are nonetheless generally deemed to be bound by the entire corpus of customary international law existing upon the date they become sovereign states.[4] Finally, unlike some treaties that by their terms permit withdrawal, customary international law does not recognize a unilateral right to withdraw from it.[5]

Second, while one might tend to think of customary international law as growing only slowly, in contrast to the more rapid formation of treaties, the actual practice of the world community in modern times suggests that the reverse is more often the case. For example, negotiations for the

---

[3] REPORT OF THE INTERNATIONAL LAW ASSOCIATION, COMMITTEE ON FORMATION OF CUSTOMARY (GENERAL) INTERNATIONAL LAW, LONDON CONFERENCE (2000), at 25.

[4] David Kaplow, *International Legal Standards and the Weaponization of Outer Space*, in SPACE: THE NEXT GENERATION – CONFERENCE REPORT, March 31– April 1, 2008, United Nations Institute for Disarmament Research (2008), at 161.

[5] Professors Bradley and Gulati criticize customary international law for failing to recognize a right to subsequent withdrawal from a customary rule in parallel with the right to withdrawal from a treaty. *See* Curtis A. Bradley and Mitu Gulati, *Customary International Law and Withdrawal Rights in an Age of Treaties*, 21 DUKE JOURNAL OF INTERNATIONAL AND COMPARATIVE LAW 1 (2010). Note, however, that not all treaties permit withdrawal. Moreover, there are situations, such as in a fundamental change of circumstances, where a state can be excused for failing to comply with a customary

Law of the Sea Convention began in 1973, the convention was concluded in 1982, and it did not enter into force until it received its sixtieth ratification in 1994 – a period of twenty-one years. Similarly, negotiations for the Vienna Convention on the Law of Treaties began in 1949, the convention was concluded in 1969, and it did not enter into force until it received its thirty-fifth ratification in 1980 – some thirty-one years. And the International Law Commission began its work on the Statute for an International Criminal Court in 1949, several preparatory committees then worked on it, and it was finally concluded in Rome in 1998 and entered into force upon receipt of its sixtieth ratification in 2002 – a span of fifty-three years from start to finish. As we shall see later, customary international law often forms at a much faster pace, especially with respect to areas of technological or other fundamental change.[6]

Finally, while one might assume that treaty law offers the benefit of greater clarity and precision in the articulation of the legal obligations, this is not always the case. Rather, the provisions of treaties, especially multinational conventions, are often subject to what H. L. A. Hart called a "penumbra of uncertainty"[7] resulting from the need to bridge language, cultural, legal, and political divides among diverse parties. It some areas, customary rules may provide greater precision since they evolve in response to concrete situations and cases and are often articulated in the written decisions of international courts.

---

rule. Hersch Lauterpacht, *The Function of Law in the International Community* 272–90 (1933).

[6] In contrast to earlier times, in the modern era of instantaneous electronic communications and a proliferation of diplomatic conferences, organizations, and other forums for multinational diplomatic exchanges, state practice is being generated at an increasing pace, while information about state practice is becoming more and more widely disseminated over the Internet. This means that the requisite quantity of claims and responses can be reached much more quickly than in the past, leading to a general acceleration of the formation of customary rules. Tullio Treves, *Customary International Law*, in MAX PLANCK ENCYCLOPEDIA OF PUBLIC INTERNATIONAL LAW (2012), at para. 25, available at www.mpepil.com (last accessed February 9, 2013).

[7] H. L. A. HART, THE CONCEPT OF LAW 121–32, 144–50 (1961).

The Definition of Customary International Law

Hugo Grotius discerned the law of nations (*jus gentium*) from custom (*usus*), the views of the learned, and the will (*voluntas*) of states.[8] In the centuries after Grotius, customary international law was deemed to constitute rules that develop through a "slow process of growth, whereby courses of conduct once thought optional become first habitual or usual, and then obligatory, and the converse process of decay, when deviations, once severely dealt with, are first tolerated and then pass unnoticed."[9]

Article 38 of the Statute of the International Court of Justice contains the modern definition of customary international law: "The Court, whose function is to decide in accordance with international law such disputes as are submitted to it, shall apply … (b) international custom, as evidence of a general practice accepted as law."[10] This text originated in the Statute of the Permanent Court of International Justice, which was drafted by the League of Nations Advisory Committee of Jurists in 1920.[11] Scholars have disparaged this text as "notoriously unclear" and as containing "serious drafting deficiencies."[12] Moreover, the drafting history of this provision indicates "that the members of the Committee did not, on the whole, have a clear idea of what exactly they meant by the phrase."[13]

---

[8] Hugo Grotius, *Belli ac Pacis*, I, xiv.

[9] H. L. A. HART, THE CONCEPT OF LAW 90 (1961).

[10] Statute of the International Court of Justice, June 26, 1945, 59 Stat. 1055, T.S. No. 993 (all member states of the United Nations are automatically parties to the Statute of the International Court of Justice).

[11] MAURICE H. MENDELSON, THE FORMATION OF CUSTOMARY INTERNATIONAL LAW 195 (1998).

[12] REPORT OF THE INTERNATIONAL LAW ASSOCIATION, COMMITTEE ON FORMATION OF CUSTOMARY (GENERAL) INTERNATIONAL LAW, LONDON CONFERENCE (2000), at 5. A more logical statement of customary international law is set forth in the European Union Guidelines of December 23, 2005, on Promoting Compliance with International Humanitarian Law [2005] OJ C327/04 at para. 7: "Customary international law is formed by the practice of States which they accept as binding upon them."

[13] MAURICE H. MENDELSON, THE FORMATION OF CUSTOMARY INTERNATIONAL LAW 195 (1998).

Yet, jurists and scholars agree that the text of Article 38 reflects the view that customary international law is composed of two elements: general state practice, termed the "objective element," and some sort of attitude toward practice (be it acknowledgment as law or consent), termed the "subjective element."[14] The judgments of the Permanent Court of International Justice and the International Court of Justice have been consistent in stating that a customary rule requires the presence of both of these elements. Thus, in the 1929 *Lotus* case, the Permanent Court of International Justice stated that international law is based on the will of states expressed in conventions or in "usages generally accepted as expressing principles of law."[15] Similarly, in the 1969 *North Sea Continental Shelf* cases, the International Court of Justice stated that the actions by states "not only must amount to a settled practice, but they must also be such, or be carried out in such as way, as to be evidence of a belief that this practice is rendered obligatory by the existence of the rule of law requiring it."[16]

Where those two elements are manifest, a rule of customary international law will be deemed to bind all states (with the exception of persistent objectors) without the necessity to show that the particular state allegedly bound by the rule has participated in its formation or has otherwise accepted it.[17] This book focuses on general custom, that is, rules that apply worldwide. There is also such a thing as regional or local customary law, which can apply in a particular geographic area (e.g., to the states surrounding a bay) or in a particular sector (e.g., all the states that possess a particular technology), but that is not the subject of this inquiry.

[14] MAURICE H. MENDELSON, THE FORMATION OF CUSTOMARY INTERNATIONAL LAW 195 (1998).

[15] S.S. *Lotus* (*France v. Turkey*) (Merits) PCIJ Rep. Series A No. 10, at 18.

[16] *North Sea Continental Shelf* cases (Germany/Denmark) (Merits) 1984 ICJ Rep. 246.

[17] MAURICE H. MENDELSON, THE FORMATION OF CUSTOMARY INTERNATIONAL LAW 218 (1998).

The Objective Element

Traditionally, jurists and scholars have put more emphasis on state conduct than on the subjective element. That is because a state's conduct is easier to ascertain than the belief of a state. With the introduction of the United Nations and other bodies where multilateral diplomacy is conducted in the open, however, the situation has in fact reversed.[18]

State practice can be reflected in the acts of the executive, the legislature, or the judiciary, as well as private persons acting on behalf of the state. It takes many different forms, including diplomatic correspondence, declarations of government policy, the advice of government legal advisers, press communiqués, official manuals dealing with legal questions, orders to the armed forces, statements and votes in international organizations, the comments of governments on draft texts produced by the International Law Commission or similar bodies, national legislation, domestic court decisions, and pleadings before international tribunals.[19]

While one might be tempted to conclude that acts count more than words because "talk is cheap," virtually all of the authorities treat the two as equal.[20] In fact, International Court of Justice Judge Richard Baxter once noted that "the firm statement by the State of what it considers to be the rule is far better evidence of its position than what can be pieced together from the actions of that country at different times and in a variety of contexts."[21] The case law of international tribunals is replete with examples of verbal acts being treated as examples of practice.[22] In

---

[18] MAURICE H. MENDELSON, THE FORMATION OF CUSTOMARY INTERNATIONAL LAW 197 (1998).

[19] IAN BROWNLIE, PRINCIPLES OF PUBLIC INTERNATIONAL LAW 5 (4th ed., 1990).

[20] REPORT OF THE INTERNATIONAL LAW ASSOCIATION, COMMITTEE ON FORMATION OF CUSTOMARY (GENERAL) INTERNATIONAL LAW, LONDON CONFERENCE (2000), at 13–14.

[21] Richard Baxter, *Multilateral Treaties as Evidence of Customary International Law*, 41 BRITISH YEAR BOOK OF INTERNATIONAL LAW 275, 300 (1965–6).

[22] E.g., S.S. *Lotus* case, (1927), PCIJ Ser. A, No. 10, pp. 23, 26–30; *Nottebohm* case (2nd phase), ICJ Rep. 1955, p. 4, at pp. 21–3; *Fisheries Jurisdiction* (Merits),

particular, diplomatic protest (or its absence) is universally viewed as important in determining whether a customary rule has been created, strengthened, amended, or superseded. Thus, in assessing the relevant behavior of states, "we look to words as well as deeds, and to silences as well as inactions."[23] Verbal acts can count as either the objective or subjective element, and the International Law Association has observed that it is possible for the same conduct to manifest both.[24] As discussed later, state votes on UN General Assembly resolutions can thus be both a form of state practice and a manifestation of the state's subjective attitude about the existence of the rule in question.[25]

State practice also includes inaction or silence, especially (but not necessarily) where a protest would be expected. Thus, in the case of the *S.S. Lotus*, the Permanent Court of International Justice (the forerunner of the ICJ) relied on the absence of protest against legislation based on the "objective territoriality" doctrine of jurisdiction in finding that such an exercise of jurisdiction was permissible under customary international law.[26] Similarly, in the *Nottebohm* case (second phase), the ICJ based its decision on the fact that many states "refrain from exercising protection in favor of a naturalized person when the latter has in fact, by his prolonged absence, severed his links with what is no longer for him anything but his nominal country."[27]

ICJ Rep. 1974, p. 3, at 24–6, paras. 55–8; *Nicaragua* case (Merits), 1986 ICJ Rep. p. 14, at 97–109, paras. 183–207; *Nuclear Weapons Advisory Opinion*, ICJ Rep. 1996, p. 226, at 259–61, paras. 86, 88; *Gabcikovo-Nagymaros* Project, ICJ Rep. 1997, at paras. 49–54, 83, 85.

[23] David Kaplow, *International Legal Standards and the Weaponization of Outer Space*, in SPACE: THE NEXT GENERATION – CONFERENCE REPORT, 31 March 31–April 1, 2008, UNITED NATIONS INSTITUTE FOR DISARMAMENT RESEARCH (2008), at 160.

[24] REPORT OF THE INTERNATIONAL LAW ASSOCIATION, COMMITTEE ON FORMATION OF CUSTOMARY (GENERAL) INTERNATIONAL LAW, LONDON CONFERENCE (2000), at 7.

[25] MAURICE H. MENDELSON, THE FORMATION OF CUSTOMARY INTERNATIONAL LAW 201 (1998).

[26] S.S. *Lotus* (1927), PCIJ, Series A, No. 10, p. 23.

[27] *Nottebohm* case, ICJ Reports 1955, p. 4, 22.

Claim and Response

Professor Myers McDougal of Yale Law School famously described the customary international law formation process as one of continuous claim and response.[28] To illustrate this process, consider the question of whether international law permits a state to use force to arrest a terrorist leader in another state without the latter's consent – a question addressed in detail in Chapter 9. The claim may be express (such as demanding that its troops be allowed to enter the territorial state to arrest the terrorist) or implicit (such as sending troops into the territorial state without its permission to apprehend the terrorist). The response to the claim may be favorable, such as consenting to or refraining from protesting the extraterritorial apprehension. In such case, the claim and response will begin the process of generating a new rule of customary international law. Some states may imitate the practice, and others, who were directly affected by the (express or implied) claim, may passively acquiesce in it.

Custom pioneers (the first states to initiate a new practice) have no guarantee that their action will actually lead to the formation of a binding custom. The response may be a repudiation of the claim. In such case, the repudiation could constitute a vigorous reaffirmation of existing law, which is strengthened thereby. Or, the claim and repudiation could constitute a kind of standoff, which could slow the formation of new customary international law. The reaction of third states is also relevant. Out of this process of claim and response, and third party reaction, rules emerge, are strengthened or degraded, or are superseded. "As pearls are produced by the irritant of a piece of grit entering an oyster's shell, so the interactions and mutual accommodations of States produce the pearl – so to speak – of customary law."[29]

---

[28] M. S. McDougal and N. A. Schlei, *The Hydrogen Bomb Tests in Perspective: Lawful Measures for Security*, 64 YALE LAW JOURNAL 648 (1955).

[29] MAURICE H. MENDELSON, THE FORMATION OF CUSTOMARY INTERNATIONAL LAW 190 (1998).

Professor Anthony D'Amato of Northwestern University has proposed an alternative formulation to explain the formation of customary rules, focusing on what he calls "articulation" and "act."[30] In
D'Amato's view, the articulation can either accompany the initial act
(what McDougal called the "claim"), or it can be embodied in a treaty,
draft instruments of the International Law Commission, or resolutions
of the UN General Assembly. Acts that follow and are consistent with
the articulation will crystallize the policy into a principle that takes on
life as a rule of customary international law.[31] In other words, once there
is a consensus articulation that states ought to conform to a given rule
of conduct, a legal custom can emerge when some level of spontaneous
compliance with the rule is manifest.

Advocates of D'Amato's approach have called it "modern custom."
In contrast with the inductive claim and response process McDougal
describes, so-called modern custom is "a deductive process that begins
with general statements of rules rather than particular instances of
practice."[32] Where McDougal's claim and response concept is back-
ward looking, D'Amato's conception is more like treaty law, proscribing
rules for the future. Yet, of the two approaches, many scholars believe
McDougal's claim and response concept better reflects the "authentic
world of politics, rather than some ideal world which may owe more to
rhetoric than to reality."[33]

General versus Constant and Uniform Practice

Although the International Court of Justice has spoken of "constant
and uniform usage" as the yardstick for ascertaining a customary

---

[30] ANTHONY A. D'AMATO, CONCEPT OF CUSTOM IN INTERNATIONAL LAW 88 (1971).

[31] ANTHONY A. D'AMATO, CONCEPT OF CUSTOM IN INTERNATIONAL LAW 88 (1971).

[32] Anthea E. Roberts, *Traditional and Modern Approaches to Customary International
Law: A Reconciliation*, 95 AMERICAN JOURNAL OF INTERNATIONAL LAW 757, 758
(2001).

[33] MAURICE H. MENDELSON, THE FORMATION OF CUSTOMARY INTERNATIONAL LAW
190–1 (1998).

rule,[34] the Court has made clear that perfect consistency is not required. On the basis of its comprehensive examination of the Court's case law, the International Law Association has observed that "general practice suffices" to generate customary rules binding on all states.[35] In the *Fisheries* case, the Court stressed that "too much importance need not be attached to the few uncertainties or contradictions" in state practice.[36] Similarly, the Court determined that although various proclamations of an exclusive economic zone were not identical, they were sufficiently similar for the Court to hold in the *Continental Shelf* cases between Tunisia and Libya, and between Libya and Malta, that the Exclusive Economic Zone (EEZ) had become part of customary international law.[37] In concluding that the rule against use of force in the territory of another state was part of customary international law in the 1986 *Nicaragua* case, the Court said it "does not consider that, for a rule to be established as customary, the corresponding practice must be in absolutely rigorous conformity with the rule. In order to deduce the existence of customary rules, the Court deems it sufficient that the conduct of States should, in general, be consistent with such rules."[38]

The International Court of Justice has also spoken of the requirement of "extensive" practice and at the same time has indicated that the most important practice is that of "States whose interests are specially affected."[39] This means discerning the existence of a customary rule is not merely a numbers game; there is an important qualitative aspect to the inquiry. In other words, it may be enough that the practice be representative, so long as it includes states whose interests are

---

[34] *Asylum* case, ICJ Reports 1951, p. 116, 131.

[35] REPORT OF THE INTERNATIONAL LAW ASSOCIATION, COMMITTEE ON FORMATION OF CUSTOMARY (GENERAL) INTERNATIONAL LAW, LONDON CONFERENCE (2000), at 24.

[36] *Fisheries* case, ICJ Reports 1951, p. 116, 138.

[37] *Continental Shelf* (Tunisia/Libya), ICJ Reports 1982, p. 18, 74, para. 100; *Continental Shelf* (Libya Malta), ICJ Reports 1985, p. 13, 33, para. 34.

[38] *Nicaragua* (merits), ICJ Reports 1986, p. 14, 98, para. 186.

[39] *North Sea Continental Shelf* cases, ICJ Reports 1969, p. 3, 43, para. 74.

specially affected. Thus, in the *Continental Shelf* case (Libya/Malta), the Court determined that, after several significant maritime states had claimed EEZs, the EEZ had ripened into a rule of customary international law despite the fact that a majority of eligible coastal states had not yet claimed an EEZ.[40] Similarly, in the *Frontier Dispute (Burkina Faso/Mali)* case, the Court held that *uti possidetis* was a rule of general customary international law, even though at the time the principle was supported only in the practice of South American and African states, which did not constitute a majority of the international community.[41]

To understand the significance of specially affected states, Professor Charles De Visscher of Ghent University likened the formation of custom to the gradual wearing of a path through a field: "Among the users are always some who mark the soil more deeply with their footprints than others, either because of their weight ... or because their interests bring them more frequently this way."[42] This metaphor helps explain why the most important states in the particular area of activity (which may or may not be the most powerful states generally) should be accorded extraordinary weight. A state especially active in an area will likely devote more resources to thinking about and developing the applicable law. Thus, as described in Chapter 5, the United States and United Kingdom were pioneers of the regime of the continental shelf because their nationals were the first to be actively engaged in offshore oil exploitation in areas beyond the territorial sea. Similarly, as described in Chapter 6, the United States and Soviet Union were pioneers of early space law since they were the first states to be capable of such flight.

Just as the practice of specially affected states can have a disproportionate influence on the formation of new rules, so too can their

---

[40] *Continental Shelf* case (Libya/Malta), ICJ Reports 1985, p.13, 33, para. 34.

[41] *Frontier Dispute* (Burkina Faso/Mali), ICJ Reports 1986, p. 554, 564–5, paras. 19–20. The *uti possidetis* principle requires that a newly independent state respect preexisting external borders.

[42] C. DE VISSCHER, THEORY AND REALITY IN PUBLIC INTERNATIONAL LAW 155 (1968).

opposition prevent a rule from coming into being. One example of this is the successful opposition of the United States and other capital-exporting countries to the replacement of the "prompt, adequate and effective" standard of compensation in cases of lawful expropriation, with a lower standard of "just compensation" advocated by a majority of states.[43]

The International Law Association has concluded that "provided that participation is sufficiently representative, it is not normally necessary for even a majority of States to have engaged in the practice, provided that there is no significant dissent."[44] According to Professor Michael Barton Akehurst of Keele University, where there is no evidence presented against a rule of customary international law, a small amount of practice is sufficient to prove the existence of such rule, resting the burden of disproving its existence on the objecting party.[45] Scholars who have carefully dissected the judgments of the International Court of Justice have concluded that "most customs are found to exist on the basis of practice by fewer than a dozen States."[46] While there is an undemocratic quality to according more weight in the formation of customary rules to specially affected states,[47] the importance given to the practice of such states does at least mean that customary rules will reflect the realities of power and therefore have a reasonable prospect of being effective.

A final consideration is whether the situation is one of initial formation of a customary rule or the alteration of existing customary law. Scholars

---

[43] M. H. Mendelson, *What Price Expropriation? Compensation for Expropriation: The Case Law*, 79 AMERICAN JOURNAL OF INTERNATIONAL LAW 414, 1041 (1985).

[44] REPORT OF THE INTERNATIONAL LAW ASSOCIATION, COMMITTEE ON FORMATION OF CUSTOMARY (GENERAL) INTERNATIONAL LAW, LONDON CONFERENCE (2000), at 25.

[45] M. Akehurst, *Custom as a Source of International Law*, 47 BRITISH YEAR BOOK OF INTERNATIONAL LAW 1, 12 (1974–5).

[46] Anthea E. Roberts, *Traditional and Modern Approaches to Customary International Law: A Reconciliation*, 95 AMERICAN JOURNAL OF INTERNATIONAL LAW 757, 767 (2001) (citing the works of Charney, Chodosh, Schacter, and Weisburd).

[47] Roberts critiques this as a "democratic deficit." Anthea E. Roberts, *Traditional and Modern Approaches to Customary International Law: A Reconciliation*, 95 AMERICAN JOURNAL OF INTERNATIONAL LAW 757, 767 (2001).

have argued that existing customs should not be lightly discarded. As Professor Bederman explained, "there should be a higher threshold of uniformity, consistency and volume of State practice in order to terminate an old, well-settled customary rule, as opposed to creating a new one in a hitherto unregulated realm of international relations."[48]

The Persistent Objector Rule

The international community is not yet ready to accept a system in which the majority can develop new rules of customary international law and bind the minority to the new rules over their objection. Thus, a state that does not wish to acquiesce in the development of a new rule of customary international law can rely on the so-called persistent objector rule. Reflecting the voluntary nature of customary international law, a state which manifests its opposition to a practice before it has developed into a rule of customary international law can, by virtue of that objection, opt out from the operation of the new rule.

While the persistent objector rule has been recognized relatively recently, it has been treated by jurists and scholars as practically axiomatic.[49] The International Court of Justice recognized the persistent objector rule in the *Asylum* case, where the Court stated, "but even if it could be supposed that such a custom existed between certain Latin-American States only, it could not be invoked against Peru which, far from having by its attitude adhered to it, has, on the contrary, repudiated it."[50] The Court also applied the rule in the *Fisheries* case, in rejecting the United Kingdom's argument that customary international law limited

---

[48] David J. Bederman, *Acquiescence, Objection and the Death of Customary International Law* 21 DUKE JOURNAL OF COMPARATIVE AND INTERNATIONAL LAW 31, 38 (2010).

[49] MAURICE H. MENDELSON, THE FORMATION OF CUSTOMARY INTERNATIONAL LAW 227 (1998) (citing the works of R. Y. Jennings, C. Rousseau, J. H. W. Verzijl, I. Brownlie, G. I. Tunkin, H. Thirlway, M. Villiger, K. Wolfke, G. Danilenko, and C. van Bynkershoek).

[50] *Asylum* case, ICJ Reports 1950, p. 266, 277–8.

closing lines in bays to a length of ten miles. The Court stated, "in any event the ten-mile rule would appear to be inapplicable to Norway, inasmuch as she has always opposed any attempt to apply it to the Norwegian coast."[51]

The persistent objector rule has certain limits. First, if a state does not make an objection at the time the general rule is emerging, it can be considered bound despite subsequent manifestations of opposition.[52] Second, customary international law rules are binding on new states and existing states that are newcomers to a particular type of activity. There is no "subsequent objector" rule available to such states.[53] Third, the rule does not apply to peremptory norms (*jus cogens*).[54] Thus, although South Africa persistently maintained that it was entitled to practice apartheid, the international community accorded no weight to this objection.

There are few instances of invocation of the persistent objector rule, but it is nonetheless considered an important safety valve that permits the "convoy" of customary international law to move forward without having to wait for the slowest member.[55] In practice, the invocation of the persistent objector rule usually serves as a short-term measure to enable dissenting states to adjust themselves to the new rule, which they eventually accept.

Treaties as Source of Custom

Treaties are binding on their parties, but they can also can generate customary rules binding on all states in three ways: First, treaties can codify

---

[51] *Fisheries* case, ICJ Reports 1951, p. 116, 131.

[52] REPORT OF THE INTERNATIONAL LAW ASSOCIATION, COMMITTEE ON FORMATION OF CUSTOMARY (GENERAL) INTERNATIONAL LAW, LONDON CONFERENCE (2000), at 27.

[53] REPORT OF THE INTERNATIONAL LAW ASSOCIATION, COMMITTEE ON FORMATION OF CUSTOMARY (GENERAL) INTERNATIONAL LAW, LONDON CONFERENCE (2000), AT. 27.

[54] REPORT OF THE INTERNATIONAL LAW ASSOCIATION, COMMITTEE ON FORMATION OF CUSTOMARY (GENERAL) INTERNATIONAL LAW, LONDON CONFERENCE (2000), at 28.

[55] MAURICE H. MENDELSON, THE FORMATION OF CUSTOMARY INTERNATIONAL LAW 240 (1998).

and elucidate customary international law. This may seem counterintuitive since traditionally, the purpose of treaties was to derogate from existing customary law, not to confirm it. In the years since its establishment by the UN General Assembly in 1945, however, the International Law Commission has promulgated a number of international conventions meant to transform customary international law into treaty law. Yet, one should not assume that every provision of a codifying treaty constitutes customary law. A particular treaty might well contain some provisions meant to reflect existing customary law, and others that constitute progressive development. Thus, in the *North Sea Continental Shelf* cases, the International Court of Justice found that Article 6 (the equal distance rule) of the Geneva Convention on the Continental Shelf did not represent customary law, but that Articles 1 and 3 (concerning the regime of the continental shelf) did.[56]

Sometimes a treaty will expressly declare that its provisions, or certain of them, are declaratory of existing customary law. For example, Article 1 of the Genocide Convention provides "the Contracting Parties confirm that genocide, whether committed in time of peace or in time of war, is a crime under international law which they undertake to prevent and to punish."[57] Such a provision is strong but not conclusive evidence, for in some cases states have strategically included such provisions to bolster their case vis-à-vis third parties.[58] On other occasions the treaty's *travaux preparatoires* (negotiating record) will indicate whether the treaty was intended as a codification or not. Even in the absence of such a provision or reference in the negotiating record, courts may find that a provision of a treaty constitutes a codification of customary law. Thus, in the *Namibia* case, the International Court of Justice held that "the rules laid down by the Vienna Convention on the Law of Treaties concerning termination of a treaty on account of breach (adopted without a

[56] *North Sea Continental Shelf* cases, ICJ Reports 1969, pp. 24–7, paras. 25–33.
[57] Convention against Genocide, 78 UN Treaty Series, p. 278.
[58] See W. E. HALL, A TREATISE ON INTERNATIONAL LAW 9 (8th ed., A. Pearce Higgins, 1924) (listing examples of such treaties).

dissenting vote) may in many respects be considered as a codification of existing customary law on the subject" and went on to apply those rules as customary law to the South-West Africa Mandate which predated the Vienna Convention.[59]

Second, the consensus formed through the process of treaty negotiation can sometimes crystallize rules of customary international law as reflected in the treaty text before the treaty goes into force. In the 1969 *North Sea Continental Shelf* case, Denmark argued that "the process of the definition and consolidation of the emerging customary law took place through the work of the International Law Commission, the reaction of governments to that work and the proceedings of the Geneva Conference [on the Law of the Sea]." While recognizing that treaty provisions could conceivably crystallize customary law, the International Court of Justice held that this was not the case with respect to Article 6 of the Geneva Convention on the Continental Shelf.[60] In contrast, in the 1982 *Continental Shelf (Tunisia/Libya)* case, the International Court of Justice found that the recently concluded, though not yet in force, 1982 Convention on the Law of the Sea "crystallizes" an "emergent rule of customary law."[61] The same principle has been applied to draft articles produced by the UN's International Law Commission experts after years of study and debate, including comments by governments. Thus, the International Court of Justice concluded in the *Gabcikova-Nagymaros* case that the requirements for invoking a state of necessity set out in the Draft Articles on State Responsibility adopted on first reading by the International Law Commission "reflect customary international law."[62]

Third, a rule enshrined in a treaty may commend itself to states generally, who then adopt it in practice even if they fail to become parties to the treaty. For example, a treaty known as the 1856 Declaration of Paris

---

[59] *Namibia* case, ICJ Reports 1971, p. 16, 47, para. 94.
[60] *North Sea Continental Shelf* cases, ICJ Reports 1969, p. 38, paras. 61–2.
[61] *Continental Shelf* (Tunisia/Libya) case, ICJ Reports 1982, p. 18, 38, para. 24.
[62] *Gabcikovo-Nagymaros* case (Hungary/Slovakia) (Merits) 1997 ICJ Reports 7, para. 52.

abolished privateering (government-sanctioned piracy against the vessels of enemy states). While very few states became parties to the instrument, it is widely recognized that the outlawry of privateering became a rule of general customary law through state practice inspired by the declaration.[63]

The Role of Judicial Decisions

Judicial decisions count both as a form of state practice within the meaning of Article 38 of the Statute of the International Court of Justice, and as a "subsidiary means for the determination of rules of law" within paragraph (d) of that article.[64] Scholars debate whether this applies not just to decisions of domestic courts, but to those of international tribunals as well.

On the one hand, Professor Maurice Mendelson, the chair of the International Law Association's Customary International Law Committee, argues that decisions of international tribunals should not be deemed state practice because international judges are supposed to act

---

[63] MAURICE H. MENDELSON, THE FORMATION OF CUSTOMARY INTERNATIONAL LAW 193 (1998).

[64] In practice, the decisions of international courts and tribunals are much greater than what emerges from Article 38(1)(d) of the ICJ Statute, which characterizes judicial decisions merely as "subsidiary means for the determination of rules of law." Despite the absence of formal *stare decisis* in this realm, international and domestic courts tend to rely on the precedents of international tribunals, and states and parties to proceedings expect them to do so. Michael P. Scharf and Margaux Day, *The International Court of Justice's Treatment of Circumstantial Evidence and Adverse Inferences*, 13 CHICAGO JOURNAL OF INTERNATIONAL LAW 123, 128 (2012). "Moreover, international courts and tribunals can assess the existence and contents of customary rules on the basis of an unparalleled amount of materials, of which they dispose because of the high technical quality of the judges and of the registries, and also because of the detailed nature of written and oral pleadings, through which States parties to the dispute present, through experienced counsel, the relevant materials, very often unearthed from archives for the purpose of the case." Tullio Treves, *Customary International Law*, MAX PLANCK ENCYCLOPEDIA OF PUBLIC INTERNATIONAL LAW (2012), at para. 55, available at www.mpepil.com (last accessed February 9, 2013).

independently of those appointing them.[65] *The Max Planck Encyclopedia of Public International Law*, on the other hand, maintains that "as the authority of international courts and tribunals to settle a dispute between States derives from agreement of the States involved, judgments of such courts and tribunals may be seen, indirectly, as manifestations of the practice of the States that have agreed to confer on them such authority and the mandate to apply international – including customary – law."[66] Moreover, as Professor Karol Wolfke of Wroclaw University in Poland points out, "the fact that States accept the judgments and opinions of judicial organs means that those decisions and opinions can themselves be regarded as a form of State practice."[67] Consistent with this, in 1950, the International Law Commission included decisions of international courts in its list of primary sources of customary international law.[68]

---

[65] Maurice H. Mendelson, The Formation of Customary International Law 200 (1998). While this may be true of some international tribunals, it is not necessarily the case with respect to the International Court of Justice. Where a case involves the judge's state of nationality, Article 31 of the statute of the ICJ provides that the opposing party may appoint an ad hoc judge to the bench so that both parties enjoy the same advantage. This implicitly recognizes that international judges are prone to be particularly sympathetic to the interests of the judge's state of nationality. Nor would Mendelson's observation apply to the Nuremberg Tribunal, which was made up of judges representing the four great powers that emerged victorious at the end of World War II. One of the criticisms of the Nuremberg Tribunal was that it represented victors' justice and that the judges were not sufficiently independent of their appointing states. See A. Brackman, The Other Nuremberg (1987), R. Conot, Justice at Nuremberg (1983), A. Tusa & J. Tusa, The Nuremberg Trial (1983).

[66] Tullio Treves, *Customary International Law*, Max Planck Encyclopedia of Public International Law (2012), at para. 53, available at: www.mpepil.com. (last accessed February 9, 2013).

[67] Comments of Professor Karol Wolfke, Report of the International Law Association, Committee on Formation of Customary (General) International Law, London Conference (2000), at 19 n. 42.

[68] The International Law Commission listed the following sources as forms of evidence of customary international law treaties; decisions of national *and international courts*, national legislation, opinions of national legal advisors, diplomatic correspondence, practice of international organizations. [1950] 2 Y.B. Int'l L. Comm'n 367, U.N. Doc. A/CN.4/Ser.A/1950/Add.1 (1957) (emphasis added).

In the *Fisheries Jurisdiction* case, the International Court of Justice stated that its role is to ascertain the existence of rules of customary international law, not to create them.[69] Yet, the Court subsequently acknowledged its broader role in contributing to the formation of customary international law in the *Nuclear Weapons* Advisory Opinion, where the Court observed: "In stating and applying the law, the Court necessarily has to specify its scope and sometimes note its general trend."[70] Thus, Professor Anthea Roberts of the London School of Economics concludes that "judicial decisions can also have a formative effect on custom by crystallizing emerging rules and thus influencing state behavior."[71]

The Subjective Element

The purpose of the subjective element (*opinio juris*) is to differentiate state actions that give rise to legal norms from actions that do not.[72] The subjective element has been described as "the philosopher's stone which transmutes the inert mass of accumulated usage into the gold of binding legal rules."[73] This element is necessary because state practice is often capable of being interpreted in various ways. Examining subjective intent is particularly important where actions (or omissions) are in and of themselves ambiguous. For example, Professor D'Amato has said that every breach of a customary law contains the seed for a new legality.[74] But that

---

[69] Fisheries Jurisdiction case (*United Kingdom v. Iceland*) (Merits) 1974 ICJ Rep. p. 3, para. 53 (the Court stressed that "the Court, as a court of law, cannot render judgment sub specie legis ferendae, or anticipate the law before the legislator has laid it down").

[70] Legality of the Threat or Use of Nuclear Weapons (Advisory Opinion), 1996 ICJ Rep 226, para. 18.

[71] Anthea E. Roberts, *Traditional and Modern Approaches to Customary International Law: A Reconciliation*, 95 AMERICAN JOURNAL OF INTERNATIONAL LAW 757, 775 (2001).

[72] REPORT OF THE INTERNATIONAL LAW ASSOCIATION, COMMITTEE ON FORMATION OF CUSTOMARY (GENERAL) INTERNATIONAL LAW, LONDON CONFERENCE (2000), at 10.

[73] H. THIRLWAY, INTERNATIONAL CUSTOMARY LAW AND CODIFICATION 47 (1972).

[74] ANTHONY A. D'AMATO, THE CONCEPT OF CUSTOM IN INTERNATIONAL LAW 97–8 (1971).

is only the case if the breaching state justifies its action on the basis of a new rule of customary law. As the International Court of Justice observed in the *Nicaragua* case, if instead the state resorts to factual or legal exceptions to justify the breach, this has the effect of confirming the general rule rather than undermining it or creating an exception to it.[75]

Moreover the subjective element can reveal actions that constitute mere comity and distinguish those taken out of convenience from those that count as precedents. Take, for example, the *Lotus* case. There, France argued that the dearth of prosecutions for collisions on the high seas other than by the flag state on board which the wrongful act took place was evidence that international law did not recognize "effects jurisdiction" in such cases. The Permanent Court of International Justice disagreed on the ground that there was no evidence of a "conscious[ness] of having a duty to abstain" from prosecuting such cases.[76] The reasons for lack of prosecution could just as easily have been based on lack of interest or lack of domestic statutory authority as on a belief that such prosecutions violated customary international law.

There are two vigorously contested schools of thought concerning the nature and role played by the subjective element. The voluntarist thesis maintains that, since states are sovereign, they cannot be bound by legal obligations (whether through treaty or customary law) without their consent. Consistent with this, voluntarists view the subjective element of customary international law as a manifestation of consent. The other approach finds the basis of custom's binding force in states' belief in the legal necessity or permissibility of the practice in question. The debate between supporters of the two approaches goes back more than two hundred years and has continued to this day.[77]

The voluntarist thesis has been criticized for adopting the legal fiction that silence is considered a form of acquiescence or tacit consent – a

---

[75] *Nicaragua* case, 1986 ICJ Rep. at 98, para. 186.

[76] S.S. *Lotus*, PCIJ, Series A, No. 10, at p. 28.

[77] MAURICE H. MENDELSON, THE FORMATION OF CUSTOMARY INTERNATIONAL LAW 246 (1998) (citing diametrically opposed articles).

fiction that is especially hard to accept in cases where the particular state was not directly affected by the conduct in question when the customary rule was being formed.[78] The approach focusing on belief, in turn, fails to explain how *opinio juris* can exist in the initial phase of state practice with respect to a new rule. If it is the first state to assert a new rule, how can the state seriously entertain the opinion that it is acting in accordance with the law? Some commentators have tried to answer this criticism by suggesting that the state could be acting in error, but "the truth is that the State which introduces a new practice has in these cases no belief that its conduct is permitted or required by existing law, and neither have the first States to respond positively or negatively to its conduct."[79] As Judge Lachs observed in his opinion in the *North Sea Continental Shelf* cases, to require a conviction that the conduct is already a matter of legal obligation is to deny the possibility of developing new rules of customary law.[80]

It is more likely in such a case that the pioneers of the customary rule believe that it would be desirable that x were the rule. They may couch their innovation in the language of existing law, even when they know they are actually breaking new ground. Thus, their invocation of the subjective element is more in the nature of advocacy for the new rule's adoption than a confirmation that they believe it already exists.

Some scholars believe that the dichotomy between the two approaches is a false one; that consent plays a role in some circumstances, and belief does in others.[81] Professor Mendelson, for example, maintains that the voluntarist thesis is the better approach to the question of the formation of customary rules, and the approach that emphasizes belief better

---

[78] REPORT OF THE INTERNATIONAL LAW ASSOCIATION, COMMITTEE ON FORMATION OF CUSTOMARY (GENERAL) INTERNATIONAL LAW, LONDON CONFERENCE (2000), at 39.

[79] MAURICE H. MENDELSON, THE FORMATION OF CUSTOMARY INTERNATIONAL LAW 279 (1998).

[80] *North Sea Continental Shelf* cases, ICJ Reports 1969, p. 218, 231.

[81] MAURICE H. MENDELSON, THE FORMATION OF CUSTOMARY INTERNATIONAL LAW 248 (1998).

explains why mature customary rules are observed.[82] Consistent with the words in Article 38 of the ICJ statute, "a general practice accepted as law," Mendelson suggests that in the early formation stage "acceptance" means consent to an emerging rule, and in the later stage "acceptance" means acknowledgment that the rule has gained the force of law.[83] Moreover, he stresses that such an acknowledgment need not be from states alone, but could emanate from a tribunal[84] or from a resolution of the UN General Assembly.[85]

The Role of General Assembly Resolutions

One of the most striking developments related to the formation of customary international law in modern times has been the year-round functioning of international organizations and their various organs. This gives states many more occasions than they used to have to express views as to customary international law. In recent years there has been a stream of resolutions from international organizations, especially the UN General Assembly, purporting to set forth, confirm, or reaffirm rules of customary international law. Consistent with the premise that words count as state practice, some jurists and scholars have argued that, when adopted unanimously or by large majorities, General Assembly resolutions can constitute both the objective and subjective elements necessary to establish customary international law and thereby can create "instant custom."[86]

---

[82] MAURICE H. MENDELSON, THE FORMATION OF CUSTOMARY INTERNATIONAL LAW 283 (1998).

[83] MAURICE H. MENDELSON, THE FORMATION OF CUSTOMARY INTERNATIONAL LAW 283 (1998).

[84] Mendelson points out that in "certain innovative decisions" such as the 1951 *Fisheries* case, the Reservations to the Genocide Convention cases, and the *Nottebohm* case, "it would not be far from the truth to say that the ICJ made new law." *Id.* at 396.

[85] MAURICE H. MENDELSON, THE FORMATION OF CUSTOMARY INTERNATIONAL LAW 283 (1998).

[86] Bin Cheng, *United Nations Resolutions on Outer Space: "Instant" International Customary Law?* 5 INDIAN JOURNAL OF INTERNATIONAL LAW 23 (1963); In his

There are five main problems with the so-called instant custom theory. The first is that the UN Charter employs the language of "recommend" in referring to the powers and functions of the General Assembly, as distinct from the powers granted to the Security Council to issue binding decisions.[87] The negotiating record of the UN Charter confirms that the drafters intended for General Assembly resolutions to be merely nonbinding recommendations. In fact, at the San Francisco conference in 1945, when the Philippines delegation proposed that the General Assembly be vested with legislative authority to enact rules of international law, the other delegations voted down the proposal by an overwhelming margin.[88]

The second problem is that General Assembly resolutions often do not clearly differentiate between *lex lata* (what the law is) and *lex ferenda* (what the law should be). Often resolutions reflect *lex ferenda* cloaked as *lex lata*. Citing the *Manila Declaration on the Peaceful Settlement of International Disputes* [89] as an example, Professor Roberts observes that General Assembly resolutions "often reflect a deliberate ambiguity between actual and desired practice, designed to develop the law and to stretch the consensus on the text as far as possible."[90]

---

dissenting opinion in the South West Africa cases (*Ethiopia v. South Africa*) (Second Phase), 1966 I.C.J. Rep. 248, 291–3, Judge Tanaka argued that when a court is trying to discern whether a certain customary norm of international law exists, General Assembly resolutions can be used as evidence of general practice. He suggested that the General Assembly can accelerate the formation of customary law by serving as a forum in which a state "has the opportunity, through the medium of the organization, to declare its position to all members of the organization and to know immediately their reaction on the same matter." *Id.* at 291.

[87] Charter of the United Nations, arts. 10, 11, June 26, 1945, 59 Stat. 1031, T.S. No. 993.

[88] Gregory J. Kerwin, *The Role of United Nations General Assembly Resolutions in Determining Principles of International Law in United States Courts*, 1983 DUKE L. J. 876, 879 (1983).

[89] GA Res. 37/20 (November 14, 1982).

[90] Anthea E. Roberts, *Traditional and Modern Approaches to Customary International Law: A Reconciliation*, 95 AMERICAN JOURNAL OF INTERNATIONAL LAW 757, 763 (2001).

The third problem is that states often vote for General Assembly resolutions to embellish their image or curry favor with other states, without the expectation that their votes will be deemed acceptance of a new
rule of law. For example, the United States initially opposed the draft of
General Assembly Resolution 1803, which mandated "appropriate compensation" following an expropriation, because the United States felt
that the correct standard should be "prompt, adequate, and effective"
compensation. Yet, the United States ultimately voted in favor of the
resolution in a spirit of compromise.[91] ICJ Judge Stephen Schwebel has
referred to this type of practice as "fake consensus."[92]

The fourth problem is that even if statements and votes in the
General Assembly can qualify as either state practice or manifestations of *opinio juris*, counting the same action as both presents a
skewed picture. Related to this, the fifth problem with an approach
that focuses exclusively on words contained in nonbinding General
Assembly resolutions is "that it is grown like a flower in a hot-house
and that it is anything but sure that such creatures will survive in the
much rougher climate of actual state practice."[93] Elsewhere I have
argued that outside situations covered by treaties with a "prosecute or
extradite" requirement, the so-called duty to prosecute crimes against
humanity, recognized in nonbinding General Assembly resolutions, is a

---

[91] *Banco Nacional de Cuba v. Chase Manhattan Bank*, 638 F.2d, 875, 890 (2d Cir. 1981)
(Opining that General Assembly Resolutions "are of considerable interest" but they
"do not have the force of law," the Court held that expropriation requires "prompt,
adequate, and effective compensation" rather than the standard of "appropriate
compensation" reflected in GA Res. 1803).

[92] Stephen Schwebel, *The Effect of Resolutions of the U.N. General Assembly on
Customary International Law*, 73 PROC. OF THE AM. SOC'Y OF INT'L L. 301, 308
(1979). Schwebel has observed that members of the UN "often vote casually.... States
often don't meaningfully support what a resolution says and they almost always do
not mean that the resolution is law. This may be as true or truer in the case of unanimously adopted resolutions as in the case of majority-adopted resolutions. It may be
truer still of resolutions adopted by consensus." *Id.* at 302.

[93] BRUNO SIMMA, INTERNATIONAL HUMAN RIGHTS AND GENERAL INTERNATIONAL
LAW: A COMPARATIVE ANALYSIS 217 (1995).

chimera.[94] A "rule" that is based only on General Assembly resolutions is unlikely to achieve substantial compliance in the real world and therefore will ultimately undermine rather than strengthen the rule of law. As Professor Roberts puts it, "deducing modern custom purely from *opinio juris* can create utopian laws that cannot regulate reality."[95]

On the other hand, General Assembly resolutions share with treaties the advantage of being written documents whose contents can be expressed with precision. While it is a radical position to argue that such resolutions constitute autonomous sources of international law, few scholars would dispute that General Assembly resolutions can codify and elucidate existing rules or inspire future development of customary international law in the same way that a multinational treaty can. More controversial is the question of whether the adoption of General Assembly resolutions can play a role in crystallizing emerging rules of customary international law[96] – a phenomenon colorfully described by Professor David Koplow of Georgetown as "helping to midwife the development of new norms of customary international law."[97] In the words of the Institute of International Law, "where a rule of customary law is (merely) emerging or there is still some doubt as to its status,

---

[94] Michael P. Scharf, *Swapping Amnesty for Peace: Was There a Duty to Prosecute International Crimes in Haiti?* 31 TEXAS INT'L. L. J. 1, 41 (1996) (citing examples of adverse state practice where amnesty is traded for peace, thus disproving the existence of a customary rule requiring prosecution in the absence of a treaty with a prosecute or extradite provision).

[95] Anthea E. Roberts, *Traditional and Modern Approaches to Customary International Law: A Reconciliation*, 95 AMERICAN JOURNAL OF INTERNATIONAL LAW 757 (2001). Similarly, Niels Petersen of the Max Planck Institute has said that the reason for requiring practice as a constituent element of customary law is that "law should not consist of abstract, utopian norms, but rather be affiliated with social reality." Niels Peterson, *Customary Law without Custom? Rules, Principles, and the Role of State Practice in International Norm Creation*, 23 AMERICAN UNIVERSITY INTERNATIONAL LAW REVIEW 301 (2008).

[96] J. Charney, *Universal International Law*, 87 AMERICAN JOURNAL OF INTERNATIONAL LAW 529, 547 (1993).

[97] David Kaplow, *International Legal Standards and the Weaponization of Outer Space*, in SPACE: THE NEXT GENERATION – CONFERENCE REPORT, March 31–April 1, 2008, UNITED NATIONS INSTITUTE FOR DISARMAMENT RESEARCH (2008), at 162.

a unanimous resolution can consolidate the custom and remove doubts which might have existed."[98]

While some scholars have argued that "customary law without custom (practice) is a contradiction in terms," the International Law Association has pointed out that since statements are a form of state practice, how a state votes and how it explains its vote in the General Assembly is a form of practice that can generate customary law.[99] And if emergent practice exists outside the resolution, the adoption of the resolution can serve as a collective expression of *opinio juris* that can crystallize the rule. In either case, "if governments choose to take their formal stance by means of a General Assembly resolution, there is no *a priori* reason why this should not count."[100] Consistent with this, in the *Legality of the Threat or Use of Nuclear Weapons* Advisory Opinion, the International Court of Justice noted "that General Assembly resolutions, even if they are not binding, may sometimes have normative value."[101]

In deciding whether to treat a particular General Assembly resolution as evidence of an emergent rule of customary international law, the International Court of Justice has stated that "it is necessary to look at its content and the conditions of its adoption."[102] In examining these factors, courts often consider the type of resolution to be significant. General Assembly resolutions fall within a spectrum, from mere "recommendations" (usually given little weight) to "Declarations" (used to impart increased solemnity) to "affirmations" (used to indicate codification or crystallization of law).[103] Courts also consider the words used in the

---

[98] 62-II *Yearbook of the Institute of International Law* (1982), at Conclusion 14.

[99] REPORT OF THE INTERNATIONAL LAW ASSOCIATION, COMMITTEE ON FORMATION OF CUSTOMARY (GENERAL) INTERNATIONAL LAW, LONDON CONFERENCE (2000), at 41.

[100] *Id.* at 63.

[101] *Legality of the Threat or Use of Nuclear Weapons*, ICJ Reports 1996, p. 226.

[102] *Legality of the Threat or Use of Nuclear Weapons*, ICJ Reports 1996, pp. 254–5.

[103] Office of International Standards and Legal Affairs, General Introduction to the Standard-Setting Instruments of UNESCO, Recommendations, available at: http://portal.unesco.org/en/ev.php-url_ID=237772&URL_DO=DO_Topic&URL_

resolution, for example, language of firm obligation versus aspiration.[104] In the same way that the amount of practice required to modify or overturn an existing rule will be greater than in cases where the matter has not previously been the subject of specific regulation in international law, General Assembly resolutions addressing "virgin territory" are better candidates for becoming law than those that counter existing rules.[105]

Another important consideration is the vote outcome. While resolutions passed unanimously or by sizable majorities could potentially have a law-generating effect, the existence of significant dissent, numerous abstentions, or even the objection of a handful of states that play an important part in the activities in question would prevent the crystallization from taking place.[106] While one might be tempted to treat consensus resolutions (adopted without an actual vote) the same as those adopted unanimously, consensus resolutions may be discounted because countries often are pressured to remain silent (even if they have objections) so as not to break consensus.[107] The International Court of Justice has also indicated that if a state expressly mentions, while voting for a particular General Assembly resolution, that it regards the text as being merely a political statement without legal content, then that resolution may not be invoked against it.[108] For these reasons, fears that conferring upon General Assembly resolutions a role in the formation of customary

---

Sectrion+201.html#4; see also Noelle Lenoir, *Universal Declaration on the Human Genome and Human Rights: The First Legal and Ethical Framework at the Global Level*, 30 COLUM. HUM. RTS. L. REV. 537, 551 (1999); Major Robert A. Ramey, *Armed Conflict on the Final Frontier: The Law of War in Space*, 48 A.F.L. REV. 1, 110n485 (2000).

[104] Robert Rosenstock, *The Declaration of Principles of International Law Concerning Friendly Relations: A Survey*, 65 AM. J. INT'L L. 713, 715–16 (1971).

[105] REPORT OF THE INTERNATIONAL LAW ASSOCIATION, COMMITTEE ON FORMATION OF CUSTOMARY (GENERAL) INTERNATIONAL LAW, LONDON CONFERENCE (2000), at 65.

[106] *Legality of the Threat or Use of Nuclear Weapons*, 1996 I.C.J. 226, 255.

[107] Stephen Schwebel, *The Effect of Resolutions of the U.N. General Assembly on Customary International Law* 73 PROC. OF THE AM. SOC'Y OF INT'L L. 301, 302 (1979).

[108] *Military and Paramilitary Activities (Nicar. v. U.S.)*, 1986 I.C.J. 106–7 (June 27).

law will transform the General Assembly into a world legislature and lead to tyranny of the majority are misplaced.

In the *Nicaragua* case, the International Court of Justice appears to have treated General Assembly Resolution 2625, the *Declaration of Principles of International Law concerning Friendly Relations and Co-operation among States,* as a resolution that generated customary international law. The Court stated that "the effect of consent to the text of such resolutions cannot be understood as merely that of a 'reiteration or elucidation' of the treaty commitment undertaken in the Charter. On the contrary, it may be understood as an acceptance of the validity of the rule or set of rules declared by the resolutions by themselves."[109]

In the TOPCO arbitration, the international arbitral panel held that a General Assembly resolution can declare international law if four conditions are met: First, the resolution must be "accepted" by all of the groups of states concerned. Second, acceptance must be demonstrated not only by the votes of the states in the General Assembly, but also by the conforming practice of those same states. Third, the state against whom enforcement is sought must not have objected to the resolution at the time of its adoption. And fourth, a resolution adopted without universal support cannot replace an existing rule of customary international law.[110]

The position of United States courts on the treatment of General Assembly resolutions, on the other hand, has been mixed. In *Filartiga v. Pena-Irala,* the United States Court of Appeals for the Second Circuit based its holding that torture abroad was a tort under international law, actionable in the United States, on General Assembly resolutions rather than state practice, which the court conceded was mixed.[111] Twenty-three

---

[109] *Nicaragua* case, ICJ Reports 1986, p. 14, 990100, para. 188.

[110] Dispute between Texaco Oversees Petroleum Co. and the Government of the Libyan Arab Republic (Compensation for Nationalized Property), 17 INTERNATIONAL LEGAL MATERIALS 1 (1978).

[111] *Filartiga v. Pena-Irala,* 630 F.2d 876 (1980). The Court appears to have been particularly swayed by the affidavit filed in the case by Professor Richard Falk, which

years later, the Second Circuit stated in *Flores v. S. Peru Copper Co.* that resolutions of the General Assembly "are not proper sources of customary international law because they are merely aspirational and were never intended to be binding on member States of the United Nations."[112]

The Sliding Scale Theory

Professor Frederic Kirgis suggests that there is a "sliding scale" relation between the amount of practice and *opinio juris* needed to produce a rule of customary international law.[113] The greater the quantity of concordant practice, he argues, the less the need for evidence of *opinio juris*. "At the other end of the scale, a clearly demonstrated *opinio juris* establishes a customary rule without much (or any) affirmative action showing that governments are consistently behaving in accordance with the asserted rule."[114] Professor Anthea Roberts criticizes Kirgis's concept because it tends to overemphasize one component at the expense of the other, potentially justifying instant customary law based solely on unanimously adopted General Assembly resolutions.[115]

Professor Mendelson believes that Kirgis's sliding scale concept is particularly apt for areas not specifically regulated in international law. Citing the UN General Assembly resolutions on the rules governing

asserted that a consensus of states can generate new norms of customary international law through the formal procedures of the United Nations. Affidavit of Richard Anderson Falk, included in Exhibit E, Affidavits of International Law Experts, *Filartiga v. Pena-Irala*, No. 79-C-917 (E.D.N.Y. 1979).

[112] *Flores v. S. Peru Copper Co.* 414 F. 3d 233, 259 (2d Cir. 2003).

[113] Frederic. L. Kirgis, Jr., *Custom on a Sliding Scale*, 81 AMERICAN JOURNAL OF INTERNATIONAL LAW 146, 149 (1987). For other scholars who have endorsed Kirgis's sliding scale concept, see John Tasioulas, *In Defense of Relative Normativity: Communitarian Values and the* Nicaragua *Case*, 16 OXFORD JOURNAL OF LEGAL STUDIES 85, 109 (1996); MAURICE H. MENDELSON, THE FORMATION OF CUSTOMARY INTERNATIONAL LAW 386 (1998).

[114] Frederic L. Kirgis Jr., *Custom on a Sliding Scale*, 81 AMERICAN JOURNAL OF INTERNATIONAL LAW 146, 149 (1987).

[115] Anthea E. Roberts, *Traditional and Modern Approaches to Customary International Law: A Reconciliation*, 95 AMERICAN JOURNAL OF INTERNATIONAL LAW 757, 774 (2001).

exploration of outer space, Mendelson states that in such areas "the solemn enunciation of rules by which States as a whole intend to conduct themselves in the future should be binding."[116] Echoing this view, referring to the legal status of General Assembly Resolution 95 (I) endorsing the Nuremberg Principles, the Israeli Supreme Court stated in the 1962 *Eichmann* case that "if fifty-eight nations [i.e., all the members of the UN at the time] unanimously agree on a statement of existing law, it would seem that such a declaration would be all but conclusive evidence of such a rule, and agreement by a large majority would have great value in determining what is existing law."[117]

The Grotian Moment Concept

Traditionally, customary international law was viewed as a slow process involving repeated acts over many years. French jurisprudence generally required the passage of at least forty years for the emergence of an international custom, while German doctrine generally required thirty years.[118]

Professor Francesco Parisi of University of Minnesota Law School has stated that "customary rules have evolved from both immemorial practice and a single act."[119] But if customary international law is in fact a product of claim and response (as characterized by Myers McDougal), by necessity there must be more than a single act and some time must elapse before a practice becomes habitual among states. Take the

---

[116] Maurice H. Mendelson, The Formation of Customary International Law 386 (1998).

[117] *Attorney-General of Israel v. Eichmann*, 36 I.L.R. 277 (29 May 1962) [*hereinafter* Eichmann II], para. 11.

[118] Francesco Parisi, *The Formation of Customary Law*, Paper Presented at the 96th Annual Conference of the American Political Science Association, August 31, 2000, at 5; G. I. Tunkin, *Remarks on the Judicial Nature of Customary Norms in International Law* 49 California Law Review 419 (1961).

[119] Franscesco Parisi, *The Formation of Customary Law*, Paper presented at the 96th Annual Conference of the American Political Science Association, August 31, 2000, at 5.

example of sovereign rights over the continental shelf, which is the subject of Chapter 5. President Truman proclaimed the continental shelf concept in 1945; the 1958 Geneva Convention on the Continental Shelf recognized this entitlement on the part of coastal states, and in 1969 the International Court of Justice acknowledged that the principle was part of customary international law in the *North Sea Continental Shelf* cases.[120] Somewhere during those twenty-four years between 1945 and 1969, the coastal states' rights over the continental shelf had crystallized into customary international law, but it would be difficult to pinpoint the exact moment that occurred.

In domestic law, we know how many stages legislation needs to go through and how many votes are needed at each stage. Likewise for international conventions, we know what formalities must be accomplished for a text to become a treaty, and how many ratifications are needed to bring it into force. In contrast, there exists no agreed-upon general formula for identifying how many states are needed and how much time must transpire to generate a rule of customary international law.[121] Yet, because lawyers yearn for certainty and predictability, they are understandably suspicious of the "I know it when I see it" type of answer.[122]

Professor Mendelson answers this quandary with the metaphor of building a house, pointing out that it is often difficult or impossible to say exactly when construction has reached the point that we can conclude a house has been created. It is neither when the first foundation stone is laid nor when the last brush of paint has been applied, but somewhere between the two. "Do we have to wait for the roof to go on, for

---

[120] *North Sea Continental Shelf* cases, ICJ Reports 1969, p. 3.
[121] ANTHONY A. D'AMATO, THE CONCEPT OF CUSTOM IN INTERNATIONAL LAW 58 (1971) (noting that there is no consensus as to how much time a practice must be maintained to evidence the existence of a custom); G. I. Tunkin, *Remarks on the Juridical Nature of Customary Norms of International Law*, 49 CALIFORNIA LAW REVIEW 419, 420 (1961) (arguing that the element of time is not dispositive as to whether a customary rule exists).
[122] MAURICE H. MENDELSON, THE FORMATION OF CUSTOMARY INTERNATIONAL LAW 172 (1998).

the windows to be put in, or for all of the utilities to be installed? So it is with customary law."[123] Rarely does a decision maker need to know the exact moment that a practice has crystallized into a binding rule, or, as Mendelson puts it, "precisely when the fruit became ripe." Instead, he concludes, "we are more interested in knowing, when we bite it, if it is now ripe or still too hard or sour."[124]

In this sense, the story recounted in this book's Introduction about the Prosecution's brief arguing that Joint Criminal Enterprise (JCE) liability existed in customary international law in 1975 is an exceptional case. While it is widely accepted that JCE liability constitutes customary international law today, proving that the JCE had crystallized prior to 1975 (when the Cambodia atrocities were committed) presented a fairly unique challenge given that the state practice prior to 1975 was limited to the establishment of the Nuremberg Tribunal, the judgment of the Tribunal, and the General Assembly Resolution affirming the Nuremberg principles.

Some scholars have maintained that "requiring repeated practice is too clumsy and slow to accommodate the fast-paced" needs of the law in modern times.[125] But experience has shown that "in rapidly evolving sectors of international law the customary process can produce rules in a timely and adequate manner."[126]

The various approaches to customary international law discussed previously focus on the ingredients of state practice and *opinio juris* in a narrow fashion, counting the numbers of states that favor or oppose a new rule and seeking to identify the positions of specially affected states. Though usually overlooked, context can be an important third ingredient

---

[123] Maurice H. Mendelson, The Formation of Customary International Law 175 (1998).

[124] Maurice H. Mendelson, The Formation of Customary International Law 176 (1998).

[125] Anthea E. Roberts, *Traditional and Modern Approaches to Customary International Law: A Reconciliation*, 95 American Journal of International Law 757, 767 (2001) (citing several scholars).

[126] *Id.* at para. 91.

that explains the sometimes accelerated formation of customary international law. Professor Parisi argues that "a flexible time requirement is
particularly necessary in situations of rapid flux."[127] Periods of fundamental change have sparked "Cambrian explosions" of customary international law, which this author labels "Grotian Moments."

The term "Cambrian explosion" describes the geologically sudden appearance of multicellular animals in the fossil record during the
Cambrian period of geologic time, a narrow window lasting no more
than 5 million years, representing an extremely small fraction of the
earth's biological history. During this period, forty-one separate phyla
first made their appearance, and almost all the major innovations in
the basic architecture of living forms occurred. Because of the sudden-
ness of the appearance of diverse animal life in the Cambrian period,
the "Cambrian explosion" has now earned titles such as "The Big Bang
of Animal Evolution" (*Scientific American*), "Evolution's Big Bang"
(*Science*), and "Biological Big Bang" (*Science News*).[128]

The Grotian Moment concept is apt for capturing the equivalent of
Cambrian explosions in customary international law that occur dur-
ing times of fundamental change. As *The Max Planck Encyclopedia of
Public International Law* observes,

> recent developments show that customary rules may come into exis-
> tence rapidly. This can be due to the urgency of coping with new
> developments of technology, such as, for instance, drilling technol-
> ogy as regards the rules on the continental shelf, or space technol-
> ogy as regards the rule on the freedom of extra-atmospheric space.
> Or it may be due to the urgency of coping with widespread senti-
> ments of moral outrage regarding crimes committed in conflicts such
> as those in Rwanda and Yugoslavia that brought about the rapid

---

[127] Franscesco Parisi, *The Formation of Customary Law*, Paper presented at the 96th
Annual Conference of the American Political Science Association, August 31, 2000,
at 6.

[128] *See* STEPHEN C. MEYER, P. A. NELSON, AND PAUL CHIEN, THE CAMBRIAN
EXPLOSION: BIOLOGY'S BIG BANG (2001), at n. 6.

formation of a set of customary rules concerning crimes committed in internal conflicts.[129]

The following chapters seek to illuminate the important role of a context of fundamental change in the accelerated formation of customary international law through an examination of six case studies: the customary international law that arose out of the Nuremberg trial (Chapter 4), the law governing the continental shelf (Chapter 5), the advent of space law (Chapter 6), the law of war applicable to internal armed conflict developed by the Yugoslavia Tribunal (Chapter 7), the legality of humanitarian intervention in the aftermath of the 1999 NATO bombing campaign in Serbia (Chapter 8), and the right to use force in self-defense against nonstate actors in the aftermath of the terrorist attacks of September 11, 2001 (Chapter 9).

[129] Tullio Treves, *Customary International Law*, MAX PLANCK ENCYCLOPEDIA OF PUBLIC INTERNATIONAL LAW (2012), at para. 24, available at: www.mpepil.com (last accessed February 9, 2013); accord REPORT OF THE INTERNATIONAL LAW ASSOCIATION, COMMITTEE ON FORMATION OF CUSTOMARY (GENERAL) INTERNATIONAL LAW, LONDON CONFERENCE (2000), at 20.

4　Nuremberg

THIS CHAPTER EXAMINES WHETHER THE PARADIGM-
shifting nature of the Nuremberg precedent, and the universal and unqualified endorsement of the Nuremberg
Principles by the UN General Assembly in 1946, constituted a Grotian
Moment, resulting in accelerated formation of customary international
law related to modes of responsibility and universal jurisdiction.

Was Nuremberg a Grotian Moment?

Nearly everyone has a passing familiarity with the events that prompted
the formation of the Nuremberg Tribunal in 1945. Between 1933 and
1940, the Nazi regime established concentration camps where Jews,
Communists, and opponents of the regime were incarcerated without
trial; it progressively prohibited Jews from engaging in employment and
participating in various areas of public life, stripped them of citizenship,
and made marriage or sexual intimacy between Jews and German citizens a criminal offense; it forcibly annexed Austria and Czechoslovakia;
it invaded and occupied Poland, Denmark, Norway, Luxembourg, the
Netherlands, Belgium, and France; and then it set in motion "the final
solution to the Jewish problem" by establishing death camps such as
Auschwitz and Treblinka, where six million Jews were exterminated.[1]

---

[1] MICHAEL P. SCHARF, BALKAN JUSTICE 3–4 (1997).

As Allied forces pressed into Germany and an end to the fighting in Europe came into sight, the Allied powers faced the challenge of deciding what to do with the surviving Nazi leaders who were responsible for these atrocities. Holding an international trial, however, was not their first preference. The British and Soviet governments initially advocated summary execution for the Nazi leaders, but the United States persuaded them to establish the world's first international criminal tribunal for four reasons: First, judicial proceedings would avert future hostilities, which would likely result from the execution, absent a trial, of German leaders. Second, legal proceedings would call German atrocities to the attention of all parts of the world, thereby legitimizing Allied conduct during and after the war. Third, they would individualize guilt by identifying specific perpetrators instead of leaving Germany with a sense of collective guilt. Finally, such a trial would permit the Allied powers, and the world, to exact a penalty from the Nazi leadership rather than from Germany's civilian population.[2]

The charter that established the Nuremberg Tribunal, and set forth its subject matter jurisdiction and procedures was negotiated by the United States, France, the United Kingdom, and the Soviet Union from June 26–August 8, 1945.[3] Nineteen other states signed onto the charter, rendering the Nuremberg Tribunal a truly international judicial institution,[4] though it was undoubtedly a victor's tribunal. The trial of twenty-two high-ranking Nazi leaders commenced on November 20, 1945, and ten months later on October 1, 1946, the tribunal issued its judgment, convicting nineteen of the defendants and sentencing eleven to death by

---

[2] *Id.* at 5.

[3] London Agreement of August 8, 1945, the Charter of the International Military Tribunal, and the Nuremberg Tribunal's Rules of Procedure are reproduced in 2 VIRGINIA MORRIS AND MICHAEL SCHARF AN INSIDER'S GUIDE TO THE INTERNATIONAL CRIMINAL TRIBUNAL FOR THE FORMER YUGOSLAVIA 675–91 (1995).

[4] Greece, Denmark, Yugoslavia, the Netherlands, Czechoslovakia, Poland, Belgium, Ethiopia, Australia, Honduras, Norway, Panama, Luxembourg, Haiti, New Zealand, India, Venezuela, Uruguay, and Paraguay.

hanging. The judgment of the Nuremberg Tribunal paved the way for the trial of more than a thousand other German political and military officers, businessmen, doctors, and jurists under Control Council Law No. 10 by military tribunals in occupied zones in Germany and in the liberated or Allied nations.[5]

While the Nuremberg trials were not without criticism, there can be no question that Nuremberg represented a paradigm-shifting development in international law. The United Nations' International Law Commission (ILC) has recognized that the Nuremberg Charter, Control Council Law Number 10, and the post–World War II war crimes trials gave birth to the entire international paradigm of individual criminal responsibility. Prior to Nuremberg, the only subjects of international law were states, and what a state did to its own citizens within its own borders was its own business. Nuremberg fundamentally altered that conception. "International law now protects individual citizens against abuses of power by their governments [and] imposes individual liability on government officials who commit grave war crimes, genocide, and crimes against humanity."[6] The ILC has described the principle of individual responsibility and punishment for crimes under international law recognized at Nuremberg as the "cornerstone of international criminal law" and the "enduring legacy of the Charter and Judgment of the Nuremberg Tribunal."[7]

Importantly, on December 11, 1946, in one of the first actions of the newly formed United Nations, the UN General Assembly unanimously affirmed the principles from the Nuremberg Charter and judgments in Resolution 95(I).[8] This General Assembly resolution had all

---

[5] MICHAEL P. SCHARF, BALKAN JUSTICE, 10 (1997).

[6] Anne-Marie Slaughter and William Burke-White, *An International Constitutional Moment*, 43 HARV. INT'L L. J. 1, 13 (2002).

[7] See, *Report of the International Law Commission on the Work of Its Forty-Eighth Session*, May 6–July 26, 1996, Official Records of the General Assembly, Fifty-First Session, Supplement No. 10, at p. 19, available at: http://www.un.org/law.ilc/index. htm (last accessed February 9, 2013).

[8] Affirmation of the Principles of International Law Recognized by the Charter of the Nuremberg Tribunal, G.A. Res. 95(I), UN GAOR, 1st Sess., U.N. Doc A/236,

the attributes of a resolution entitled to great weight as a declaration of customary international law: it was labeled an "affirmation" of legal principles; it dealt with inherently legal questions; it was adopted by a unanimous vote; and none of the members expressed the position that it was merely a political statement.[9]

Despite the fact that Nuremberg and its Control Council Law Number 10 progeny consisted of only a few dozen cases tried by a handful of courts over a period of just three years, the International Court of Justice,[10] the International Criminal Tribunal for the Former Yugoslavia,[11]

December 11, 1946, pt. 2, at 1144, available at: http://untreaty.un.org/cod/avl/ha/ga_95-I/ga_95-I.html (last accessed February 9, 2013). The resolution states in whole:

The General Assembly,

Recognizes the obligation laid upon it by Article 13, paragraph 1, sub-paragraph a, of the Charter, to initiate studies and make recommendations for the purpose of encouraging the progressive development of international law and its codification;

Takes note of the Agreement for the establishment of an International Military Tribunal for the prosecution and punishment of the major war criminals of the European Axis signed in London on 8 August 1945, and of the Charter annexed thereto, and of the fact that similar principles have been adopted in the Charter of the International Military Tribunal for the trial of the major war criminals in the Far East, proclaimed at Tokyo on 19 January 1946;

Therefore,

Affirms the principles of international law recognized by the Charter of the Nuremberg Tribunal and the judgment of the Tribunal;

Directs the Committee on the codification of international law established by the resolution of the General Assembly of 11 December 1946, to treat as a matter of primary importance plans for the formulation, in the context of a general codification of offenses against the peace and security of mankind, or of an International Criminal Code, of the principles recognized in the Charter of the Nuremberg Tribunal and in the judgment of the Tribunal.

[9] See *supra* Chapter 3, notes 102–108.
[10] Legal Consequences of the Construction of a Wall in Occupied Palestinian Territory, Advisory Opinion, 2004 I.C.J. 136, 172 (July 9).
[11] ICTY (*Tadic*, Opinion and Judgment, Trial Chamber, May 7, 1997, para. 623; and *Tadic*, Decision on the Defense Motion for Interlocutory Appeal on Jurisdiction, Appeals Chamber, October 2, 1995, para. 141).

the European Court of Human Rights,[12] and several domestic courts[13] have cited the General Assembly resolution affirming the principles of the Nuremberg Charter and judgments as an authoritative declaration of customary international law. As mentioned in Chapter 3, in reference to General Assembly Resolution 95 (I), the Israeli Supreme Court stated that "if fifty-eight nations [i.e., all the members of the UN at the time] unanimously agree on a statement of existing law, it would seem that such a declaration would be all but conclusive evidence of such a rule, and agreement by a large majority would have great value in determining what is existing law."[14]

Nuremberg, then, constitutes a prototypical Grotian Moment. The tribunal's formation was in response to the most heinous atrocity in the history of humankind – the extermination of six million Jews and several million other "undesirables" by the Nazi regime. From a conventional view of customary international law formation, the amount of state practice was quite limited, consisting only of the negotiation of the Nuremberg Charter by four states, its accession by nineteen others, the judgment of the tribunal, and a General Assembly resolution endorsing

[12] The European Court of Human Rights recognized the "universal validity" of the Nuremberg principles in *Kolk and Kislyiy v. Estonia*, in which it stated: "Although the Nuremberg Tribunal was established for trying the major war criminals of the European Axis countries for the offences they had committed before or during the Second World War, the Court notes that the universal validity of the principles concerning crimes against humanity was subsequently confirmed by, *inter alia*, resolution 95 of the United Nations General Assembly (11 December 1946) and later by the International Law Commission." *Kolk and Kislyiy v. Estonia*, Decision on Admissibility, January 17, 2006.

[13] The General Assembly resolution Affirming the Nuremberg Principles has been cited as evidence of customary international law in cases in Canada, Bosnia, France, and Israel. See *R. v. Finta*, Supreme Court of Canada (1994), 1 S.C.R. 701; *Prosecutor v. Ivica Vrdoljak*, Court of Bosnia and Herzegovina, July 10, 2008); Leila Sadat Wexler, *The Interpretation of the Nuremberg Principles by the French Court of Cassation: From Touvier to Barbie and Back Again*, 32 COLUM. J. TRANSNAT'L L., 289 (1994) (summarizing *Touvier* and *Barbie* cases in French courts).

[14] *Attorney-General of Israel v Eichmann*, 36 I.L.R. 277 (May 29, 1962) [*hereinafter Eichmann II*], para. 11.

(though not enumerating) its principles. Moreover, the period from the end of the war to the General Assembly endorsement of the Nuremberg Principles was a mere year, a drop in the bucket compared to the amount of time it ordinarily takes to crystallize customary international law. Yet, despite the limited state practice and minimal time, the International Court of Justice, European Court of Human Rights, and four international criminal tribunals have confirmed that the Nuremberg Charter and judgment immediately ripened into customary international law.

The Grotian Moment concept rationalizes this outcome. Nuremberg reflected a novel solution to unprecedented atrocity in the context of history's most devastating war. Beyond the Nuremberg trial, there was a great need for universal implementation of the Nuremberg Principles. Yet, on the eve of the Cold War, it was clear that a widely ratified multilateral convention would not be a practicable near-term solution. In fact, it would take half a century before the international community was able to conclude a widely ratified treaty transforming the Nuremberg model into a permanent international criminal court. It is this context of fundamental change and great need for a timely response that explains how Nuremberg could so quickly and universally be accepted as customary international law.

Did Nuremberg Establish JCE as Customary International Law?

What are the consequences of characterizing Nuremberg as a Grotian Moment, thereby recognizing the Nuremberg Principles as having rapidly crystallized into customary international law? Some aspects of the Nuremberg Principles have been uncontroversial, such as recognition that individuals can be responsible for violations of international law and the rejection of the act of state and obedience to orders defenses.[15]

---

[15] In an effort to flesh out what the General Assembly had endorsed in 1946, in 1950, the International Law Commission enumerated the following "Nuremberg Principles":

Principle I: Any person who commits an act which constitutes a crime under international law is responsible therefore and liable to punishment.

Others have been subject to great debate, such as whether the customary international law generated from Nuremberg provides a basis for the theory of liability known as Joint Criminal Enterprise (JCE), which has been applied by modern international criminal tribunals.

The Nuremberg Charter and judgment never specifically mention the term "Joint Criminal Enterprise." Yet, a close analysis of the Nuremberg

Principle II: The fact that internal law does not impose a penalty for an act which constitutes a crime under international law does not relieve the person who committed the act from responsibility under international law.

Principle III: The fact that a person who committed an act which constitutes a crime under international law acted as Head of State or responsible Government official does not relieve him from responsibility under international law.

Principle IV: The fact that a person acted pursuant to order of his Government or of a superior does not relieve him from responsibility under international law, provided a moral choice was in fact possible to him.

Principle V: Any person charged with a crime under international law has the right to a fair trial on the facts and law.

Principle VI: The crimes hereinafter set out are punishable as crimes under international law:

(a) Crimes against peace:

(i) Planning, preparation, initiation or waging of a war of aggression or a war in violation of international treaties, agreements or assurances; (ii) Participation in a common plan or conspiracy for the accomplishment of any of the acts mentioned under (i).

(b) War crimes:

Violations of the laws or customs of war include, but are not limited to, murder, ill-treatment or deportation to slave-labour or for any other purpose of civilian population of or in occupied territory, murder or ill-treatment of prisoners of war, of persons on the seas, killing of hostages, plunder of public or private property, wanton destruction of cities, towns, or villages, or devastation not justified by military necessity.

(c) Crimes against humanity:

Murder, extermination, enslavement, deportation and other inhuman acts done against any civilian population, or persecutions on political, racial or religious grounds, when such acts are done or such persecutions are carried on in execution of or in connexion with any crime against peace or any war crime.

Principle VII: Complicity in the commission of a crime against peace, a war crime, or a crime against humanity as set forth in Principle VI is a crime under international law.

The ILC's Nuremberg Principles are available at: http://www.icrc.org/ihl.nsf/full/390 (last accessed February 9, 2013).

judgment and the holdings of several Control Council Law Number 10 cases[16] reveal that the Nuremberg Tribunal and its progeny applied a concept analogous to JCE, which they called the "common plan" or "common design" mode of liability.

Prior to Nuremberg, liability for participation in a common plan had existed in some form in the national legislation or jurisprudence of a handful of common law and civil law countries since the nineteenth century. Modes of coperpetration similar to JCE included conspiracy,[17] the felony murder doctrine,[18] the concept of *association de malfaiteurs*,[19] and numerous other doctrines of coperpetration.[20]

---

[16] This law was based on the Nuremberg Charter and governed subsequent war crimes trials. Control Council Law Number 10, in *Official Gazette of the Control Council for Germany* (1946), Vol. 3, at 50. Because Control Council Law Number 10 sought to "establish a uniform legal basis in Germany for the prosecution of war criminals," Article I of the law explicitly incorporated the Nuremberg Tribunal Charter as an "integral part" of the Law. Pursuant to Article I, all the military commissions (U.S., British, Canadian, and Australian) adopted implementing regulations, rendering a defendant responsible under the principle of "concerted criminal action" for the crimes of any other member of that "unit or group." UN War Crimes Commission, *XV Law Reports of Trials of War Criminals* 92 (1949).

[17] See *Pinkerton v. U.S.*, 328 U.S. 640 (1946) (establishing the Pinkerton rule, in which a conspirator can be convicted of the reasonably foreseeable consequence of the unlawful agreement).

[18] The Felony murder doctrine, first enunciated by Lord Coke in 1797, has been applied in the United Kingdom, the United States, New Zealand, and Australia. Antonio Cassese, *International Criminal Law* (2nd ed., 2008), at 202. The rule allows a defendant to be "held accountable for a crime because it was a natural and probable consequence of the crime which that person intended to aid or encourage." WAYNE LAFAVE & AUSTIN SCOTT, CRIMINAL LAW (1972), at p. 515–16.

[19] Professor van Sliedregt notes that the concept of "association de malfaiteurs," which has been used in France and the Netherlands to deal with mob violence by overcoming causality problems, "inspired the drafters of the Nuremberg Statute to penalize membership of a criminal organization." Elies van Sliedregt, *Joint Criminal Enterprise as a Pathway to Convicting Individuals for Genocide*, 5 JOURNAL OF INT'L CRIM. J. 184, 199 (2006).

[20] The Indian Penal Code of 1860 imposed individual liability for unlawful acts committed by several persons in furtherance of a common plan. Walter Morgan and A. G. MacPherson, *Indian Penal Code* (XLV, 1860) (London: GC Hay, 1861). Similarly, Section 61(2) of the *Canadian Criminal Code* of 1893 punishes persons who "form

The drafters of the Nuremberg Charter, like the drafters of the Yugoslavia Tribunal (ICTY) Statute forty-eight years later, recognized that the unique nature of atrocity crimes justifies and requires a correspondingly unique mode of liability. This was explained by the Appeals Chamber of the ICTY in the *Tadic* case:

> Most of the time these crimes do not result from the criminal propensity of single individuals but constitute manifestations of collective criminality: the crimes are often carried out by groups of individuals acting in pursuance of a common criminal design. Although only some members of the group may physically perpetrate the criminal act (murder, extermination, wanton destruction of cities, towns or villages, etc.), the participation and contribution of the other members of the group is often vital in facilitating the commission of the offence in question. It follows that the moral gravity of such participation is often no less – or indeed no different – from that of those actually carrying out the acts in question.[21]

This passage has been quoted in a number of subsequent judgments of the ICTY[22] and ICTR.[23] Similarly, Antonio Cassese, former president of the ICTY, opined:

> International crimes such as war crimes, crimes against humanity, genocide, torture, and terrorism share a common feature: they tend

---

a common intention to prosecute any unlawful purpose" and makes each "a party to every offense committed by any one of them in the prosecution of such common purpose." Section 21(2) of the Criminal Code, R.S.C. 1970, C-34.

[21] Tadic Appeals Chamber Judgment, para. 191.

[22] See, e.g., *Prosecutor v. Kvacka et al.*, Appeal Judgment, Case No.IT-98–30/1-A, February 28, 2005, para. 80; *Prosecutor v. Krnojelac*, Appeal Judgment, Case No. IT-97–25-A, September 17, 2003, para. 29; *Prosecutor v. Blagojevic and Jokic*, Trial Judgment, Case. No. IT-02–60-T, January 17, 2005, para. 695.

[23] In *Karemera* the ICTR Trial Chamber articulated a similar rationale for the JCE doctrine:

"To hold criminally liable as a perpetrator only the person who materially performs the criminal act would disregard the role as co-perpetrators of all those who in some way made it possible for the perpetrator physically to carry out that criminal act. At the same time, depending upon the circumstances, to hold the latter liable only as aiders and abettors might understate the degree of their criminal responsibility."

> to be expression of collective criminality, in that they are perpetrated by a multitude of persons, military details, paramilitary units or government officials acting in unison or, in most cases, in pursuance of a policy. When such crimes are committed, it is extremely difficult to pinpoint the specific contribution made by each individual participant in the criminal enterprise or collective crime.... The notion of joint criminal enterprise denotes a mode of criminal liability that appears particularly fit to cover the criminal liability of all participants in a common criminal plan.[24]

Thus, application of common design or JCE liability was seen as justified by both the unique threats posed by organized criminality and the unique challenge of prosecuting such perpetrators.

Consistent with the doctrine's historic origins in an international agreement (the 1945 London Charter establishing the Nuremberg Tribunal) and the jurisprudence of international judicial bodies (the Nuremberg and Control Council Law Number 10 Tribunals), Professor Elies van Sliedregt concludes that "JCE is a merger of common law and civil law. JCE in international law is a unique (*sui generis*) concept in that it combines and mixes two legal cultures and systems."[25] Specifically, the major powers sought to create a scheme in the Nuremberg Charter that would combine the Anglo-American conspiracy doctrine with the approach to co-perpetration in France and the Soviet Union, where conspiracy was not recognized as a crime.[26] Thus, Article 6 of the London Charter implemented a modified form of the initial American proposal to include conspiracy, providing that "leaders, organizers, instigators and

Prosecutor v. Eduard Karemera, Mathieu Ngirumpatse, Joseph Nzirorera and Andre Rwamakuba, Decision on the Preliminary Motions by the Defense Challenging Jurisdiction in Relation to Joint Criminal Enterprise, ICTY Trial Chamber III, Case No. ICTR-98-44-T, May 14, 2004, para. 36.

[24] ANTONIO CASSESE, *INTERNATIONAL CRIMINAL LAW* (2nd ed., 2008), p. 189–91.

[25] Elies van Sliedregt, *Joint Criminal Enterprise as a Pathway to Convicting Individuals of Genocide*, 5 J. INT'L CRIM. JUST. 184, 199 (2007).

[26] Stanislaw Pomorski, *Conspiracy and Criminal Organizations in* GEORGE GINSBURGS & V. N. KUDRIAVTSEV, EDS., THE NUREMBERG TRIAL AND INTERNATIONAL LAW, 213 (1990), p. 216.

accomplices participating in the formulation or *execution of a common plan* or conspiracy to commit any of the foregoing crimes are responsible for all acts performed by any persons in execution of such plan."[27]

During the Nuremberg Trial, Justice Robert Jackson, the chief U.S. negotiator of the Nuremberg Charter and chief U.S. prosecutor at Nuremberg, explained to the tribunal the meaning of "common plan," as distinct from the U.S. concept of conspiracy:

> The Charter did not define responsibility for the acts of others in terms of "conspiracy" alone. The crimes were defined in non-technical but inclusive terms, and embraced formulating and executing a "common plan" as well as participating in a "conspiracy." It was feared that to do otherwise might import into the proceedings technical requirements and limitations which have grown up around the term "conspiracy." There are some divergences between the Anglo-American concept of conspiracy and that of either Soviet, French, or German jurisprudence. It was desired that concrete cases be guided by the broader considerations inherent in the nature of the social problem, rather than controlled by refinements of any local law.[28]

In harmony with this statement, the Nuremberg Tribunal[29] and the Control Council Law Number 10 Tribunals adopted their own version of the "common design or plan" concept, thereby transforming it into what has now become known as the doctrine of JCE. These tribunals found that "the difference between a charge of conspiracy and one of acting in pursuance of a common design is that the first would claim that an agreement to commit offences had been made while the second would allege not only the making of an agreement but the performance

---

[27] Agreement for the Prosecution and Punishment of Major German War Criminals of the European Axis, Art. 6, 59 Stat. 1544, 82 U.N.T.S. 279.

[28] Robert H. Jackson, "The Law under Which Nazi Organizations Are Accused of Being Criminal," argument by Robert H. Jackson, February 28, 1946, reprinted in THE NURNBERG CASE: AS PRESENTED BY ROBERT JACKSON (1971), p. 108.

[29] See *International Military Tribunal Judgment*, in TRIAL OF THE MAJOR WAR CRIMINALS BEFORE THE INTERNATIONAL MILITARY TRIBUNAL, NUREMBERG, Vol. 1 (1947), p. 226.

of acts pursuant to it."[30] In other words, conspiracy is a crime in its own right, while acting in pursuance of a common design or plan, like JCE, is a mode of liability that attaches to substantive offenses. In developing JCE liability from preexisting practices in domestic jurisdictions, the Nuremberg Tribunal declared that its conclusions were made "in accordance with well-settled legal principles, one of the most important of which is that criminal guilt is personal and that mass punishments should be avoided."[31]

The Nuremberg judgment contained several passages that laid the foundation for modern application of JCE. For example, in convicting Albert Speer of offenses associated with enslavement because he contributed to the context that precipitated them, the tribunal stated that although Speer was not "directly concerned with the cruelty in the administration of the slave labor program," he knew of its occurrence. In particular, he was aware that his demands for labor led to "violent methods in recruiting," of which he was thus liable.[32]

While the Nuremberg Tribunal tried the twenty-two highest-ranking surviving members of the Nazi regime, Control Council Law Number 10 was jointly promulgated by the Allied Powers to govern subsequent trials of the next level of suspected German war criminals by U.S., British, Canadian, and Australian military tribunals, as well as German courts, in occupied Germany. Under the authority of Control Council Law Number 10, the tribunals were to follow the charter and jurisprudence of the Nuremberg Tribunal.[33] As such, the case law from those tribunals

[30] *XV Law Reports of Trials of War Criminals 97–98*, UN War Crimes Commission, 1948 (summarizing the jurisprudence of the Nuremberg and Control Council Law Number 10 trials).

[31] International Military Tribunal, Judgment in the Trial of the Major War Criminals before the International Military Tribunal: Nuremberg, November 14, 1945, October 1, 1947, p. 256.

[32] International Military Tribunal, Judgment in the Trial of the Major War Criminals before the International Military Tribunal: Nuremberg, November 14, 1945, October 1, 1947, pp. 332–3.

[33] Control Council Law Number 10, in *Official Gazette of the Control Council for Germany*, 1946, Vol. 3, p. 50.

has been viewed as an authoritative interpretation of the Nuremberg Charter and judgment and a reflection of customary international law.[34]

An analysis of several of the Control Council Law Number 10 cases supports the conclusion that the JCE doctrine was in fact employed by those tribunals in 1946–7. Although the Nuremberg Charter had confined "common plan" liability to crimes against peace, the Control Council Law Number 10 tribunals applied a version of it that they called "common design" to other international crimes.

As recognized by the modern international criminal tribunals, there are three forms of JCE.[35] The first requires proof that the perpetrators shared a common intent to commit the crimes in question. The second imputes such a common intent to the unique circumstances of those involved in running a death or torture camp. The third type (the extended form) is similar to the American felony murder rule, under which a cofelon can be held responsible for the reasonably foreseeable crimes of his confederates. In reaching its conclusion that JCE has existed in customary international law since the Nuremberg judgments, the Appeals Chamber of the Yugoslavia Tribunal in *Tadic* relied partly on ten different post–World War II cases – six regarding JCE I,[36] two

---

[34] *Prosecutor v. Kupreskic*, Judgment, Case No: IT-95–16-A, ICTY Trial Chamber, January 14, 2000, para. 541: "It cannot be gainsaid that great value ought to be attached to decisions of such international criminal courts as the international tribunals of Nuremberg and Tokyo, or to national courts operating by virtue, and on the strength, of Control Council Law Number 10, a legislative act jointly passed in 1945 by the four Occupying Powers and thus reflecting international agreement among the Great Powers on the law applicable to international crimes and the jurisdiction of the courts called upon to rule on those crimes. These courts operated under international instruments laying down provisions that were either declaratory of existing law or which had been gradually transformed into customary international law."

[35] ICTY (*Tadic*, Opinion and Judgment, Trial Chamber, May 7, 1997, para. 623; and *Tadic*, Decision on the Defense Motion for Interlocutory Appeal on Jurisdiction, Appeals Chamber, October 2, 1995, para. 141).

[36] *Trial of Otto Sandrock and Three Others*; *Hoelzer and Others*; *Gustav Alfred Jepsen and Others*; *Franz Schonfeld and Others*; *Feurstein and Others*; *Otto Ohlenforf and Others* (JCE I requires proof that the perpetrators share a common criminal purpose).

regarding JCE II,[37] and two regarding JCE III.[38] Most of these cases were published in summary form in the 1949 Report of the UN War Crimes Commission.[39] All of these cases clarified the meaning of Nuremberg's common plan liability – the forerunner of JCE. Summing up this extensive case law and explaining the difference between common design and simple coperpetration, the UN War Crimes Commission Report states that "the prosecution has the additional task of providing the existence of a common design, [and] once that is proved the prosecution can rely upon the rule which exists in many systems of law that those who take part in a common design to commit an offence which is carried out by one of them are all fully responsible for that offence in the eyes of the criminal law."[40] Consistent with this explanation, the Appeals Chamber of the Yugoslavia Tribunal in the *Milutinovic* case, after considering extensive filings by the parties on whether JCE is part of customary international law, found that JCE and common plan liability are one and the same.[41]

In its 2011 decision in Case 002, the Trial Chamber of the Extraordinary Chambers in the Courts of Cambodia (ECCC) followed its sister tribunals in recognizing that the first and second forms of JCE

---

[37] *Dachau Concentration Camp Case* (Trial of Martin Gottfied Weiss and Thirty-nine Others); the *Belsen Case* (Trial of Josef Kramer and Forty-four Others). (JCE II applies in the setting of concentration camps, where all members of the camp's staff are presumed to share a common criminal purpose).

[38] *Essen Lynching* case; *Borkum Island* case. For JCE III, the Appeals Chamber also cited several unpublished Italian decisions.

[39] Notably, the JCE III *Borkum Island* case was not included in the Report of the UN War Crimes Commission, but the charging instrument, transcript, and other documents of the case have been publicly available from the United States Archives. See Publication Number M1103, "Records of United States Army War Crimes Trials," *United States of America v. Goebel*, et al., February 6–March 21, 1946. In addition, a detailed account and analysis of the *Borkum Island* case was published in 1956 in Maxilimian Koessler, *Borkum Island Tragedy and Trial*, 47 JOURNAL OF CRIMINAL LAW 183–96 (1956).

[40] UN War Crimes Commission, Law Reports of Trials of War Criminals, UNWCC, Vol. XV (1949), p. 96.

[41] Milutinovic Decision, para. 36.

were clearly founded in the customary international law arising out of Nuremberg, but the chamber found that the extended form of JCE lacks sufficiently clear and unambiguous support in the case law of the Nuremberg and Control Council Law Number 10 Tribunals to conclude that it too reflects customary international law.[42]

Given that the extended form of JCE (similar to the felony murder rule) is the most controversial type of JCE liability, the three Control Council Law Number 10 cases dealing with that mode of JCE liability are worth examining in some detail. The first is the trial of Erich Heyer and six others – known as the *Essen Lynching* case. According to the official summary of the trial published in the UN War Crimes Commission Report, this case concerned the lynching of three British prisoners of war by a mob of Germans.[43] Though the case was tried by a British military court, it did so under the authority of Control Council Law Number 10, and it was therefore "not a trial under English law." One of the accused, Captain Heyer, had placed three prisoners under the escort of a German soldier, Koenen, who was to take them for interrogation. As Koenen left, Heyer, within earshot of a waiting crowd, ordered Koenen not to intervene if German civilians molested the prisoners and stated that the prisoners deserved to be and probably would be shot. The prisoners were beaten by the crowd and one German corporal fired a revolver at a prisoner, wounding him in the head. One died instantly when they were thrown over a bridge and the remaining two were killed by shots from the bridge and by members of the crowd who beat them to death. The defense argument that the prosecution needed to prove that each of the accused – Heyer, Koenen, and five civilians – had intended to kill the prisoners was not accepted by the court. The prosecution argued that in order to be convicted, the accused had to have been "concerned in the killing" of the prisoner. Both Heyer and

---

[42] Decision on the Applicability of Joint Ciminal Enterprise, Ieng Sary et al., Case 002, EEEC Trial Chamber, September 12, 2011.

[43] *Trial of Erich Heyer and Six Others*, British Military Court for the Trial of War Criminals, Essen, December 18–19 and 21–2, 1945, UNWCC, Vol. 1 (1949), p. 88.

Koenen were convicted of committing a war crime in that they were concerned in the killing of the three prisoners, as were three of the five accused civilians. Even though it was not proven which of the civilians delivered the fatal shots or blows, they were convicted because "from the moment they left those barracks, the men were doomed and the crowd knew they were doomed and every person in that crowd who struck a blow was both morally and criminally responsible for the deaths of the three men."[44]

A second example (surprisingly not cited in *Tadic)*, which the UN War Crimes Commission specifically found analogous to the *Essen Lynching* case, is the *Trial of Hans Renoth and Three Others*.[45] In that case, two policemen (Hans Ronoth and Hans Pelgrim) and two customs officials (Friedrich Grabowski and Paul Nieke) were accused of committing a war crime in that they "were concerned in the killing of an unknown Allied airman, a prisoner of war." According to the allegations, the pilot crashed on German soil unhurt and was arrested by Renoth, then attacked and beaten with fists and rifles by a number of people while the three other defendants witnessed the beating but took no active part to stop it or to help the pilot. Renoth also stood by for a while and then shot and killed the pilot. "The case for the prosecution was that there was a common design in which all four accused shared to commit a war crime, [and] that all four accused were aware of this common design and that all four accused acted in furtherance of it."[46] All the accused were found guilty, presumably on the basis of the foreseeability that the pilot would eventually be killed during the beating at the hands of the crowd or by one of them.

A third example is the case of *Kurt Goebell et al.* (the *Borkum Island* case). Although it was not published in the Report of the UN War Crimes Commission, a case review was published by the U.S. Judge

[44] *Id*. at 97.
[45] *Trial of Hans Ronoth and Three Others*, British Military Court, January 9–10, 1946, UNWCC, Vol. XV (1949), pp. 76–7.
[46] *Id*. at 76.

Advocate General in 1947,[47] the records of the case are publicly available through the U.S. National Archives Microfilm Publications,[48] and a detailed report of the trial (based on trial transcripts) was published in the *Journal of Criminal Law* in 1956.[49] According to the 1956 publication, the mayor of Borkum, the garrison commander, and several German military officers and soldiers were convicted of the assault and killing of seven American airmen who had crash-landed. Garrison Commander Goebell had instructed his subordinates to offer the prisoners no protection, facilitating a mob attack, which ended with the prisoners' shooting at the hands of one of the soldiers. The prosecution argued that the accused were "cogs in the wheel of common design, all equally important, each cog doing the part assigned to it." It further argued that "it is proved beyond a reasonable doubt that each one of the accused played his part in mob violence which led to the unlawful killings," and "therefore, under the law each and every one of the accused is guilty of murder." After deliberating in closed session, the judges rendered an oral verdict in which they convicted the mayor and several officers of the killings and assaults. From the arguments and evidence submitted, it is apparent that the accused were convicted pursuant to a form of common design liability equivalent to the extended form of JCE. Essentially, the court decided that though certain defendants had not participated in the murder nor intended for it to be committed, they were nonetheless liable because it was a natural and foreseeable consequence of their treatment of the prisoners. In confirming the convictions, the reviewing officers stated in regard to each defendant, "all who join as participants in a plan

---

[47] Case Review, *United States v. Goebell et al.* (Deputy Judge Advoc. 1947), available at: http://www.online.uni-marburg.de/icwc/dachau/000–012–0489.pdf (last accessed February 9, 2013).

[48] The United States Archives, Publication Number M1103, "Records of United States Army War Crimes Trials," *United States of America v. Goebell et al.*, February 6–March 21, 1946. The Appeals Chamber in *Tadic* states that a copy of these case materials is on file in the ICTY's Library. Tadic Appeals Chamber Decision, p. 93.

[49] Maxilimian Koessler, *Borkum Island Tragedy and Trial*, 47 JOURNAL OF CRIMINAL LAW 183–96 (1956).

to commit an unlawful act, the natural and probable consequences of the execution of which involves the contingency of taking human life, are legally responsible as principals for a homicide committed by any of them in pursuance of or in furtherance of the plan."[50]

International judicial decisions, like domestic court cases, can evince state practice and *opinio juris*, establishing customary international law.[51] In objecting to the use of JCE before the Cambodia Tribunal, the attorneys for the Khmer Rouge defendants protested that these Control Council Law Number 10 cases are "unpublished cases" or, in some instances, mere summaries of unwritten verdicts. The suggestion is that the court could not validly rely on them to glean the substance of customary international law because defendants could not be deemed to have constructive knowledge of unpublished works with respect to the doctrine of *ignorantia juris non excusat* (ignorance of the law is no excuse). It is significant, however, that two of the three Control Council Law Number 10 JCE cases described earlier were published in summary form in the official UN War Crimes Commission Report in 1949. According to the UN publication's Foreword, the "main object of these Reports [was] to help to elucidate the law, i.e., that part of International Law which has been called the law of war."[52] This authoritative and widely disseminated multivolume account of the trials, in which the war

---

[50] Case Review, *United States v. Goebell et al.* (Deputy Judge Advoc. 1947), at 21, 22, 24, 26, 28–9, 32–3, 35, 38–43, available at: http://www.online.uni-marburg.de/icwc/dachau/000–012–0489.pdf (last accessed February 9, 2013).

[51] In 1950, the International Law Commission listed the following sources as forms of evidence of customary international law: "treaties, decisions of national and international courts, national legislation, opinions of national legal advisors, diplomatic correspondence, practice of international organizations." ([1950] 2 Y.B. INT'L L. COMM'N 367, U.N. Doc. A/CN.4/Ser.A/1950/Add.1 [1957]).

[52] Foreword, *Law Reports of Trials of War Criminals*, XV UNWCC, p. vii (1949). While the UN War Crimes Commission recognizes that where "there is no reasoned judgment [...] it is difficult in some cases to specify precisely the grounds on which the courts gave their decision," the commission goes on to state: "the difficulty is, however, to a large extent surmounted in [such cases] by examining carefully the indictment, the speeches of the counsel on both sides and the judgment."

crimes tribunals recognized and applied JCE liability, supports the argument that the Khmer Rouge leaders had sufficient constructive notice in
1975–9 that their mass atrocity crimes would attract criminal responsibility under the JCE doctrine. In objecting that the case synopses in
the UN War Crimes Commission's volumes are mere two- to three-page
summaries rather than lengthy and detailed decisions, the attorneys for
the Khmer Rouge defendants overlook the fact that in most countries
around the world, particularly those of the civil law tradition, judicial
opinions are often of this length and form.

While the *Borkum Island* case was not included in the Report of the
UN War Crimes Commission, it is significant that the case review, charging instrument, transcript (including oral bench judgment), and other
documents of the case have been publicly available from the United
States Archives.[53] In addition, as mentioned, a detailed account and
analysis of the *Borkum Island* case was published in 1956 in the *Journal
of Criminal Law*.[54] It may be an open question, however, whether a judgment that was the subject of a scholarly article in a widely read presti-
gious publication and that was available in public archives years before
the Khmer Rouge launched their genocidal campaign can be viewed as
a published judicial decision for this purpose.

The Cambodia Tribunal's Appeal Chamber will ultimately decide
whether the Nuremberg precedent did in fact include JCE III. In doing
so, it may turn to the Jerusalem District Court and Israeli Supreme
Court's decisions in the *Eichmann* case. Those decisions demonstrate that, as of 1961, domestic courts recognized JCE as developed
by the jurisprudence of Nuremberg and its progeny.[55] The Jerusalem

---

[53] See Publication Number M1103, "Records of United States Army War Crimes
Trials," *United States of America v. Goebel et al.*, February 6–March 21, 1946.

[54] Maxilimian Koessler, *Borkum Island Tragedy and Trial*, 47 JOURNAL OF CRIMINAL
LAW 183–96 (1956).

[55] *Attorney-General of Israel v. Eichmann*, 36 I.L.R.5 (December 11, 1961) [*hereinafter
Eichmann*] affirmed by *Attorney-General of Israel v Eichmann*, 36 I.L.R. 277 (29
May 1962) [*hereinafter Eichmann II*].

District Court's approach to determining Adolf Eichmann's individual responsibility for participating in a common criminal plan to extinguish the Jews in Europe closely resembled that applied by the Control Council Law Number 10 cases cited previously (several of which were cited by the Jerusalem District Court). This can be seen clearly in its statement:

> Hence, everyone who acted in the extermination of Jews, knew about the plan for the Final Solution and its advancement, is to be regarded as an accomplice in the annihilation of the millions who were exterminated during the years 1941–1945, irrespective of the fact of whether his actions spread over the entire front of the extermination, or over only one or more sectors of that front. His responsibility is that of a "principal offender" who perpetrated the entire crime in co-operation with the others.[56]

The District Court found that Eichmann was made aware of the criminal plan to exterminate the Jews in June of 1941; he actively furthered this plan via his central role as referent for Jewish affairs in the Office for Reich Security as early as August of 1941; and he possessed the requisite intent (specific intent here, because the goal was genocide) to further the plan as evidenced by "the very breadth of the scope of his activities" undertaken to achieve the biological extermination of the Jewish people.[57] On the basis of these findings, Eichmann was held criminally liable for the "general crime" of the Final Solution, which encompassed acts constituting the crime "in which he took an active part in his own sector *and the acts committed by his accomplices to the crime in other sectors* on the same front."[58] In so holding, the District Court ruled that full awareness of the scope of the plan's operations was not necessary, noting that many of the principal perpetrators, including the defendant, may have possessed only compartmentalized

---

[56] *Eichmann*, para. 194.
[57] *Id.*, para. 182.
[58] *Id.*, para. 197 (emphasis added).

knowledge.[59] Particularly significant is the fact that the Israeli Supreme Court cited the 1946 General Assembly resolution affirming the Nuremberg Principles for authority in applying the forerunner of the JCE doctrine.[60]

One might wonder whether the customary international law growing out of the Nuremberg judgments and General Assembly Resolution 95(1) encompasses the theories of liability as well as the substantive crimes applied at Nuremberg. Indeed, when the International Law Commission began its project of formulating the Principles of International Law Recognized in the Charter of the Nuremberg Tribunal and in the judgment of the tribunal, it initially made a distinction between (1) the principles *strict sensu* (which included the liability of accomplices, the precedence of international law over inconsistent domestic law, the denial of immunity for individuals who acted in an official capacity, the prohibition of the defense of superior orders, and the right to a fair trial) and (2) the substantive offenses (crimes against peace, war crimes, and crimes against humanity).[61] This distinction was, however, abandoned by the International Law Commission when it enumerated the seven Nuremberg Principles in 1950,[62] which include substantive offenses, modes of liability, and limitations on certain defenses, all of which have been applied by the modern international tribunals. Although the ILC's 1950 formulation neither specifically references nor specifically excludes Joint Criminal Enterprise liability, it does make clear that anyone who "commits" a crime against peace, a war crime, or crime against humanity, is criminally liable. It is of note in this regard that the ICTY, ICTR, SCSL, and

[59] *Id.*, para. 193.

[60] *Eichmann II*, para. 11 (concerning universal jurisdiction for crimes against humanity), para. 14 (concerning rejection of the act of state defense), and para. 15 (concerning rejection of the superior orders defense).

[61] International Law Commission, Report on the formulation of Nürnberg principles, by Mr. Spiropoulos (A/CN.4/22, April 12 1950), at 131–3, available at:.http://untreaty.un.org/ilc/publications/yearbooks/Ybkvolumes(e)/ILC_1949_v1_e.pdf.

[62] The ILC's Nuremberg Principles are available at: http://www.icrc.org/ihl.nsf/full/390 (last accessed February 9, 2013).

STL have all read the word "committed" in their statutes as including participation in the realization of a common design or purpose.[63]

The UN General Assembly did not pass a resolution endorsing the International Law Commission's 1950 enumeration of the Nuremberg Principles because the General Assembly had four years earlier already confirmed the status of the Nuremberg Principles as international law. Instead, it directed the commission to codify them in an "International Code of Offences against the Peace and Security of Mankind."[64] Although the commission's 1950 enumeration of the Nuremberg Principles did not include explicit reference to the common plan mode of liability, six years later, in the ILC's draft International Code of Offenses, the commission specifically included "the principle of individual criminal responsibility for formulating a plan or participating in a common plan or conspiracy to commit a crime"[65] – thus indicating that the commission perceived the common plan concept to be part of the Nuremberg Principles.

[63] See *e.g.*, *CDF Case*, Decision on Motions for Judgment of Acquittal Pursuant to Rule 98, Case No. SCSL-04–14-T, October 21, 2005, para. 130: "The Chamber recognizes, as a matter of law, generally, that Article 6(1) of the Statute of the Special Court does not, in its proscriptive reach, limit criminal liability to only those persons who plan, instigate, order, physically commit a crime or otherwise aid and abet in its planning, preparation or execution. Its proscriptive ambit extends beyond that to prohibit the commission of offenses through a joint criminal enterprise, in pursuit of the common plan to commit crimes punishable under the Statute." See also Interlocutory Decision on the Applicable Law: Terrorism, Conspiracy, Homicide, Perpetration, Cumulative Charging, Special Tribunal for Lebanon Appeals Chamber, Case No. STL-11–01/I, February 16, 2011, available at: http://www. stl-tsl.org/x/file/TheRegistry/Library/CaseFiles/chambers/20110216_STL-11–01_R176bis_F0010_AC_Interlocutory_Decision_Filed_EN.pdf (last accessed February 9, 2013).

[64] On the recommendation of the Sixth Committee, the General Assembly, by a vote of 42 to 0, with 6 abstentions, adopted Resolution 488 (V) on November 14, 1950. By this resolution, the General Assembly decided to send the formulation of the Nuremberg Principles to the governments of member states for comments and requested the ILC, in preparing the draft Code of Offences against the Peace and Security of Mankind, to take account of the observations received from governments. The ILC did not submit the draft code to the General Assembly until 1996.

[65] See *Report of the International Law Commission on the Work of Its Forty-Eighth Session*, May 6–July 26, 1996, Official Records of the General Assembly, Fifty-First

In sum, it was the paradigm-shifting nature of the Nuremberg precedent in response to atrocities of an unprecedented scale and the universal and unqualified endorsement of the Nuremberg Principles by the
nations of the world in 1946 that crystallized (at least the first two forms
of) JCE into a mode of individual criminal liability under customary
international law despite the initially limited number of cases reflecting
state practice.[66] The significance of this example of a Grotian Moment
extends beyond the application of JCE liability in international criminal
tribunals. Because the international tribunals have recognized that JCE
became customary international law in 1946, in accordance with Article
15(2) of the International Covenant on Civil and Political Rights, hybrid
and domestic courts, as well as international tribunals, may lawfully try
international crimes using internationally recognized modes of liability
including JCE whether or not such crimes or forms of liability were recognized in the domestic law at the time of their commission.[67]

Did Nuremberg Establish Aggression as a Universal Jurisdiction Crime?

While JCE's provenance (especially the extended form) remains somewhat contentious, an even more controversial question is whether the

Session, Supplement No. 10, at p. 21 available at: http://www.un.org/law.ilc/index.htm
(last accessed February 9, 2013).

[66] See Frank Lawrence, *The Nuremberg Principles: A Defense for Political Protesters*,
40 HASTINGS L. J. 397, (1989), pp. 397, 408–10 (disputing the argument that "more
than a single event is necessary for a proposed principle to be considered part of
customary international law"). In 2006, the European Court of Human Rights recognized the "universal validity" of the Nuremberg Principles: *Kolk and Kislyiy v.
Estonia*, Decision on Admissibility, January 17, 2006.

[67] ICCPR, Art. 15(2): "Nothing in this article shall prejudice the trial and punishment of
any person for any act or omission which, at the time it was committed, was criminal
according to the general principles of law recognized by the community of nations."
Prosecutor v. Milan Milutinovic, Nikola Sainovic & Dragoljub Odjanic, Appeals
Chamber Decision on Ojdanic's Motion Challenging Jurisdiction – Joint Criminal
Enterprise, Case No.: IT-99-37-AR72, May 21, 2003, paras. 41–2 [*hereinafter* Ojdanic
JCE Decision] (noting that application of JCE to crimes in Bosnia was legitimate even
though the former Yugoslavia did not recognize that mode of liability).

customary international law that emerged from the Nuremberg Grotian
Moment provides states the right to exercise universal jurisdiction over
the crime of aggression. This question arose during the International
Criminal Court Review Conference in Kampala, Uganda, in June 2010,
when the United States delegation expressed trepidation that adding
aggression to the jurisdiction of the ICC might stimulate states to enact
implementing statutes giving their domestic Courts universal jurisdiction over the crime of aggression.[68]

This was a quite legitimate concern given that five countries
(Azerbaijan, Belarus, Bulgaria, the Czech Republic, and Estonia)
already have enacted laws giving their Courts universal jurisdiction over
the crime of aggression,[69] and eighteen countries have statutes giving
their courts universal jurisdiction generically over "offenses against
international law" under international treaties as well as customary
international law.[70] In an attempt to prevent such an outcome, the United
States and a few allies persuaded the delegates at Kampala to adopt an
"understanding" to accompany the amendments, stipulating that "it is
understood that the amendments shall not be interpreted as creating the
right or obligation to exercise domestic jurisdiction with respect to an act
of aggression committed by another State."[71]

[68] Claus Kress and Leonie von Holtendorff, *The Kampala Compromise on the Crime of
Aggression*, 8 J. INT'L CRIM. JUSTICE 1179, 1216 (2010).

[69] REPORT OF THE SECRETARY-GENERAL PREPARED ON THE BASIS OF COMMENTS
AND OBSERVATIONS OF GOVERNMENTS ON THE SCOPE AND APPLICATION OF THE
PRINCIPLE OF UNIVERSAL JURISDICTION, UN Doc. a/65/181, July 29, 2010, at 29.

[70] Amnesty International, UNIVERSAL JURISDICTION: A PRELIMINARY SURVEY
OF LEGISLATION AROUND THE WORLD, October 2011, at 1; REPORT OF THE
SECRETARY-GENERAL PREPARED ON THE BASIS OF COMMENTS AND OBSERVATIONS
OF GOVERNMENTS ON THE SCOPE AND APPLICATION OF THE PRINCIPLE OF UNIVERSAL
JURISDICTION, UN Doc. a/65/181, July 29, 2010, at 11, 12.

[71] Resolution RC/Res.6, Annex III, para. 5, June 28, 2010. The resolution specifically
"adopt[s] the understandings regarding the interpretation of the above mentioned
amendments contained in annex III of the present resolution." Resolution RC/
Res.6, para. 3. The adopted understandings therefore formed a critical component
of the negotiated solution to various substantive difficulties and should be considered an important part of the travaux preparatoires (negotiating record) entitled to

This language, however, will have little dissuasive effect if states conclude that they already have an existing right under customary international law, based on the customary international law generated from the Nuremberg Trials, to prosecute foreign nationals for the crime of aggression.[72] In this context, eight years before the Kampala Review Conference, ad litem ICJ Judge Van den Wyngaert of Belgium wrote in her opinion in the *Belgian Arrest Warrant* case: "The Rome Statute does not establish a new legal basis for third States to introduce universal jurisdiction. It does not prohibit it but does not authorize it either. This means that, as far as crimes in the Rome Statute are concerned (war crimes, crimes against humanity, genocide *and in the future perhaps aggression* and other crimes), pre-existing sources of international law retain their importance."[73] This section explores whether the Nuremberg Grotian Moment established a customary international law right of states to exercise universal jurisdiction over the crime of aggression.

Nuremberg Prosecutor Robert Jackson felt that confirming and prosecuting the crime of aggression was the most important outcome of the Nuremberg trials.[74] The international community codified the prohibition on launching wars of aggression in the UN Charter[75] and adopted

great weight in interpreting the Aggression amendments consistent with the rule of treaty interpretation provided by Article 31 of the Vienna Convention on the Law of Treaties, May 23, 1969, 1155 UNTS 331.

[72] Several states that provided reports to the UN secretary-general on universal jurisdiction in 2010 had taken the position that customary international law extended universal jurisdiction to the crime of aggression. REPORT OF THE SECRETARY-GENERAL PREPARED ON THE BASIS OF COMMENTS AND OBSERVATIONS OF GOVERNMENTS ON THE SCOPE AND APPLICATION OF THE PRINCIPLE OF UNIVERSAL JURISDICTION, UN Doc. a/65/181, July 29, 2010, at 8–9.

[73] Case Concerning the Arrest Warrant of April 11, 2000 (*Democratic Republic of the Congo v. Belgium*), 2002 ICJ 3, February 14, 2002 (dissenting opinion of Judge Van den Wygaert), at para. 66 (emphasis added).

[74] Report to the President by Mr. Justice Robert Jackson, June 6, 1945, available at: http://avalon.law.yale.edu/imt/jack63.asp.

[75] UN Charter, Art. 2(4): "All Members shall refrain in there international relations from the threat or use of force against the territorial integrity or political independence of any state, or in any other manner inconsistent with the Purposes of the United Nations." There are two exceptions to this prohibition: the inherent right of

by consensus a definition of the crime in 1974.[76] Nevertheless, the modern international tribunals established by the Security Council were not granted jurisdiction over this crime; rather the Security Council confined their jurisdiction to war crimes, crimes against humanity, and genocide. The decision to exclude aggression reflected the drafters' recognition that aggression is a different species of offense as it is based on *jus ad bellum* (the legality of the war itself), whereas the crimes within the tribunals' jurisdiction are based on *jus in bello* (the legality of the conduct of the war). Moreover, the members of the Security Council viewed jurisdiction over aggression as antithetical to their interests in an era in which they, themselves, were constantly being accused of having committed acts of aggression throughout the world.[77]

Yet, at the 1988 Rome Diplomatic Conference to establish the ICC, three elderly Nuremberg prosecutors – Whitney Harris, Henry King, and Ben Ferencz – used their unique moral authority, dogged persistence, and formidable skills of persuasion to convince the delegates to include the crime of aggression in the Court's statute.[78] This was widely

---

individual or collective self-defense (Article 51) and collective security measures authorized by the Security Council (the entirety of chapter vii).

[76] Annex to UN Doc. A/ES/3314 (XXIX), December 14, 1974 (Res. 3314) (adopted by consensus).

[77] Professor Michael Glennon has written that had the crime of aggression applied to the United States during "the last several decades, every U.S. President since John F. Kennedy, hundreds of U.S. legislators and military leaders, as well as innumerable military and political leaders from other countries could have been subject to prosecution." Michael J. Glennon, *The Blank-Prose Crime of Aggression*, 35 YALE J. INT'L L. 71, 73 (2010). Glennon cites as examples, the 2008 Russian invasion of Georgia, the 2003 U.S. invasion of Iraq, the 2001 NATO invasion of Afghanistan, the 1999 NATO bombing operations against Serbia, the 1998 U.S. air strikes against Afghanistan and Sudan, the 1993 U.S. air strikes against Iraq, the 1989 U.S. invasion of Panama, the 1986 U.S. air strikes against Libya, the 1983 U.S. invasion of Grenada, the 1979 Soviet invasion of Afghanistan, the 1965 U.S. invasion of the Dominican Republic, the 1970 U.S. bombing of Cambodia, the 1962 U.S. blockade of Cuba, and the 1961 U.S. invasion of Cuba at the Bay of Pigs. *Id.* at 91–5.

[78] Michael P. Scharf and Philip S. Hadji, *Foreword and Dedication: The International Criminal Court and the Crime of Aggression*, 41 CASE W. RES. J. INT'L L. 267, 267(2009).

viewed as a symbolic victory, however, since the ICC Statute stipulated in Article 5(2) that before the Court can exercise jurisdiction over this crime, the states parties must adopt amendments at a review conference setting forth a definition of aggression and the conditions under which the Court could exercise its jurisdiction over it.[79] Nevertheless, from 2003 to 2009, delegates of the Special Working Group on the Crime of Aggression made slow progress toward an acceptable definition and trigger mechanism for aggression, laying the foundations for eventual success at Kampala in June 2010.[80]

As a result of the Kampala amendments, the crime of aggression is defined in new Article 8 bis as "planning, preparation, initiation or execution, by a person in a position effectively to exercise control over or to direct the political or military action of a State, of an act of aggression which, by its character, gravity and scale, constitutes a manifest violation of the Charter of the United Nations."[81] The meaning of "act of aggression" in turn is drawn directly from the list of seven acts enumerated in the 1974 General Assembly resolution defining aggression.[82] Once the amendments enter into force (no sooner than January 1, 2017), the

---

[79] Rome Statute of the International Criminal Court, U.N. Doc. A/CONF.183.9, July 17, 1998, reprinted in CHERIF BASSIOUNI, THE STATUTE OF THE INTERNATIONAL CRIMINAL COURT 39 (1998).

[80] Claus Kress and Leonie von Holtendorff, *The Kampala Compromise on the Crime of Aggression*, 8 J. INT'L CRIM. JUSTICE 1179, (2010). For an account of the previous negotiations in the International Law Commission, legal, special, ad hoc, and preparatory committees, working and special working groups, see BEN FERENCZ, DEFINING INTERNATIONAL AGGRESSION: THE SEARCH FOR WORLD PEACE (1975).

[81] Resolution RC/Res.6, Annex I, Art. 8 bis (1), June 28, 2010.

[82] Resolution RC/Res.6, Annex I, Art. 8 bis (2), June 28, 2010:

The invasion or attack by the armed forces of a State of the territory of another State, or any military occupation, however temporary, resulting from such invasion or attack, or any annexation by the use of force of the territory of another State or part thereof;

Bombardment by the armed forces of a State against the territory of another State or the use of any weapon by a State against the territory of another State;

The blockade of the ports or coasts of a State by the armed forces of another State;

Court can exercise jurisdiction over the crime of aggression committed by any state when the Security Council refers a situation to the Court. The Court can also exercise jurisdiction over the crime of aggression committed by state parties either when the Security Council has made a determination that an act of aggression has been committed or, where no determination is rendered by the council within six months of an incident, the ICC's Pre-trial Division authorizes the prosecutor to proceed with an investigation.[83]

The consensus reached at Kampala in the early hours of June 12, 2010, was the result of several delicate compromises negotiated by the president of the Assembly of State Parties, Ambassador Christian Wenaweser, and his deputy, Stephen Barriga, of Liechtenstein. One of the most important of these was the adoption of a U.S.-proposed understanding providing that the aggression amendments "shall not be interpreted as creating the right or obligation to exercise domestic jurisdiction with respect to an act of aggression committed by another State."[84] The U.S.-proposed understanding is based on the view that states do not have an existing right under customary international law to exercise universal jurisdiction over the crime of aggression. In the following pages, we will examine whether that view overlooks the significance of the Nuremberg precedent.

> An attack by the armed forces of a State on the land, sea or air forces, or marine and air fleets of another State;
> The use of armed forces of one State which are within the territory of another State with the agreement of the receiving State, in contravention of the conditions provided for in the agreement or any extension of their presence in such territory beyond the termination of the agreement;
> The action of a State in allowing its territory, which it has placed at the disposal of another State, to be used by that other State for perpetrating an act of aggression against a third State;
> The sending by or on behalf of a State of armed bands, groups, irregulars or mercenaries, which carry out acts of armed force against another State of such gravity as to amount to the acts listed above, or its substantial involvement therein.

[83] Resolution RC/Res.6, Annex I, para. 3, Art. 15 bis, June 28, 2010.
[84] Resolution RC/Res.6, Annex III, para. 5, June 28, 2010.

The term "jurisdiction" refers to the legitimate assertion of authority to affect legal interests. Jurisdiction may describe the authority to make law applicable to certain persons, territories, or situations (prescriptive jurisdiction); the authority to subject certain persons, territories, or situations to judicial processes (adjudicatory jurisdiction); or the authority to compel compliance and to redress noncompliance (enforcement jurisdiction).[85] There are five types of jurisdiction recognized under international law: territorial (based on the location of the acts or effects), nationality (based on the citizenship of the accused), passive personality (based on the citizenship of the victim), protective (based on essential security interests), and universal.[86]

Universal jurisdiction provides every state with jurisdiction over a limited category of offenses generally recognized as of universal concern, regardless of where the offense occurred, the nationality of the perpetrator, or the nationality of the victim.[87] While other bases of jurisdiction require connections between the prosecuting state and the offense, the perpetrator, or the victim, the universality principle assumes that every state has a sufficient interest in exercising jurisdiction to combat egregious offenses that states universally have condemned.[88]

There are two premises underlying universal jurisdiction.[89] The first involves the gravity of the crime. Many of the crimes subject to the universality principle are so heinous in scope and degree that they offend the interest of all humanity, and any state may, as humanity's agent, punish the offender. The second involves the *locus delicti* (place of the act). Many of the crimes subject to the universality principle occur in territory over which no country has jurisdiction or in

---

[85] See Kenneth C. Randall, *Universal Jurisdiction under International Law*, 66 Tex. L. Rev. 785, 786 (1988).

[86] *Id.*

[87] *Id.* at 788.

[88] *Id.* at 787.

[89] See Lee A. Steven, *Genocide and the Duty to Extradite or Prosecute: Why the United States Is in Breach of Its International Obligations*, 39 Va. J. Int'l L. 425, 435 (1999).

situations in which the territorial state is unlikely to exercise jurisdiction, because, for example, the perpetrators are state authorities or agents of the state.[90]

The first widely accepted crime of universal jurisdiction was piracy. For more than three centuries, states have exercised jurisdiction over piratical acts on the high seas, even when neither the pirates nor their victims were nationals of the prosecuting state.[91] Piracy's fundamental nature and consequences explained why it was subject to universal jurisdiction. Piracy often consists of heinous acts of violence or depredation, which are committed indiscriminately against the vessels and nationals of numerous states.[92] Moreover, pirates can quickly flee across the seas, making pursuit by the authorities of particular victim states difficult.[93] In 1820, the U.S. Supreme Court upheld the exercise of universal jurisdiction by U.S. courts over piracy in *United States v. Smith*.[94] The Court reasoned that "pirates being *hostis humani generis* [enemies of all humankind], are punishable in the tribunals of all nations. All nations are engaged in a league against them for the mutual defense and safety of all."[95]

---

[90] Leila Sadat Wexler & S. Richard Carden, *The New International Criminal Court: An Uneasy Revolution*, 88 GEORGETOWN L.J. 381, 407 n. 156 (2000).

[91] Like other international criminals, pirates can retain their nationality and still be subject to universal jurisdiction. See Kenneth C. Randall, *Universal Jurisdiction under International Law*, 66 TEX. L. REV. 785, 794 (1988).

[92] Hari M. Osofsky, *Domesticating International Criminal Law: Bringing Human Rights Violators to Justice*, 107 YALE L. J. 191, 194 (1997).

[93] *Id.* at 194, n.18.

[94] 18 U.S. (5 Wheat.) 153 (1820). The Piracy Statute of 1819 provided "if any person or persons whatsoever, shall, on the high seas, commit the crime of piracy, as defined by the law of nations, and ... shall afterwards be brought into or found in the United States, every such offender ... shall, upon conviction ... be punished with death." The Supreme Court upheld this statute over the objection that it failed to define the crime with sufficient particularity. See *id.* at 162.

[95] *United States v. Smith*, 18 U.S. (5 Wheat.) 153, 156 (1820). Accord *U.S. v. Klintock*, 18 U.S. (5 Wheat) 144 (1820), in which the Supreme Court stated:

A pirate, being *hostis humani generis*, is of no nation or state.... All the states of the world are engaged in a tacit alliance against them. An offense committed by them

In the aftermath of the atrocities of the Second World War, the international community extended universal jurisdiction to war crimes and crimes against humanity. Trials of World War II war criminals based on this type of jurisdiction took place in international tribunals at Nuremberg and Tokyo, as well as domestic courts. Some individuals faced trial in the states in which they had committed their crimes, but others were tried by the state in which they were later captured, surrendered, or found – including such far-off countries as Canada[96] and Australia.[97] Thus, on the basis of universal jurisdiction, Israel tried Adolph Eichmann in 1961[98]

against any individual nation, is an offense against all. It is punishable in the courts of all. So, in the present case, the offense committed on board a piratical vessel, by a pirate, against a subject of Denmark, is an offense against the United States, which the courts of this country are authorized and bound to punish. *Id.* at 147–8.

[96] See *R. v. Imre Finta*, [1994] 28 C.R. (4th) 265 (S.C.) (Canada) (reaffirming universal jurisdiction over crimes against humanity committed against Jews in Hungary during Second World War but finding that the available evidence did not meet the requisite standard for such crimes).

[97] See *Polyukhovich v. Commonwealth*, 172 C.L.R. 501 (Austl. 1991) (Australia) (reaffirming universal jurisdiction over crimes against humanity and war crimes committed against Jews in the Ukraine during Second World War).

[98] Israel kidnapped Adolph Eichmann in Argentina and prosecuted him in Jerusalem in 1961 for crimes against humanity and war crimes. As chief of the Gestapo's Jewish Section, Eichmann had primary responsibility over the persecution, deportation, and extermination of hundreds of thousands of Jews. Although the Security Council condemned Israel for violating Argentina's territorial sovereignty in apprehending Eichmann, there was no averment that Israel lacked jurisdiction to try him. In upholding the District Court's conviction and death sentence, the Supreme Court of Israel stated:

There is full justification for applying here the principle of universal jurisdiction since the international character of crimes against humanity ... dealt with in this case is no longer in doubt.... The basic reason for which international law recognizes the right of each state to exercise such jurisdiction in piracy offenses ... applies with even greater force to the above-mentioned crimes. Not only do all the crimes attributed to the appellant bear an international character, but their harmful and murderous effects were so embracing and widespread as to shake the international community to its very foundations. The State of Israel therefore was entitled, pursuant to the principle of universal jurisdiction and in the capacity of a guardian of international law and an agent for its enforcement, to try the appellant.

and John Demjanjuk in 1988[99] for Nazi atrocities committed before Israel even existed as a state.

In the years since the Nuremberg and Tokyo prosecutions, there have been several notable domestic prosecutions outside the context of World War II atrocities based on the universality principle.[100] The United Kingdom, for example, relied on universal jurisdiction in finding former President of Chile Augusto Pinochet extraditable to Spain for acts of torture committed in Chile in the 1980s,[101] courts of Denmark and Germany have relied on the universality principle in trying Croatian and Bosnian Serb nationals for war crimes and crimes against humanity

> That being the case, no importance attaches to the fact that the State of Israel did not exist when the offenses were committed.

Attorney General of Israel v. Eichmann, 36 I.L.R. 277, 299, 304 (Isr. Sup. Ct. 1962).

[99] The United States granted Israel's request for the extradition of John Demjanjuk, a retired autoworker accused of being the infamous Treblinka Nazi death camp guard "Ivan the Terrible." See *Demjanjuk v. Petrovsky*, 776 F. 2d 571 (6th Cir. 1985). The Court held that Israel had the right to try Demjanjuk under universal jurisdiction for crimes committed at the Treblinka concentration camp during 1942 or 1943, prior to the establishment of the Israeli state. See id. at 582–3. Demjanjuk was found guilty and sentenced to death for crimes against humanity by the Israeli court, but his conviction was subsequently overturned when new evidence discovered after the collapse of the Soviet Union was considered by the Israeli Supreme Court. See Cr. A. 347/88, *Demjanjuk v. State of Israel* 395–6 (Special Issue); Mordechai Kremnitzer, The Demjanjuk Case, in War Crimes in International Law 321, 323 (Yoram Dinstein and Mala Tabory eds., 1996). Ultimately, Demjanjuk was tried and convicted by Germany in 2011 on charges stemming from his participation in crimes at a different concentration camp (Sobibor).

[100] Since World War II there have been prosecutions for crimes under international law based on universal jurisdiction in seventeen states (Argentina, Australia, Austria, Belgium, Canada, Denmark, Finland, France, Germany, Israel, Netherlands, Norway, Spain, Sweden, Switzerland, United Kingdom, and the United States). Amnesty International Report, Universal Jurisdiction: UN General Assembly Should Support this Essential International Justice Tool, IOR 53/015/2010, October 5, 2010, at 19, available at: http://www.amnesty.org/fr/library/info/IOR53/015/2010/ en (last accessed February 9, 2013).

[101] In the Pinochet case, the UK House of Lords found the former president of Chile extraditable to Spain for prosecution under the universality principle enshrined in the Torture Convention. *Regina v. Bow Street Metropolitan Stipendiary Magistrate, ex parte Pinochet Ugarte*, [1999] 2 W.L.R. 272 (H.L.), 38 I.L.M. 430 (1999).

committed in Bosnia in 1992,[102] courts in Belgium and Canada have cited the universality principle as a basis for prosecuting persons involved in the atrocities in Rwanda in 1994,[103] and the United States employed universal jurisdiction in prosecuting Charles Taylor Jr. for torture committed in Sierra Leone in the 1990s.[104]

Yet, it has been sixty years since anyone has been prosecuted for the crime of aggression under customary international law. The lack of modern prosecutions and the Security Council's decision to exclude the crime from the jurisdiction of the modern ad hoc international criminal tribunals are viewed by some as indicating that Nuremberg did not establish a right to prosecute aggression under universal jurisdiction.

---

[102] In the 1994 case of *Director of Public Prosecutions v. T*, the defendant was tried by a Danish court for war crimes committed against Bosnians in the territory of the former Yugoslavia. See Mary Ellen O'Connell, *New International Legal Process*, 93 Am. J. Int'l L. 334, 341 (1999). On April 30, 1999, the German Federal Supreme Court upheld the conviction of a Bosnian Serb convicted for committing acts of genocide in Bosnia. See 5 International Law Update 52 (May 1999). A press release on this case – Number 39/1999 – is available on the German Federal Supreme Court's Web site: www.unikarlsruhe.de/-bgh. The U.S. Second Circuit Court of Appeals similarly relied on universal jurisdiction in a tort case arising under the Alien Tort Claims Act and the Torture Victim Protection Act against Radovan Karadzic, the Bosnian Serb leader accused of crimes against humanity and war crimes in Bosnia. See *Kadic v. Karadzic*, 70 F.3d 232, 240 (2d Cir. 1995).

[103] Dessire Munyaneza was tried and found guilty in Canada in 2009 of seven counts of genocide, crimes against humanity, and war crimes committed in Rwanda and sentenced to life in prison. See R. C. Munyaneza, No. 500–73–002500–052, May 29, 2009. See *also* Theodor Meron, *International Criminalization of Internal Atrocities*, 89 Am. J. Int'l L. 554, 577 (1995) (while several of the warrants involved the killing of Belgian peacekeepers, one of the warrants was issued against a Rwandan responsible for massacres of other Rwandans in Rwanda).

[104] *United States v. Belfast* (a.k.a. Chuckie Taylor), 611 F.3d 783 (2010) (upholding a 97 year sentence for conviction of acts of torture committed by a citizen of Liberia against other citizens of Liberia in the territory of Liberia). The United States has statutes granting its courts universal jurisdiction over grave breaches of the Geneva Conventions, genocide, torture, the recruitment or use of child soldiers, and trafficking in persons. Amnesty International Report, Universal Jurisdiction: UN General Assembly Should Support This Essential International Justice Tool, IOR 53/015/2010, October 5, 2010, at notes 28–30, available at: http://www.amnesty.org/fr/library/info/IOR53/015/2010/en (last accessed February 9, 2013).

Courts and commentators often cite to the Nuremberg precedent as crystallizing universal jurisdiction for international crimes under customary international law.[105] It is significant that Nuremberg did not confine itself to war crimes and crimes against humanity; it also applied its jurisdiction to the crime of aggression ("then known as crimes against peace"), which it considered the most important crime within its jurisdiction. As the Nuremberg Tribunal concluded, "To initiate a war of aggression, therefore, is not only an international crime; it is the supreme international crime differing only from other war crimes in that it contains within itself the accumulated evil of the whole."[106] In his report to the president, Nuremberg Prosecutor Robert Jackson stated that at Nuremberg the prohibition of aggressive war, by force of "a judicial precedent," had become "a law with a sanction."[107]

The charter establishing the Nuremberg Tribunal provided the tribunal jurisdiction over war crimes, crimes against humanity, and "crimes against peace," which it defined as the "planning, preparation, initiation or waging of a war of aggression, or a war in violation of international treaties, agreements or assurances, or participating in a common plan or conspiracy for the accomplishment of any of the foregoing."[108] The

---

[105] *Prosecutor v. Tadic*, Interlocutory Appeal on Jurisdiction, IT-94–1AR72, October 2, 1995, para. 62; *Prosecutor v. Ntuyuhaga*, Decision on the Prosecutor's Motion to Withdraw the Indictment, ICTR-96–40-T, March 18, 1999; *Prosecutor v. Kallon and Kamara*, Decision on Challenge to Jurisdiction: Lome Accord Amnesty, SCSL-2004–15 AR72(E) and SCSL-2004–16-AR72(E), March 13, 2004, paras. 67–71; cf. Interlocutory Decision on the Applicable Law: Terrorism, Conspiracy, Homicide, Perpetration, Cumulative Charging, STL-11–01/1, February 16, 2011, para. 103 (citing *Tadic* for test for establishing a crime under customary international law).

[106] Judgment, 1 Trial of the Major War Criminals before the International Military Tribunal, Nuremberg November 14, 1945–October 1, 1946, at 13 (1946), reprinted in 41 Am. J. Int'l L. 172, 186 (1947).

[107] Report to the President by Mr. Justice Robert Jackson, June 6, 1945, available at: http://avalon.law.yale.edu/imt/jack63.asp.

[108] London Agreement and the Nuremberg Charter annexed thereto, August 8, 1945, Art. 6, 82 UNTS 280, reproduced in 2 Virginia Morris and Michael P. Scharf, An Insider's Guide to the International Criminal Tribunal for the Former Yugoslavia 675 (1995).

crime of aggression did not exist in customary international law prior to Nuremberg. In its judgment, the tribunal maintained that, because the charter made war of aggression a crime, "it is therefore not strictly necessary to consider whether and to what extent aggressive war was a crime before the execution of the London Agreement."[109]

Of the twenty-two high-ranking Nazi leaders tried at Nuremberg from November 20, 1945, to October 1, 1946, twelve were convicted of the crime of aggression. The crime of aggression was subsequently prosecuted by the American Control Council Law Number 10 Tribunals at Nuremberg in the *I. G. Farben, Krupp, High Command*, and *Ministries* cases,[110] as well as by the Supreme National Tribunal of Poland in the *Greiser* case, and the Chinese War Crimes Military Tribunal in the *Sakai* case.[111] Most recently, in 2006, the British High Court confirmed that on the basis of the Nuremberg precedent, the crime of aggression had crystallized into a crime under customary international law.[112]

In 1996, the International Law Commission finished its decades-long project of drafting the Code of Crimes against the Peace and Security of Mankind. Article 16 of that document confirmed that the crime of aggression constitutes a crime under international law, though it did not spell out the elements of the crime.[113] Some commentators take the position that unlike the other offenses tried at Nuremberg, the crime of aggression was not sufficiently defined by the Nuremberg Tribunal or subsequent developments to have become a customary international law crime.[114] As former U.S. Ambassador at Large for War Crimes Issues

---

[109] The Trial of Major War Criminals: Proceedings of the International Military Tribunal Sitting at Nuremberg Germany, Part 22, 445, 447 (1950).

[110] Mark A. Drumbl, *The Push to Criminalize Aggression: Something Lost amid the Gains?* 41 CASE W. RES. J. INT'L L. 291, 296 (2009).

[111] *Id.* at 299.

[112] *R. v. Jones et al.* (2006), UKHL 16, sections 12 and 19 (Lord Bingham), 44 and 59 (Lord Hoffmann), 96 (Lord Rodger), 97 (Lord Carswell), and 99 (Lord Mance).

[113] Code of Crimes against the Peace and Security of Mankind, Art. 16, UN Doc. A/51/10 (1996).

[114] Noah Weisbord, *Prosecuting Aggression*, 49 HARV. INT'L L. J. 161, 168 (2008).

David Scheffer, stated on the eve of the Kampala conference, "aggression had to be more sharply defined than the U.N. Charter's prohibition of 'the threat or use of force against the territorial integrity or political independence of any state,' which describes everything from pinprick attacks to massive invasions."[115] Others have observed that the 1974 UN Definition of Aggression was designed only to act as a guide for the Security Council and was not usable for prosecution.[116] In particular, they take exception to Article 4 of the 1974 resolution, which provides that "[t]he acts enumerated above are not exhaustive and the Security Council may determine that other acts constitute aggression under the provisions of the Charter."[117]

This approach, however, is not unique to the crime of aggression. Crimes against humanity as defined in the statutes of the ad hoc tribunals and ICC have a comparable "semiopen" clause. Thus, Article 7(1)(K) of the ICC Statute speaks of "other inhumane acts of a similar character intentionally causing great suffering, or serious injury to body or to mental or physical health."[118] Moreover, the concern is undercut by the historic treatment of piracy, the precursor to the modern crimes of universal jurisdiction. Although piracy is the oldest of the crimes of universal jurisdiction recognized under customary international law, until quite recently there was no authoritative definition of piracy. "It was not settled, for example, whether *animus furandi*, an intent to rob, was a necessary element, whether acts by insurgents seeking to overthrow their government should be exempt, as were acts by state vessels and by recognized belligerents, and whether the act had to be by one ship against another or could be on the same ship."[119] The historic debate

---

[115] David Scheffer, *Aggression Is Now a Crime*, INTERNATIONAL HAROLD TRIBUNE, July 1, 2010.

[116] Noah Weisbord, *Prosecuting Aggression*, 49 HARV. INT'L L. J. 161, 168 (2008).

[117] Annex to UN Doc. A/ES/3314 (XXIX), December 14, 1974 (Res. 3314).

[118] Rome Statute of the International Criminal Court, Art. 7(1)(K), UN Doc. A/CONF.183.9, July 17, 1998.

[119] Malvina Halberstam, *Terrorism on the High Seas: The Achille Lauro, Piracy and the IMO Convention on Maritime Safety*, 82 AMER. J. INT'L L. 269, 272 (1988).

over the definition of the crime of piracy suggests that disagreement over the scope or contours of a universal crime may not deprive the offense of its universal character.

While acknowledging that the Nuremberg Principles constitute customary international law, some commentators question whether Nuremberg actually applied a collective form of universal jurisdiction delegated by the countries that ratified the London Agreement establishing the Nuremberg Tribunal. Instead, they argue that Nuremberg should be viewed as a court of the occupying powers applying the territorial jurisdiction of Germany over the accused Nazis. If that is the case, then Nuremberg and its progeny would not provide a customary international law basis for the domestic assertion of universal jurisdiction over the crime of aggression.

This view finds support in the fact that the four Allied states that established the Nuremberg tribunal had assumed supreme authority in Germany. As stated in the *Berlin Declaration* of June 5, 1945:

> The Governments of the United States of America, The Union of Soviet Socialist Republics and the United Kingdom, and the Provisional Government of the French Republic, hereby assume supreme authority with respect to Germany, including all the powers possessed by the German Government, the High Command and any state, municipal, or local government or authority.[120]

From this language, some commentators have concluded that the "Nuremberg tribunal prosecutions were actually an exercise of national jurisdiction by the effective German sovereign, the Allies."[121] Yet, there

---

[120] *Berlin Declaration*, June 5, 1945, 60 Stat. 1649, 1650; see also Agreement between the Governments of the United States of America and the Union of Soviet Socialist Republics and the United Kingdom and the Provisional Government of the French Republic on Certain Additional Requirements to Be Imposed on Germany, September 20, 1945, 3 Bevans 1254 (delineating further the powers to be exercised by the Allies including prosecutions for war crimes).

[121] Madeline Morris, *High Crimes and Misconceptions: The ICC and Non Party States*, 64 LAW & CONTEMP. PROBS 13, 38(2001). As Hans Kelsen stated, "the criminal prosecution of Germans for illegal acts of their state could have been based on national

are several reasons to conclude that the better (or at least equally valid) view was that Nuremberg was an international tribunal applying universal jurisdiction.

To begin with, in his seminal 1946 article on the Nuremberg Tribunal, Professor Egon Schwelb listed the following features that evince that the Nuremberg tribunal was not a mere occupation court but rather an international judicial body applying universal jurisdiction over the Axis country war criminals: (a) the name given to the court, the International Military Tribunal; (b) the reference in the preamble to the fact that the four signatories are "acting in the interests of all the United Nations"; (c) the provision in Article 5 of the agreement giving any government of the United Nations the right to adhere to the agreement; (d) the provision of Article 6 of the charter, according to which the jurisdiction of the tribunal is not restricted to German major war criminals, but, in theory at least, comprises the right to try and punish the major war criminals of all other European Axis countries; and (e) the provision of Article 10 of the charter providing for the binding character, in proceedings before courts of the signatory states, of a declaration by the tribunal that a group or organization is criminal.[122]

Moreover, it is telling that the opening statements of both the U.S. Prosecutor Robert Jackson[123] and UK Prosecutor Sir Hartley

---

law, enacted for this purpose by the competent authorities. These authorities were the four occupant powers exercising their joint sovereignty in a condominium over the territory and the population of subjugated Germany through the Control Council as the legitimate successor of the last German Government." Hans Kelsen, *Will the Judgment in the Nuremberg Trial Constitute a Precedent in International Law?* 1 INT'L L. Q. 153, 167 (1947). Similarly Georg Schwarzenberger concluded, "In substance, ... [the Nuremberg] Tribunal is a municipal tribunal of extraordinary jurisdiction which the four Contracting Powers share in common." Georg Schwarzenberger, *The Problem of an International Criminal Law*, 3 CURRENT LEGAL PROBS. 263, 290, 291 (1950); see also Georg Schwarzenberger, *The Judgment of Nuremberg*, 21 TUL. L. REV. 329, 334–5 (1947).

[122] Egon Schwelb, *Crimes against Humanity*, 23 BRITISH Y.B. INT'L L. 178, 208 (1946).
[123] See Robert H. Jackson, The Nurnberg Case 88 (1947, 2nd printing, 1971) ("The principle of individual responsibility for piracy and brigandage, which have long been

Shawcross[124] drew an analogy between the right to prosecute pirates under universal jurisdiction and the legitimacy of the Nuremberg Tribunal's exercise of jurisdiction over war crimes, crimes against humanity, and the crime of aggression. Like piracy, the Nazi offenses during the war involved violent and predatory action and were typically committed in locations where they would not be prevented or punished through other bases of jurisdiction.[125] As Colonel Willard Cowles wrote on the eve of the establishment of the Nuremberg Tribunal:

> Basically, war crimes are very similar to piratical acts, except that they take place usually on land rather than at sea. In both situations there is, broadly speaking, a lack of any adequate judicial system operating on the spot where the crime takes place – in the case of piracy it is because the acts are on the high seas and in the case of war crimes because of a chaotic condition or irresponsible leadership in time of war. As regards both piratical acts and war crimes there is often no well-organized police or judicial system at the place where the acts are committed, and both the pirate and the war criminal take advantage of this fact, hoping thereby to commit their crimes with impunity.[126]

In addition, the Nuremberg judgment contains an oft-cited passage indicating that the Court itself perceived that its jurisdiction was based on the universality principle:

> The Signatory Powers created this Tribunal, defined the law it was to administer, and made regulations for the proper conduct of the trial.

recognized as crimes punishable under International Law, is old and well established. That is what illegal warfare is.").

[124] See 3 Trial of the Major War Criminals before the International Military Tribunal 106 (1995) ("Nor is the principle of individual international responsibility for offenses against the law of nations altogether new. It has been applied not only to pirates. The entire law relating to war crimes, as distinct from the crime of war, is based upon the principle of responsibility.").

[125] See Kenneth C. Randall, *Universal Jurisdiction under International Law*, 66 TEX. L. REV. 785, 793 (1988).

[126] Willard B. Cowles, *Universality of Jurisdiction over War Crimes*, 33 CAL. L. REV. 177, 194 (1945).

In doing so, they have done together what any one of them might
have done singly; for it is not to be doubted that any nation has the
right thus to set up special courts to administer law.[127]

While this passage can be read in varying ways, it is of particular significance that the definitive report on the Nuremberg Trials submitted by the
United Nations secretary-general in 1949 concluded that Nuremberg's
jurisdiction was analogous to the exercise of universal jurisdiction of
piracy. As the secretary-general explained:

> It is possible that the Court meant that the several signatory Powers
> had jurisdiction over the crimes defined in the Charter because these
> crimes threatened the security of each of them. The Court may, in
> other words, have intended to assimilate the said crimes, in regard
> to jurisdiction, to such offences as the counterfeiting of currency. On
> the other hand, it is also possible and perhaps more probable, that
> the Court considered the crimes under the Charter to be, as inter-
> national crimes, subject to the jurisdiction of every state. The case
> of piracy would then be the appropriate parallel. This interpretation
> seems to be supported by the fact that the Court affirmed that the
> signatory Powers in creating the Tribunal had made use of a right
> belonging to any nation. But it must be conceded, at the same time,
> that the phrase "right thus to set up special courts to administer law"
> is too vague to admit of definite conclusion.[128]

Fifty years later, in its Report to the Security Council, the UN
Commission of Experts on Violations of International Humanitarian
Law in the Former Yugoslavia reaffirmed that Nuremberg's jurisdiction
had been based on the universality principle of jurisdiction.[129]

---

[127] 22 Trial of the Major War Criminals before the International Military Tribunal 461,
466 (1995).

[128] The Charter and Judgment of the Nuremberg Tribunal 80, U.N. Doc. A/CN.4/5, U.N.
Sales No. 1949 V.7 (1949) (memorandum submitted by the secretary-general).

[129] Interim Report of the Independent Commission of Experts Established Pursuant to
Security Council Resolution 780 (1992), P 73, U.N. Doc. S/25274 (1993), reprinted
in 2 Virginia Morris & Michael P. Scharf, An Insider's Guide to the
International Criminal Tribunal for the Former Yugoslavia 311 (1995).

If the Nuremberg judgment itself was somewhat vague about the underpinnings of the court's jurisdiction, it is noteworthy that the Control Council Law Number 10 Tribunals[130] unambiguously referred to their jurisdiction as applying the universality principle in their judgments. A prominent example is the case of *In re List*, which involved the prosecution of German officers who had commanded the execution of hundreds of thousands of civilians in Greece, Yugoslavia, and Albania.[131] In describing the basis of its jurisdiction to punish such offenses, the U.S. CCL10 tribunal in Nuremberg indicated that the defendants had committed "international crimes" that were "universally recognized" under existing customary and treaty law.[132] The tribunal explained that "an international crime is ... an act universally recognized as criminal,

The UN Commission of Experts stated: "States may choose to combine their jurisdictions under the universality principle and vest this combined jurisdiction in an international tribunal. The Nuremberg International Military Tribunal may be said to have derived its jurisdiction from such a combination of national jurisdiction of the States parties to the London Agreement setting up that Tribunal."

[130] On December 20, 1945, the Allied Control Council of Germany, composed of the commanders in chief of the occupying forces of each of the Four Powers, issued Control Council Law No. 10, which was intended to "establish a uniform legal basis in Germany for the prosecution of war criminals and other similar offenders, other than those dealt with by the International Military Tribunal." See Matthew Lippman, *The Other Nuremberg: American Prosecutions of Nazi War Criminals in Occupied Germany*, 3 IND. INT'L & COMP. L. REV. 1, 8 (1992). CCL 10 and the Rules of Procedure for the CCL 10 proceedings are reproduced in 2 Morris & Scharf, Rwanda Tribunal, supra note 90, at 494, 497. By its terms, CCL 10 made the London Agreement and Nuremberg Charter an "integral part" of the law and provided for the creation of tribunals established by the four occupying powers in their zones of control in Germany to try the remaining German economic, political, military, legal, and medical leaders accused of war crimes and crimes against humanity. *Id.* CCL 10 arts. 1, 3. General Telford Taylor, the chief prosecutor of the U.S. CCL 10 trials, has written that the trials "were held under a comparable authorization from the same four powers that signed the London Charter." TELFORD TAYLOR, NUREMBERG AND VIETNAM: AN AMERICAN TRAGEDY 81 (1970).

[131] 11 Trials of War Criminals 757 (1946–9) (U.S. Mil. Trib. – Nuremberg 1948). In re List is known as the Hostage case because civilians were taken hostage and then killed.

[132] *Id.* at 1235.

which is considered a grave matter of international concern and for some valid reason cannot be left within the exclusive jurisdiction of the state that would have control over it under ordinary circumstances."[133] The tribunal concluded that a state that captures the perpetrator of such crimes either may "surrender the alleged criminal to the state where the offense was committed, or ... retain the alleged criminal for trial under its own legal processes."[134] Other decisions rendered by the CCL10 Tribunals that similarly rely on the universality principle include the *Hadamar* trial of 1945,[135] the *Zyklon B* case of 1946,[136] and the *Einsatzgruppen* case of 1948.[137] On the basis of these precedents, the United States Court of Appeals for the Sixth Circuit concluded in *Demjanjuk v. Petrovsky* that "it is generally agreed that the establishment of these

---

[133] *Id*. at 1241.

[134] *Id*. at 1242.

[135] 1 Law Reports of Trials of War Criminals 46 (1949) (U.S. Mil. Commission – Wiesbaden 1945). In asserting the universality principle as one of its bases of jurisdiction in a case involving allegations that the defendants had executed by lethal injection nearly 500 Polish and Russian civilians at a sanatorium in Hadamar, Germany, the United States Military Commission in the *Hadamar* trial case claimed jurisdiction irrespective of the nationalities of the defendants and their victims and "of the place where the offence was committed, particularly where, for some reason, the criminal would otherwise go unpunished." *Id*. at 53. The prosecution had argued that "an offense against the laws of war is a violation of the law of nations and a matter of general interest and concern.... War crimes are now recognized as of special concern to the United Nations, which states in the real sense represent the civilized world." Trial of Afons Klein, Adolf Wahlmann, Heinrich Ruoff, Karl Willig, Adolf Merkle, Irmgard Huber, and Philipp Blum 9 (The Hadamar Trial) (Earl W. Kintner, ed., 1949) (reply by the prosecutor).

[136] 1 Law Reports of Trials of War Criminals 93 (1949) (British Mil. Ct. – Hamburg 1946). In a case involving three German industrialists charged with having knowingly supplied poison gas used for the extermination of Allied nations (which did not include British victims), the British military court in Hamburg noted that jurisdictional support derived from the universality principle, under which every state has jurisdiction to punish war criminals. See *id*. at 103.

[137] The *Einsatzgruppen* case involved the trial before a U.S. Tribunal in Nuremberg of the commanders of killing squads that shadowed the German troops advancing into Poland and Russia. Citing the universality principle as one of the bases for the tribunal's jurisdiction, the tribunal stated:

[World War II] tribunals and their proceedings were based on universal jurisdiction."[138]

While the case for characterizing Nuremberg as a court applying universal jurisdiction is a strong one, we need not definitively decide the age-old debate since Nuremberg could have been based on multiple and overlapping types of jurisdiction. Thus, Professor Roger Clark writes, "the power of the Allies to set up the Tribunal may be said to flow either from their authority as the de facto territorial rulers of a defeated Germany, or more congenially, as exercising the authority of the international community operating on a type of universal jurisdiction."[139] Professor Schwelb similarly concluded: "If the Tribunal based the legislative powers of the signatories of the Charter on the unconditional surrender of Germany and the right to legislate for occupied territory, it did not exclude the construction that the Nuremberg proceedings had, in addition to this territorial basis, also a wider foundation in the provisions of international law and the Court the standing of an international judicial body."[140] As such, it is reasonable for states to conclude that Nuremberg and its progeny provide a customary international law basis for prosecuting the crime of aggression under the universality principle.

> They are being tried because they are accused of having offended against society itself, and society, as represented by international law, has summoned them for explanation.... It is the essence of criminal justice that the offended community inquires into the offense involved.... There is no authority which denies any belligerent nation jurisdiction over individuals in its actual custody charged with violation of international law. And if a single nation may legally take jurisdiction in such instances, with what more reason may a number of nations agree, in the interest of justice, to try alleged violations of the international code of war?
>
> *United States v. Otto Ohlendorf*, reprinted in IV Trials of War Criminals before the Nuremberg Military Tribunals under Control Council Law No. 10, at 411, 462 (1950).

[138] *Demjanjuk v. Petrovsky*, 776 F.2d 571, 582 (6th Cir. 1985) (referring to the IMT and CCL10 tribunals).

[139] Roger Clark, *Nuremberg and Tokyo in Contemporary Perspective*, in THE LAW OF WAR CRIMES, NATIONAL AND INTERNATIONAL APPROACHES 172 (Timothy L. H. McCormack & Gerry J. Simpson, eds. 1997).

[140] Egon Schwelb, *Crimes against Humanity*, 23 BRITISH Y.B. INT'L L. 178, 210 (1946).

The adoption of the crime of aggression at Kampala has been her-
alded as one of the major developments in international law in modern
times. Great developments are never risk free, and the United States
was right to be concerned that an unintended consequence of Kampala
would be a proliferation of state laws providing for universal jurisdiction over the crime of aggression. However, the preceding analysis suggests that the U.S.-proposed understanding may do little to prevent that
from occurring. If the United States and its allies truly want to prevent
the Kampala amendments from prompting states to add the crime of
aggression to the offenses subject to their universal jurisdiction, they
should seek an amendment to the Kampala text that renders the crime
of aggression subject to the exclusive jurisdiction of the International
Criminal Court. Such an amendment will not prevent nonparties from
prosecuting the crime of aggression, but it would apply to the 122 states
(i.e., the parties to the ICC Statute) that are most likely to adopt universal jurisdiction for the crime. In the years before a final decision is made
to bring the aggression amendments into force, there will be opportuni-
ties to consider adoption of an exclusive jurisdiction amendment in one
form or another.

* * *

This chapter has established that despite the paucity of state practice, consistent with the Grotian Moment concept the Nuremberg Principles rapidly
ripened into customary international law. While debate continues over the
content of those principles, we have seen that the unique mode of liability
developed at Nuremberg known as JCE is now applied by international and
hybrid criminal tribunals and may soon be adopted by national courts. In
addition, since Nuremberg has been widely viewed as providing the foundation for states to exercise universal jurisdiction over genocide, crimes
against humanity, and war crimes, states are likely to cite Nuremberg as
the foundation of a customary international law right to exercise universal
jurisdiction over the crime of aggression as well, now that the ICC has
adopted a modern definition and elements of the crime.

5 The Truman Proclamation on the Continental Shelf

THIS CHAPTER EXAMINES THE EFFECT OF U.S. PRESIDENT
Harry S. Truman's executive order on September 28, 1945,
proclaiming that the resources on the continental shelf
contiguous to the United States belonged to the United States. This was
a radical departure from the existing approach, under which the two
basic principles of the law of the sea had been a narrow strip of coastal
waters under the exclusive sovereignty of the coastal state and an unregulated area beyond that known as the high seas. The speed at which
Truman's continental shelf concept was recognized through emulation
or acquiescence led Sir Hersch Lauterpacht to declare in 1950 that it represented virtually "instant custom."[1] This chapter focuses on the conflu-
ence of postwar economic needs and technological changes that made
this accelerated formation of customary international law concerning
the continental shelf possible.

Customary International Law of the Sea prior to the Truman Proclamation

Prior to conclusion of the 1958 Law of the Sea Conventions, this area of
law was governed mainly by custom. The Romans considered the seas as

---

[1] Hersch Lauterpacht, *Sovereignty over Submarine Areas* 27 BRITISH YEAR BOOK OF
INTERNATIONAL LAW 377 (1950).

res communis – belonging to everyone, and therefore open to use but not appropriation.[2] After the fall of Rome, state practice tended toward an alternate approach, treating the seas as *res nullius* – belonging to no one, and therefore open to claim.[3] This approach reached its zenith in 1493, when the major powers of the day, Spain and Portugal, purported to divide most of the world's oceans between them, claiming exclusive navigation rights in a joint act of appropriation ratified by Pope Alexander VI.[4]

During the next century, however, English and Dutch naval power began to challenge the Spanish and Portuguese claims. In 1608 Hugo Grotius published an influential pamphlet, *Mare Liberum* (The Free Sea), in which he attacked the *mare clausum* (closed sea) concept and argued instead for the "freedom of the seas."[5] According to Grotius, "The sea can in no way become the private property of any one, because nature not only allows but enjoins its common use.... Nature does not give a right to anybody to appropriate such things as may inoffensively be used by everybody and are inexhaustible, and therefore, sufficient for all."[6]

The Grotian doctrine was accepted by the international community for three hundred years, and the idea of *mare clausum* retreated to a narrow belt of territorial sea bordering a state's coast.[7] During the eighteenth, nineteenth, and most of the twentieth century, the limit of territorial waters was fixed at the distance that a cannon could shoot from shore, that is, three miles seaward from the coast.[8] By 1945, the

---

[2] BARRY BUZAN, SEABED POLITICS 1 (Praeger Publishers, 1976).

[3] *Id.*

[4] JAMES B. MORELL, THE LAW OF THE SEA: AN HISTORICAL ANALYSIS OF THE 1982 TREATY AND ITS REJECTION BY THE UNITED STATES 1 (McFarland & Co., 1992).

[5] HUGO GROTIUS, MARE LIBERUM (1608), English translation available at: http://oll.libertyfund.org/index.php?option=com_staticxt&staticfile=show. php%3Ftitle=552&Itemid=27 (last accessed February 9, 2013).

[6] JAMES B. MORELL, THE LAW OF THE SEA: AN HISTORICAL ANALYSIS OF THE 1982 TREATY AND ITS REJECTION BY THE UNITED STATES 2 (McFarland & Co., 1992).

[7] BARRY BUZAN, SEABED POLITICS 2 (Praeger Publishers, 1976).

[8] JAMES B. MORELL, THE LAW OF THE SEA: AN HISTORICAL ANALYSIS OF THE 1982 TREATY AND ITS REJECTION BY THE UNITED STATES 2 (McFarland & Co., 1992).

width of the territorial sea had been extended to six miles by six states, to nine miles by one state, and to twelve miles by two states, but the great majority of states continued to hold to the three mile jurisdictional limit.[9]

Although the Truman Proclamation is widely viewed as a singular turning point, long before 1945 coastal states had made legal claims to the resources of the seabed and subsoil beyond the territorial sea.[10] Thus, Ceylon, Venezuela, Panama, and France asserted jurisdiction over the oyster and pearl beds well off their coast, while Tunisia laid claims to sponge fishing grounds beyond its territorial waters.[11] Yet these were viewed as unique historic claims and accepted as limited exceptions to the three mile limit on coastal state jurisdiction rather than precedent for a new juridical concept.[12]

Nor was the United States the first country in modern times to claim jurisdiction over the entire continental shelf. In February 1942, Venezuela and the United Kingdom signed the Treaty of Paria, which divided the seabed in the Gulf of Paria between Venezuela and British Trinidad.[13] Although the term "continental shelf" did not appear anywhere in the treaty, some regard this as the first treaty on the continental shelf because of "reference to off shore installation for the drilling of petroleum and provisions assuring freedom of navigation."[14] Yet, "in the general furor of the war," this precedent had little impact on the development of customary international law.[15] Rather, it was the Truman

---

[9] James B. Morell, The Law of the Sea: An Historical Analysis of the 1982 Treaty and Its Rejection by the United States 4 (McFarland & Co., 1992). Under the 1982 Law of the Sea Treaty, the territorial sea was extended to twelve nautical miles.

[10] Suzette V. Suarez, The Outer Limits of the Continental Shelf: Legal Aspects of Their Establishment 21 (Springer, 2008).

[11] Barry Buzan, Seabed Politics 2 (Praeger Publishers, 1976).

[12] Id.

[13] Barry Buzan, Seabed Politics 7 (Praeger Publishers, 1976).

[14] Suzette V. Suarez, The Outer Limits of the Continental Shelf: Legal Aspects of Their Establishment 89 (Springer, 2008).

[15] Barry Buzan, Seabed Politics 7 (Praeger Publishers, 1976).

Proclamation of September 28, 1945, "that gave birth to the modern concept of the continental shelf."[16]

The Politics behind the Truman Proclamation

There were actually two law of the sea proclamations simultaneously
issued by President Truman on September 28, 1945.[17] The better remem-
bered proclamation, which is the focus of this chapter, asserted U.S.
jurisdiction and control over the natural resources of the continental
shelf contiguous to the United States. It also called for the determination of boundaries with adjacent states (namely, Mexico) on the basis of
equitable principles and for the retention of the high seas character of
the waters above the continental shelf. The proclamation was carefully
worded, avoiding any mention of sovereignty and claiming jurisdiction
only over resources. Neither did it claim the waters superjacent to the
continental shelf.

The Truman Proclamation was the first claim by a major maritime
power to jurisdiction over the continental shelf beyond the territorial
sea. The pathbreaking proclamation was driven by "the emergence of
influential new transnational interest groups within the United States –
particularly scientists, ecologists, and the oil and mining industries."[18]
By the mid-1930s, technological capabilities had reached the stage where
the prospects for offshore oil were generating widespread interest.[19]
Moreover, the drain on American resources caused by the war and the

---

[16] Suzette V. Suarez, The Outer Limits of the Continental Shelf: Legal
Aspects of Their Establishment 25 (Springer, 2008).

[17] The second of the two proclamations declared a U.S. right to establish conservation
zones for the protection of fisheries in certain areas of the high seas contiguous to
the United States where fishing activities had been or would be maintained on a substantial scale. Ann L. Hollick, U.S. Foreign Policy and the Law of the Sea 18
(Princeton University Press, 1981).

[18] James B. Morell, The Law of the Sea: An Historical Analysis of the 1982
Treaty and Its Rejection by the United States 4 (McFarland & Co., 1992).

[19] Ann L. Hollick, U.S. Foreign Policy and the Law of the Sea 28 (Princeton
University Press, 1981).

rapid growth following the war had triggered increasing interest in continental shelf resources.[20] Exploratory drilling had indicated that deposits of offshore oil were substantial.[21] Today, drilling in the continental shelf of the southern states accounts for 30 percent of the United State's total oil production, generates 400,000 jobs, and yields $20 billion in annual fees paid to the federal government.[22]

Within the U.S. government, the main proponent of the extension of jurisdiction over the continental shelf was Secretary of the Interior Harold L. Ickes, who sent President Franklin Delano Roosevelt a letter on June 5, 1943, which said:

> The War has impressed us with the necessity for an augmented supply of natural resources. In this connection I draw your attention to the importance of the Continental Shelf.... The Continental Shelf extending some 100 or 150 miles from our shores ... contains ore and other resources similar to those found in our States. I suggest the advisability of laying the groundwork now for availing ourselves fully of the riches in this submerged land.[23]

President Roosevelt responded favorably to Ickes's initiative. On June 10, Roosevelt sent a memo to the secretary of state, Cordell Hull, in which he stated:

> I think Harold Ickes has the right slant on this. For many years, I have felt that the old three-mile limit or twenty-mile limit should be superseded by a rule of common sense. For instance, the Gulf of Mexico is bounded on the south by Mexico and on the north by the United States. In parts of the Gulf, shallow water extends very many miles off shore. It seems to me that the Mexican Government

[20] BARRY BUZAN, SEABED POLITICS 7 (Praeger Publishers, 1976).

[21] Id. at 28.

[22] HIS GLOBAL INSIGHT, SPECIAL REPORT, THE ECONOMIC IMPACT OF THE GULF OF MEXICO OFFSHORE OIL AND NATURAL GAS INDUSTRY AND THE ROLE OF INDEPENDENTS, July 21, 2010.

[23] ANN L. HOLLICK, U.S. FOREIGN POLICY AND THE LAW OF THE SEA 34 (Princeton University Press, 1981) (citing Foreign Relations 1945, II, 1481).

should be entitled to drill for oil in the southern half of the Gulf and
we in the northern half of the Gulf. That would be far more sensible
than allowing some European nation, for example, to come in there
and drill.[24]

President Roosevelt recognized that the new policy would constitute a
departure from existing international law. In a memorandum addressed
to the attorney general and secretaries of state, navy, and interior, he
wrote, "I recognize that new principles of international law might have
to be asserted but such principles would not in effect be wholly new,
because they would be based on the consideration that inventive genius
has moved jurisdiction out to sea to the limit of inventive genius."[25]

The State Department, meanwhile, expressed concern about the
international reaction to a unilateral assertion of jurisdiction over the
continental shelf. An internal memorandum from the Office of Economic
Affairs to the secretary of state warned that it could "lead to misunder-
standing, suspicion, and opposition on the part of many other countries"
and stressed that the United States "should not announce this policy
without some form of international consultation with at least the countries that would feel themselves interested in and affected thereby."[26] As
a compromise to gain the Department of State's support, Ickes proposed
the following formulation for President Roosevelt's approval: "Within a
period of two months from the date of your approval *and after consultation with the foreign governments* concerned, the necessary documents
will be submitted for signature and promulgation by you."[27] President
Roosevelt approved the policy on March 31, 1945, while in the final

[24] ANN L. HOLLICK, U.S. FOREIGN POLICY AND THE LAW OF THE SEA 35 (Princeton
University Press, 1981) (citing *Foreign Relations* 1945), II, 1482.
[25] ANN L. HOLLICK, U.S. FOREIGN POLICY AND THE LAW OF THE SEA 30 (Princeton
University Press, 1981) (citing Unpublished, National Archives Record
Group), 48.
[26] ANN L. HOLLICK, U.S. FOREIGN POLICY AND THE LAW OF THE SEA 41 (Princeton
University Press, 1981).
[27] ANN L. HOLLICK, U.S. FOREIGN POLICY AND THE LAW OF THE SEA 43 (Princeton
University Press, 1981) (emphasis added).

stages of illness. Less than two weeks later, Roosevelt died, leaving it for his vice president, Harry Truman, to issue the proclamation.

The Legal Rationale for the Truman Proclamation

The most comprehensive analysis of the legal basis for the Truman Proclamation was set forth in a memorandum prepared by William Bishop of the State Department Office of the Legal Advisor.[28] The explanatory statement was drafted for use in the consultations with other governments that would precede the promulgation of the proclamation.

The legal adviser's memorandum began with the following definition of the continental shelf : "The continental shelf extends seaward for varying distances off the shores, and in most places terminates in a fairly definite drop off." It went on to say the continental shelf "is that part of the undersea land mass adjacent to the coast, over which the sea is not more than 100 fathoms (600 feet) in depth." The term "shelf" was to include "the shallow waters around this nation's islands as well as all the continental United States." The memorandum stressed that the U.S. claim to continental shelf resources was not to affect the high seas status of the superjacent waters.[29]

The legal adviser's memorandum then offered six distinct legal arguments for why "it was reasonable and just" for the United States to lay claim to the resources in its continental shelf:

> (a) The continental shelf may be regarded on geographic and physical grounds as an extension of the land mass of the coastal state and thus naturally appurtenant to it; (b) these resources often form part of a pool or deposit extending seaward from within the State and their

[28] ANN L. HOLLICK, U.S. FOREIGN POLICY AND THE LAW OF THE SEA 45–6 (Princeton University Press, 1981).

[29] ANN L. HOLLICK, U.S. FOREIGN POLICY AND THE LAW OF THE SEA 49 (Princeton University Press, 1981) (citing Explanatory Statement on the Protection and Conservation of Coastal Fisheries, Foreign Relations 1945, II, 1496–7).

utilization may affect resources therein; (c) the effectiveness of measures which may be adopted to utilize or conserve these resources would be contingent upon cooperation and protection from the coastal State; (d) self-protection compels the coastal State to keep close watch over activities off its shores which are of the nature and relative permanence necessary for utilization of resources of the subsoil and seabed of the continental shelf; (e) prudent conservation and practical utilization of these resources are dependent upon a clear government policy defining their jurisdictional status; and (f) the government of the country to whose shores the resources are contiguous is clearly the logical government to exercise jurisdiction and control over these resources.[30]

In sum, the legal rationale was based on geological reality, technological developments, national security, economic necessity, conservation, and the efficacy of coastal state regulation. The United States recognized that it was acting as a legal pioneer, but it couched its justification in legal terms that would render the action easier to accept and replicate by other states. Thus, the legal adviser's memo invited other governments to join the United States in the "practical application of the principles set forth above."[31]

Did the Truman Proclamation Constitute a Grotian Moment?

The Truman Proclamation has been described as "a conceptual breakthrough."[32] At the time it was issued, the area beyond the narrow territorial sea, including the seabed, was universally considered to be the high seas, open to all. The proclamation gave great weight to the principle emphasized in its preamble that the mere existence of the continental shelf as "an extension of the land mass to the coastal nation and thus

[30] ANN L. HOLLICK, U.S. FOREIGN POLICY AND THE LAW OF THE SEA 48 (Princeton University Press, 1981).
[31] ANN L. HOLLICK, U.S. FOREIGN POLICY AND THE LAW OF THE SEA 49 (Princeton University Press, 1981).
[32] BARRY BUZAN, SEABED POLITICS 8 (Praeger Publishers, 1976).

naturally appurtenant to it" was a sufficient legal basis for a claim by the coastal state to areas that had previously been considered beyond the state's jurisdiction.[33]

Despite its radical nature, the Truman Proclamation encountered no public opposition from any state.[34] One scholar asserts that this reflected the successful behind-the-scenes diplomacy that the U.S. State Department engaged in during the months prior to the announcement of the proclamation in September 1995.[35] In fact, the State Department had consulted only four states (Canada, Mexico, the United Kingdom, and the Soviet Union), and the communications were more in the nature of advance notifications than actual consultations. With the exception of the United Kingdom, which indicated that it was not prepared to support a broad statement of principle on the continental shelf, none of the states consulted even issued a reply.[36]

---

[33] Proclamation 2667 of September 28, 1945, Policy of the United States with Respect to the Natural Resources of the Subsoil and Sea Bed of the Continental Shelf, 10 Fed. Reg. 12,305 (1945). The preamble of the Truman Proclamation states: "Whereas it is the view of the Government of the United States that the exercise of jurisdiction over the natural resources of the subsoil and sea bed of the continental shelf by the contiguous nation is reasonable and just, since the effectiveness of measures to utilize or conserve these resources would be contingent upon cooperation and protection from the shore, since the continental shell may be regarded as an extension of the land-mass of the coastal nation and thus naturally appurtenant to it, since these resources frequently form a seaward extension of a pool or deposit lying within the territory, and since self-protection compels the coastal nation to keep close watch over activities off its shores which are of the nature necessary for utilization of these resources."

[34] BARRY BUZAN, SEABED POLITICS 8 (Praeger Publishers, 1976).

[35] D. P. O'CONNELL, THE INTERNATIONAL LAW OF THE SEA, 31–2 n. 58 (Oxford University Press, 1983).

[36] ANN L. HOLLICK, U.S. FOREIGN POLICY AND THE LAW OF THE SEA n.158 (Princeton University Press, 1981). The British communiqué, dated August 31, 1945, stated: "His Majesty's Government do not wish to be associated with this Decision and would prefer that, when it is announced, no reference should be made to prior consultation with His Majesty's Government." ANN L. HOLLICK, U.S. FOREIGN POLICY AND THE LAW OF THE SEA 58 (Princeton University Press, 1981) (citing letter from the second secretary of the British embassy to Mr. William Bishop, assistant to the legal adviser, August 31, 1945, *Foreign Relations* 1945, II, 1527).

Another scholar has asserted that the lack of protest concerning the Truman Proclamation merely reflected the fact that "U.S. offshore resources were not in danger of foreign exploitation in 1945."[37] It was true that the first commercially viable oil well located beyond the United States' three mile territorial sea was not drilled until 1947. However, by 1945, deep water drilling technology had progressed far enough to indicate that such drilling would soon be feasible.[38]

Other scholars have stated that the United States avoided protest by making clear to other governments that it was willing to lease rights to drill for oil on its continental shelf to foreign nationals and corporations on equal footing with U.S. nationals.[39] Others noted that the proclamation was not threatening to foreign interests since it made clear that "freedom of navigation and of the high seas fishing were not compromised."[40] Still others believed that "in 1945 the nations of the world were too enfeebled by six years of war or too pre-occupied with the pressing problem of repairing the havoc of war or too dependent on the United States to challenge the doctrine or reveal its flaws."[41]

Not only was there an absence of protest, but other coastal states quickly grasped the economic and security benefits of the continental shelf concept in the Truman Proclamation and declared that it constituted a legally valid precedent. Within five years of the Truman Proclamation, jurisdiction was extended farther offshore by more than thirty coastal States, several of which claimed expanded territorial sovereignty as

---

[37] ANN L. HOLLICK, U.S. FOREIGN POLICY AND THE LAW OF THE SEA 61 (Princeton University Press, 1981).

[38] National Commission on the BP Deep Water Horizon Oil Spill and Offshore Drilling, Staff Working Paper #1 (2011), at 2, available at http://www.cs.ucdavis.edu/~rogaway/classes/188/materials/bp.pdf (last accessed February 9, 2013).

[39] BARRY BUZAN, SEABED POLITICS 8 (Praeger Publishers, 1976).

[40] SUZETTE V. SUAREZ, THE OUTER LIMITS OF THE CONTINENTAL SHELF: LEGAL ASPECTS OF THEIR ESTABLISHMENT 23 (Springer, 2008) (citing various publicists).

[41] SUZETTE V. SUAREZ, THE OUTER LIMITS OF THE CONTINENTAL SHELF: LEGAL ASPECTS OF THEIR ESTABLISHMENT 28 (Springer, 2008) (citing remarks by the president of the third UN Conference on the Law of the Sea).

far as two hundred miles from shore.[42] The Truman Proclamation was unquestionably the catalyst that set off this round of unilateral claims to the continental shelf. But it did not become the exclusive model on which all the claims were based. While Britain, Mexico, Guatemala, Iran, and the Philippines followed the United States formula of claiming only functional jurisdiction over resources, most of the Latin American countries claimed the shelf as part of their sovereign territory.[43] And while the Truman Proclamation was based on geological contiguity of the shallow shelf, in the 1952 *Santiago Declaration*, Chile, Ecuador, and Peru made claims based wholly upon adjacency to the territorial sea, regardless of the existence of a geological shelf in the area.[44]

Commentators have noted that despite these developments, in the 1949 Abu Dhabi Oil Arbitration case, a distinguished international arbitrator declined to recognize the emerging "continental shelf doctrine" as an established rule of international law.[45] The question in the Abu Dhabi case, however, was whether the continental shelf concept reflected customary international law in 1939 at the time the contract in question was signed, six years before the issuance of the Truman Proclamation. And while holding that the continental shelf principle was not yet customary law in 1939, the arbitrator, Lord Asquith, was nevertheless "of the opinion that its adoption into the corpus of international law was an imminent future possibility."[46]

One year later, in 1950, the spate of unilateral state declarations and the absence of protests from other states prompted renowned

---

[42] JAMES B. MORELL, THE LAW OF THE SEA: AN HISTORICAL ANALYSIS OF THE 1982 TREATY AND ITS REJECTION BY THE UNITED STATES 2 (McFarland & Co., 1992).

[43] BARRY BUZAN, SEABED POLITICS 9 (Praeger Publishers, 1976).

[44] SUZETTE V. SUAREZ, THE OUTER LIMITS OF THE CONTINENTAL SHELF: LEGAL ASPECTS OF THEIR ESTABLISHMENT 28 (Springer, 2008).

[45] *The Abu Dhabi Oil Arbitration*, in C. B. BOURNE AND L. G. JAHNKE, CASES AND MATERIALS ON PUBLIC INTERNATIONAL LAW 7–43 to 7–47 (University of British Columbia Press, 1972).

[46] Edwin J. Cosford, Jr., *The Continental Shelf and the Abu Dhabi Oil Arbitration*, 1 McGILL LAW JOURNAL 109, 126–7 (1953).

international legal scholar Sir Hersch Lauterpacht to conclude that the concept of the continental shelf had become virtually "instant" customary international law.[47] As Professor Lauterpacht put it, "seldom has an apparent major change in international law been accomplished by peaceful means more rapidly and amidst more general acquiescence and approval than in the case of the claims to submarine areas – the sea-bed and its subsoil – adjacent to the coast of littoral states."[48]

Soon after the United Nations General Assembly created the International Law Commission (ILC) in 1947, the fifteen members of the commission conferred high priority on the challenge of defining the continental shelf on the basis of the rapid development of international recognition of the concept.[49] Professor Lauterpacht observed that the members of the International Law Commission considered the elaboration of the principles governing the continental shelf second only in importance to the formulation of the principles of the Nuremberg Charter[50] – the subject of the previous chapter.

Just as the ILC considered its task with the Nuremberg Principles to elaborate the customary international law that arose out of the Nuremberg Charter and trial, so it considered the continental shelf concept arising from the Truman Proclamation to represent customary international law and perceived its task as developing a universally acceptable definition of the continental shelf. By 1951, the International Law Commission had produced a set of draft articles, which were refined after comment by UN member states in 1953 and further refined in 1956.[51] The commission's draft articles were important both as a set of proposals on which the UN diplomatic conference on the law of the sea could base its deliberations,

---

[47] Hersch Lauterpacht, *Sovereignty over Submarine Areas* 27 BRITISH YEAR BOOK OF INTERNATIONAL LAW 376, 394 (1950).

[48] Hersch Lauterpacht, *Sovereignty over Submarine Areas* 27 BRITISH YEAR BOOK OF INTERNATIONAL LAW 376 (1950).

[49] BARRY BUZAN, SEABED POLITICS 19 (Praeger Publishers, 1976).

[50] Hersch Lauterpacht, *Sovereignty over Submarine Areas* 27 BRITISH YEAR BOOK OF INTERNATIONAL LAW 377 (1950).

[51] BARRY BUZAN, SEABED POLITICS 20–2 (Praeger Publishers, 1976).

and as a statement of the emerging international consensus on the definition of the continental shelf.[52]

Only thirteen years after the Truman Proclamation, the concept of the continental shelf had become so widely accepted that the United Nations decided it merited an entire multinational convention for itself – the 1958 Convention on the Continental Shelf.[53] In 1958, the first UN Conference on the Law of the Sea concluded the convention based on the articles drafted by the U.N. International Law Commission. Article 1 of the convention defines the continental shelf as

> the seabed and subsoil of the submarine areas adjacent to the coast but outside the area of the territorial sea, to a depth of 200 meters or, beyond that limit, to where the depth of the superjacent waters admits of the exploitation of the natural resources of the said areas; and also to the seabed and subsoil of similar submarine areas adjacent to the coasts of islands.[54]

Article 2 of the convention stipulates that the rights of a coastal state over its continental shelf are exclusive and do not depend on effective or notional occupation or on any explicit proclamation.[55] The 1958 convention was ratified by fifty-eight states and remains in force for those parties that did not later ratify the 1982 Law of the Sea Convention, namely, Belarus, Cambodia, Colombia, Dominican Republic, Israel, Lesotho, Malawi, Switzerland, Thailand, the United States, and Venezuela.[56]

The 1958 Convention on the Continental Shelf amounted to formal international affirmation of the Truman Proclamation. Even before the convention entered into force in 1964, however, acceptance

---

[52] BARRY BUZAN, SEABED POLITICS 24 (Praeger Publishers, 1976).

[53] SUZETTE V. SUAREZ, THE OUTER LIMITS OF THE CONTINENTAL SHELF: LEGAL ASPECTS OF THEIR ESTABLISHMENT 29 (Springer, 2008).

[54] 1958 Convention on the Continental Shelf, Art.1, adopted April 29, 1958, entry into Vol. 499, p. 311.

[55] 1958 Convention on the Continental Shelf, Art.2, adopted April 29, 1958, entry into Vol. 499, p. 311.

[56] SUZETTE V. SUAREZ, THE OUTER LIMITS OF THE CONTINENTAL SHELF: LEGAL ASPECTS OF THEIR ESTABLISHMENT 34 (Springer, 2008).

of the continental shelf as part of customary international law was no longer in doubt.

In the 1969 *North Sea Continental Shelf* case, the International Court of Justice confirmed that the continental shelf concept as articulated in the Truman Proclamation was enshrined in customary international law and was therefore applicable to the Federal Republic of Germany, which had not yet ratified the 1958 Convention on the Continental Shelf. In doing so, the Court recognized that the Truman Proclamation has "a special status" as "the starting point of positive law on the subject, and the chief doctrine it enunciated, namely that of the coastal State as having an original, natural, and exclusive (in short a vested) right to the continental shelf off its shores, came to prevail over all others"[57] and "must be considered as having propounded the rules of law in this field."[58] Notably, the International Court of Justice observed that customary norms can sometimes ripen quite rapidly, and that a short period is not a bar to finding the existence of a new rule of customary international law.[59] But rather than apply the equidistance principle set forth in Article 6 of the 1958 Continental Shelf Convention,[60] the International Court of Justice held that customary international law reflected the two concepts for determining the boundaries of the continental shelf set out in the Truman Proclamation,

---

[57] *North Sea Continental Shelf* (*Federal Republic of Germany v. Denmark*; *Federal Republic of Germany v. Netherlands*), Merits, 20 February 1969, ICJ Rep. 3, *North Sea Continental Shelf* case, I.C.J. Reports (1969), pp. 33–4, para. 47.

[58] *Id.*, p. 48, para. 86.

[59] *Id.*, p. 43, para. 74.

[60] While affirming that Articles 1 through 3 of the 1958 Continental Shelf Convention (concerning the legal definition of the continental shelf, the nature of rights of the coastal state over the continental shelf, and the legal status of the superjacent waters and the airspace over those waters) had the status of established customary international law, the Court held that the equidistance principle contained in Article 6 of the convention did not constitute a rule of customary international law because unlike Articles 1 through 3, Article 6 could be subject to reservation and few states that were not parties to the convention had recognized and applied the equidistance principle. *Id.* at pp. 40–1, paras. 71–4.

namely, "of delimitation by mutual agreement and delimitation in accordance with equitable principles."[61]

As described in Chapter 1, Grotian Moments are marked by a context of fundamental technological or social change and recognition that the rule has acquired customary law status despite a dearth and short period of state practice. With respect to the Truman Proclamation, we have seen that developments in offshore drilling, paired with the great need for oil, gas, and other resources following World War II, set the stage for a radical change in the customary law of the sea. Within five years of the Truman Proclamation, thirty coastal states had followed the lead of the United States in asserting jurisdiction over the continental shelf. Though that number represented less than half of the world's coastal states, as a result of the unique technological and economic factors that contributed to its development, "its incubation period as a legal concept was very short."[62] Indeed, by 1950, one of the world's leading international law scholars, who would be elected two years later to be a judge on the International Court of Justice, concluded that the concept represented virtually instant customary international law.[63] We can conclude, then, that the Truman Proclamation has all of the hallmarks of a legitimate Grotian Moment.

Although the continental shelf concept remains governing law today, the definition of the juridical continental shelf has evolved since the Truman Proclamation. While the Truman Proclamation had grounded its jurisdictional claim upon the geographic adjacency of the shelf, in the 1960s and 1970s further technological advances prompted states to base their claims on the criterion of exploitability contained in the 1958 convention.[64] Fearing that this unrestricted approach would ultimately result

---

[61] *Id.*, at p. 33, para. 47.

[62] SUZETTE V. SUAREZ, THE OUTER LIMITS OF THE CONTINENTAL SHELF: LEGAL ASPECTS OF THEIR ESTABLISHMENT 38 (Springer, 2008).

[63] Hersch Lauterpacht, *Sovereignty over Submarine Areas* 27 BRITISH YEAR BOOK OF INTERNATIONAL LAW 377 (1950).

[64] JAMES B. MORELL, THE LAW OF THE SEA: AN HISTORICAL ANALYSIS OF THE 1982 TREATY AND ITS REJECTION BY THE UNITED STATES 11 (McFarland & Co., 1992).

in creeping jurisdiction extending to the entirety of the ocean floors, the international community decided to revisit the definition of the continental shelf. The result was the 1982 Convention on the Law of the Sea, which entered into force in 1994 and now has 162 state parties. Under the new formula contained in Article 76 of the 1982 convention, every state is entitled to a 200 nautical mile juridical continental shelf. A state's continental shelf may exceed 200 nautical miles until the natural prolongation of its geological continental shelf ends. However, it may never exceed 350 nautical miles from the baseline; or it may never exceed 100 nautical miles beyond the 2,500 meter isobath (the line connecting the depth of 2,500 meters).[65] In this manner, the continental shelf example is similar to that of Nuremberg. Both reflect instances of rapid emergence of customary international law where definitional ambiguities continued to be worked out in later years.

---

[65] United Nations Convention on the Law of the Sea, Art.76, December 10, 1982, in force November 16, 1994, United Nations, *Treaty Series*, vol. 1833, p. 3.

6 Outer Space Law

THIS CHAPTER EXAMINES THE CUSTOMARY INTERNATIONAL law rules that grew out of the U.S. and Soviet development of the ability to launch satellites and manned rockets into earth orbit and outer space in the 1960s.[1] In response to this new technological development, in 1963 the UN General Assembly adopted the *Declaration of Legal Principles Governing the Activities of States in the Exploration and Use of Outer Space*, which provided that the provisions of the UN Charter, including limitations on the use of force, apply to outer space; outer space and celestial bodies are not subject to national appropriation by claim of sovereignty; states bear responsibility for parts of space vehicles that land on the territory of other states; the state of registry of a spacecraft has exclusive jurisdiction over it and any personnel it carries; and states shall regard astronauts as envoys and shall accord them assistance and promptly return them to the state of registry.[2] Though state practice was limited in the early

---

[1] Space law is not a separate field of law but rather that part of international law relating to outer space, natural and man-made objects in outer space, astronauts, and man's activities in outer space or affecting outer space.

[2] United Nations General Assembly Resolution 1962 (XVIII), *Declaration of Legal Principles Governing the Activities of States in the Exploration and Use of Outer Space*, December 13, 1963, available at: http://www.oosa.unvienna.org/oosa/en/SpaceLaw/gares/html/gares_18_1962.html (last accessed February 9, 2013).

years of space exploration, ICJ Judge Manfred Lachs concluded that "it is difficult to regard the 1963 Declaration as a mere recommendation: it was an instrument which has been accepted as law."[3] The chapter analyzes whether the dawn of space law culminating in the 1963 declaration constituted a Grotian Moment, or whether the principles enshrined in the 1963 declaration should be discounted because the international community concluded a binding treaty on principles governing the activities of states in outer space in 1967, which some might argue has supplanted the 1963 declaration in the regulation of outer space activities.

Early History of Space Flight

The space age was inaugurated on October 4, 1957, when the Soviet Union launched *Sputnik 1*, the world's first artificial satellite, which was followed by the launch of the U.S. satellite *Explorer 1*, a year later.[4] In 1961, Soviet cosmonaut Yuri Gagarin became the first man to reach outer space. Between 1957 and 1967, when the Outer Space Treaty was concluded, the Soviet Union space program included *Luna* missions to the moon, *Zond* flyby missions to Mars, and *Venera* flyby missions to Venus, as well as manned *Vostock*, *Voskhod*, and *Soyuz* flights to earth orbit. Keeping pace with the Soviets, the U.S. space program included unmanned *Ranger*, *Lunar Orbiter*, and *Surveyor* missions to the moon; *Pioneer* flyby missions to Venus; and *Mariner* flyby missions to Mars; as well as manned *Mercury*, *Gemini*, and *Apollo* flights to earth orbit in preparation for Neil Armstrong's first steps on the surface of the moon in 1969.

---

[3] MANFRED LACHS, THE LAW OF OUTER SPACE: AN EXPERIENCE IN CONTEMPORARY LAW-MAKING 138 (1972).

[4] Ricky J. Lee, *Reconciling International Space Law with the Commercial Realities of the Twenty-First Century*, 4 SINGAPORE JOURNAL OF INTERNATIONAL & COMPARATIVE LAW 194 (2000).

Altogether between 1957 and 1967 there were a total of eighty-three space flights – fifty-seven unmanned flights[5] and twenty-six manned

[5] Unmanned Space flights 1957–67: *Sputnik 1* (USSR) (Oct. 4, 1957) (first artificial satellite); *Sputnik 2* (USSR) (Nov. 3, 1957) (carried first animal into space); *Explorer 1* (USA) (Jan. 31, 1958) (first U.S. satellite); *Pioneer 0* (USA) (Aug. 17, 1958) (lunar orbiter – exploded during first stage); *Pioneer 1* (USA) (Oct. 11, 1958) (lunar orbiter – failed to reach escape velocity); *Pioneer 3* (USA) (Dec. 6, 1958) (lunar flyby – failed to reach escape velocity); *Luna 1* (USSR) (Jan 2, 1959) (lunar flyby – still in solar orbit); *Pioneer 4* (USA) (Mar. 3, 1959) (lunar flyby – still in solar orbit); *Luna 2* (USSR) (Sept. 12, 1959) (lunar lander – impacted moon); *Luna 3* (USSR) (Oct. 4, 1959) (lunar flyby – returned the first photograph of far side of the moon); *Pioneer 5* (USA) (Mar. 11, 1960) (solar monitor – still in solar orbit); *Mars 1960A* (USSR) (Oct. 10, 1960) (Mars probe – failed to reach earth orbit); *Mars 1960B* (USSR) (Oct. 14, 1960) (Mars probe – failed to reach earth orbit); *Venera 1* (USSR) (Feb. 12, 1961) (Venus flyby – now in solar orbit); *Ranger 1* (USA) (Jan. 26, 1962) (lunar lander – missed the moon and is now in solar orbit); *Ranger 4* (USA) (Apr. 23, 1962) (lunar lander – first U.S. impact on the moon); *Mariner 2* (USA) (Aug. 27, 1962) (Venus flyby – now in solar orbit); *Ranger 5* (USA) (Oct. 18, 1962) (lunar flyby); *Mars 1962A* (USSR) (Oct. 24, 1962) (Mars flyby – failed to leave earth orbit); *Mars 1* (USSR) (Nov. 1, 1962) (Mars flyby – lost communications); *Mars 1962B* (USSR) (Nov. 4, 1962) (failed to leave earth orbit); *Luna 4* (USSR) (Apr. 2, 1963) (lunar lander); *Ranger 6* (USA) (Jan. 30, 1964) (lunar lander); *Zond 1* (USSR) (Apr. 2, 1964) (Venus flyby); *Ranger 7* (USA) (July 28, 1964) (lunar lander); *Mariner 3* (USA) (Nov. 5, 1964) (Mars flyby); *Mariner 4* (USA) (Nov. 28, 1964) (Mars fly-by); *Zond 2* (USSR) (Nov. 30, 1964) (Mars flyby); *Ranger 8* (USA) (Feb. 17, 1965) (lunar lander); *Ranger 9* (USA) (Mar. 21, 1965) (lunar lander); *Luna 5* (USSR) (May 9, 1965) (lunar lander); *Luna 6* (USSR) (June 8, 1965) (lunar lander); *Zond 3* (USSR) (July 18, 1965) (lunar flyby); *Luna 7* (USSR) (Oct. 4, 1965) (lunar lander); *Venera 2* (USSR) (Nov. 12, 1965) (Venus flyby); *Venera 3* (USSR) (Nov. 16, 1965) (Venus probe); *Luna 8* (USSR) (Dec. 3, 1965) (lunar lander); *Pioneer 6* (USA) (Dec. 16, 1965) (solar probe); *Luna 9* (USSR) (Jan. 31, 1966) (lunar lander); *Luna 10* (USSR) (Mar. 31, 1966) (lunar orbiter); *Surveyor 1* (USA) (Apr. 30, 1966) (lunar lander); *Lunar Orbiter 1* (USA) (Aug. 10, 1966) (lunar orbiter); *Pioneer 7* (USA) (Aug. 17, 1966) (solar probe); *Luna 11* (USSR) (Aug. 24, 1966) (lunar orbiter); *Surveyor 2* (USA) (Sept. 20, 1966) (lunar lander); *Luna 12* (USSR) (Oct. 22, 1966) (lunar orbiter); *Lunar Orbiter 2* (USA) (Nov. 6, 1966) (lunar orbiter); *Luna 13* (USSR) (Dec. 21, 1966) (lunar lander); *Lunar Orbiter 3* (USA) (Feb. 5, 1967); *Surveyor 3* (USA) (Apr. 17, 1967); *Lunar Orbiter 4* (USA) (May 4, 1967) (lunar orbiter); *Venera 4* (USSR) (June 12, 1967) (Venus probe); *Mariner 5* (USA) (June 14, 1967) (Venus flyby); *Surveyor 4* (USA) (July 14, 1967) (lunar lander); *Lunar Orbiter 5* (USA) (Aug. 1, 1967) (lunar orbiter); *Surveyor 5* (USA) (Sept. 8, 1967) (lunar lander); *Surveyor 6* (Nov. 7, 1967) (lunar lander); *Pioneer 8* (USA) (Dec. 13, 1967) (solar probe). See, American Public University, A History of Satellites and Robotic Space Missions, available at: http://www.windows2universe.org/space_missions/unmanned_table.html (last accessed February 9, 2013).

flights.[6] Prior to the launch of these rockets, satellites, and space probes, there were no legal rules governing activities in outer space. This led Professor John C. Cooper, "the dean of all air and space law scholars," to write in 1961 that "today the legal status of outer space is as vague and uncertain as was the legal status of the high seas in the centuries before Grotius, in the *Mare Liberum*, focused attention on the need of the world to accept the doctrine of the freedom of the seas."[7]

---

[6] Manned Space flights 1961–7: *Vostok 1* (USSR) (Apr. 12, 1961) (Garagin became first human in space); *Mercury 3* (USA) (May 5, 1961) (Shepard became first American in space); *Mercury 4* (USA) (July 21, 1961 (Grissom reaches altitude of 126 miles); *Vostok 2* (USSR) (Aug. 6, 1961) (Titov is first to spend an entire day in space); *Mercury 6* (USA) (Feb. 20, 1962) (Glenn is first American to orbit the earth); *Mercury 7* (USA) (May 24, 1962) (Carpenter orbits earth three times); *Vostok 3* (USSR) (Aug. 11, 1962) (Nikolayev spends four days in space); *Vostok 4* (USSR) (Aug. 12, 1962) (Popovich pilots *Vostok 4* within five miles of *Vostok 3*); *Mercury 8* (USA) (Oct. 3, 1962) (Schirra orbits earth six times); *Mercury 9* (USA) (May 15, 1963) (Cooper spends thirty-four hours in space); *Vostok 5* (USSR) (June 14, 1963) (Bykovsky spends five days in space); *Vostok 6* (USSR) (June 16, 1963) (Tereshkova becomes first woman in space); *Voskhod* (USSR) (Oct. 12, 1964) (first three person space flight); *Voskhod 2* (USSR) (Mar. 18, 1965) (Leonov becomes first person to walk in space); *Gemini-Titan 3* (USA) (Mar. 23, 1965) (start of *Gemini* program with two U.S. astronauts, and first spacecraft to carry a computer); *Gemini-Titan 4* (USA) (June 3, 1965) (White is first American to walk in space); *Gemini-Titan 5* (USA) (Aug. 21, 1965) (Cooper and Conrad spend a record five days in space); *Gemini-Titan 7* (USA) (Borman and Lovell spend a record thirteen days in space and accomplish first rendezvous with another manned spacecraft, *Gemini 6*); *Gemini-Titan 6-A* (USA) (Dec. 15, 1965) (Schirra and Stafford rendezvous with *Gemini 7*); *Gemini-Titan 8* (USA) (Mar. 16, 1966) (Armstrong and Scott perform first docking in space); *Gemini-Titan 9-A* (USA) (June 3, 1966) (Stafford and Cernan rendezvous with Augmented Target Docking Adapter); *Gemini-Titan 10* (USA) (July 18, 1966) (Young and Collins reach record altitude of 468 miles and perform two space walks); *Gemini-Titan 11* (USA) (Sept. 12, 1966) (Conrad and Gordon reach record altitude of 850 miles and make first autopilot reentry and landing); *Gemini-Titan 12* (USA) (Nov. 11, 1966) (Aldrin makes three space walks, totaling five hours); *Apollo-Saturn 204* (USA) (Jan. 27, 1967) (Grissom, White, and Chaffee are killed by fire on launch pad); *Soyuz 1* (USSR) (Apr. 23, 1967) (Komarov is killed on reentry). See, American Public University, A History of Manned Space Flights, available at: http://www.windows2universe.org/space_missions/manned_table.html (last accessed February 9, 2013).

[7] John C. Cooper, *The Rule of Law in Outer Space*, 47 AMERICAN BAR ASSOCIATION JOURNAL 25, 24 (1961).

In those early days, scholars were wondering whether states would have the right to demand that their permission must be obtained for spaceflights that passed over their airspace on the way to or back from outer space. Would equatorial states be entitled to charge a fee for the right of foreign states to station satellites in geosynchronous orbit directly above their territory permanently? Would astronauts and cosmonauts be treated as trespassers or spies if they landed in the territory of another state? Could states salvage foreign technology if they were the first to arrive at a space capsule's splashdown site? Who would be liable and under what standard if falling space debris caused injury or damage to nationals or property of another state? Could the space-faring states place military installations in orbit and militarize outer space with weapons of mass destruction? And could space-faring states claim portions of the moon or asteroids as national territory under the principle of *territorium nullius*, just as the colonial powers carved up the new world in the decades following the journeys of Christopher Columbus? These important questions were soon answered as customary international law governing spaceflight "emerged in a historically short time span."[8]

Development of the Rules Governing Spaceflight

In the early years of spaceflight, only two countries – the Soviet Union and United States – sent rockets and satellites into outer space.[9] One might be tempted to conclude that two states are not a sufficient number to establish customary international law for the entire community of nations. But that would ignore the nature of spaceflight, in which rockets

---

[8] V. S. Verschchetin, The *Law of Outer Space in the General Legal Field (Commonality and Particularities)*, REVISTA BRASILIERA DE DIREITO AERONAUTICO E ESPACIAL, April 2010, at 42.

[9] Outer space is widely accepted as meaning the region at and above the line determined by the lowest perigee of satellites so far placed in orbit (approximately 100 kilometers above sea level). Vladlen S. Vershchetin and Gennady M. Danilenko, *Custom as a Source of International Law of Outer Space*, 13 JOURNAL OF SPACE LAW 22, 27 (1985).

and satellites fly directly over many states on the way to and back from outer space.[10] Consequently, the reaction (including lack of protest) of those states over the course of eighty-three launches from 1957 to 1967 is a source of widespread state action and *opinio juris*.[11]

From the start of the space age, the Soviet Union and United States did not request permission from the states over whose territories the rockets flew. As the flights were quite conspicuous and often treated as public relations spectacles, the "overflown" states were fully aware of this activity. Yet they did not protest or complain, or request fees, or advocate regulation. Instead, the nations of the world "robustly applauded the scientific achievements" and acquiesced to the Soviet and American assertion of rights related to spaceflight.[12] Professor David Koplow of Georgetown University has suggested that this lack of protest might have been due to the fact that the overflown states "were largely unaware of the full extent of the potential rights they were sleeping on, and insufficiently focused on the nature of the novel legal regime" that was being generated.[13]

Whatever the reason for their silence, their tacit acceptance quickly crystallized into a new set of customary international law rules. Those rules were codified by the United Nations, which established a Committee on the Peaceful Uses of Outer Space in 1961 and in 1963 adopted the *Declaration of Legal Principles Governing the Activities of*

---

[10] The issue of overflight generated recent controversy when North Korea attempted to launch a satellite from a rocket that would fly over Japan on the way to earth orbit. See Reuters, *North Korea Readies Longer Range Rocket, Japan, South Korea Wary*, April 9, 2012, available at: http://www.reuters.com/article/2012/04/09/us-korea-nort h-rocket-idUSBRE83802D20120409 (last accessed February 9, 2013).

[11] MAURICE H. MENDELSON, THE FORMATION OF CUSTOMARY INTERNATIONAL LAW 386 n. 644 (1998).

[12] David A. Koplow, *ASAT-isfaction: Customary International Law and the Regulation of Anti-Satellite Weapons*, 30 MICHIGAN JOURNAL OF INTERNATIONAL LAW 1187, 1232 (2008).

[13] David A. Koplow, *ASAT-isfaction: Customary International Law and the Regulation of Anti-Satellite Weapons*, 30 MICHIGAN JOURNAL OF INTERNATIONAL LAW 1187, 1232 (2008).

States in the Exploration and Use of Outer Space, which was drafted by
the committee. The declaration provides:

1. The exploration and use of outer space shall be carried on for the
   benefit and in the interests of all mankind.
2. Outer space and celestial bodies are free for exploration and use
   by all States on a basis of equality and in accordance with international law.
3. Outer space and celestial bodies are not subject to national appropriation by claim of sovereignty, by means of use or occupation, or by
   any other means.
4. The activities of States in the exploration and use of outer space shall
   be carried on in accordance with international law, including the
   Charter of the United Nations, in the interest of maintaining international peace and security and promoting international co-operation
   and understanding.
5. States bear international responsibility for national activities in
   outer space, whether carried on by governmental agencies or by
   non-governmental entities, and for assuring that national activities
   are carried on in conformity with the principles set forth in the present Declaration. The activities of non-governmental entities in outer
   space shall require authorization and continuing supervision by the
   State concerned. When activities are carried on in outer space by
   an international organization, responsibility for compliance with the
   principles set forth in this Declaration shall be borne by the international organization and by the States participating in it.
6. In the exploration and use of outer space, States shall be guided by
   the principle of co-operation and mutual assistance and shall conduct all their activities in outer space with due regard for the corresponding interests of other States. If a State has reason to believe that
   an outer space activity or experiment planned by it or its nationals
   would cause potentially harmful interference with activities of other
   States in the peaceful exploration and use of outer space, it shall

undertake appropriate international consultations before proceeding with any such activity or experiment. A State which has reason to believe that an outer space activity or experiment planned by another State would cause potentially harmful interference with activities in the peaceful exploration and use of outer space may request consultation concerning the activity or experiment.

7. The State on whose registry an object launched into outer space is carried shall retain jurisdiction and control over such object, and any personnel thereon, while in outer space. Ownership of objects launched into outer space, and of their component parts, is not affected by their passage through outer space or by their return to the earth. Such objects or component parts found beyond the limits of the State of registry shall be returned to that State, which shall furnish identifying data upon request prior to return.

8. Each State which launches or procures the launching of an object into outer space, and each State from whose territory or facility an object is launched, is internationally liable for damage to a foreign State or to its natural or juridical persons by such object or its component parts on the earth, in air space, or in outer space.

9. States shall regard astronauts as envoys of mankind in outer space, and shall render to them all possible assistance in the event of accident, distress, or emergency landing on the territory of a foreign State or on the high seas. Astronauts who make such a landing shall be safely and promptly returned to the State of registry of their space vehicle.[14]

One of the most important of the provisions is the "free use" principle contained in the second paragraph of the declaration, which has been interpreted as confirming that states cannot interfere with the right of

---

[14] United Nations General Assembly Resolution 1962 (XVIII), *Declaration of Legal Principles Governing the Activities of States in the Exploration and Use of Outer Space*, December 13, 1963, available at: http://www.oosa.unvienna.org/oosa/en/SpaceLaw/gares/html/gares_18_1962.html (last accessed February 9, 2013).

other states to launch rockets and satellites that fly over their territory for peaceful uses of outer space. Another important provision is the "non-appropriation principle" contained in paragraph three of the declaration. This provision makes clear that outer space and celestial bodies are not subject to national appropriation by claim of sovereignty. While the text leaves room for interpretation, the overwhelming majority of states consider that this only prohibits the appropriation of areas and does not prohibit commercial exploitation.[15] The principle of "peaceful uses," set forth in paragraph four, requires that space activities comport with international law and the UN Charter, including the prohibition on the use of force subject to the exception of self-defense. Notably, this provision has not been viewed as prohibiting military activity in space that is compatible with general international law and the UN Charter.[16] This means that military spy satellites, for example, are not prohibited. The 1967 Outer Space Treaty, however, clarifies that states are prohibited from placing nuclear weapons and weapons of mass destruction in outer space. Finally, the principle of "responsibility and liability" found in paragraph eight makes it clear that the launching state can be held liable under international law for damage caused by its spacecraft. The Liability Convention of 1972 later clarified that with respect to damage on the ground this is a principle of strict liability, justified by the ultrahazardous nature of space activity. Damage by an object in space to another object in space, on the other hand, is subject only to the regime of fault-based liability.[17]

---

[15] Steven Hobe, Proceedings, Disseminating and Developing International and National Space Law: The Latin American and Caribbean Perspective, *Proceedings of the UN/Brazil Workshop in Space Law*, ST/SPACE/28, UN Office for Outer Space Affairs (UN Office at Vienna), United Nations 2005, at 6.

[16] BIN CHENG, STUDIES IN INTERNATIONAL SPACE LAW 515 (1997).

[17] Steven Hobe, Proceedings, Disseminating and Developing International and National Space Law: The Latin American and Caribbean Perspective, *Proceedings of the UN/Brazil Workshop in Space Law*, ST/SPACE/28, UN Office for Outer Space Affairs (UN Office at Vienna), United Nations 2005, at 8.

The 1963 declaration was adopted by a unanimous vote. The negotiating record indicates that the United States, Soviet Union, and many
of the other members of the United Nations considered the declaration
to be a consensus codification of the key rules of customary international law governing outer space activity. Thus, upon adoption of the
declaration, the U.S. representative to the United Nations stated that
"the American government considered that the legal principles contained in the Draft Declaration of Principles Governing the Activities
of States in Space reflected international law as accepted by Members
of the United Nations."[18] The Soviet delegate added, "the Soviet
Union, for its part will also respect the principles contained in this
declaration."[19]

The view that the declaration reflected binding obligations was not,
however, unanimous. The French delegate said, "my delegation could
not for the moment give this declaration more value than that of a declaration of intention. We do not, in fact, consider that a resolution of the
General Assembly, even though adopted unanimously, can in this case
create juridical obligations incumbent upon Member States. Such obligations can flow only from international agreements."[20]

In part to mollify those who shared the French position, the principles contained in the declaration were later incorporated in the Outer
Space Treaty, which entered into force in October 1967[21]; the Agreement
on the Rescue of Astronauts, the Return of Astronauts and the Return

---

[18] David A. Koplow, *ASAT-isfaction: Customary International Law and the Regulation of Anti-Satellite Weapons*, 30 MICHIGAN JOURNAL OF INTERNATIONAL LAW 1187, 1234 n152 (2008).

[19] OGUNSOLA O. OGUNBANWO, INTERNATIONAL LAW AND OUTER SPACE ACTIVITIES 19 (Martinus Nijhoff, 1975) (citing verbatim record of the General Assembly).

[20] OGUNSOLA O. OGUNBANWO, INTERNATIONAL LAW AND OUTER SPACE ACTIVITIES 19 (Martinus Nijhoff, 1975) (citing verbatim record of the General Assembly).

[21] Treaty on Principles Governing the Activities of States in the Exploration and Use of Outer Space, including the Moon and Outer Celestial Bodies, October 10, 1967, 21 O.O.S.A. (UN Office for Outer Space Affairs) 2222.

of Objects Launched into Outer Space, which entered into force in December 1968[22]; and the Convention on International Liability for Damage Caused by Space Objects, which entered into force in September 1972.[23]

Was the Development of Space Law in the 1960s a Grotian Moment?

It is difficult to ascertain the exact moment the various rules governing activities in outer space crystallized into customary international law because there was no authoritative judgment on point from the International Court of Justice or any other competent tribunal. Some would pin the date on the conclusion of the 1967 Outer Space Treaty, while others believe the treaty merely recodified the rules that had been recognized as customary international law in the 1963 *Declaration of Legal Principles Governing the Activities of States in the Exploration and Use of Outer Space*. As Professor Stephan Hobe, the director of the Institute of Air and Space Law at the University of Cologne, put it, "the Outer Space Treaty, the Magna Charta for outer space activities, was but a consecration of the 1963 United Nations General Assembly Resolution."[24]

Professor Koplow similarly concludes that the principles inscribed in the 1963 declaration "were probably all embedded as accepted propositions of customary international law even before they were written into the Outer Space Treaty." He adds that "these principles, asserted as solemn pronouncements by the international community, had attained

---

[22] Agreement on the Rescue of Astronauts, the Return of Astronauts, and the Return of Objects Launched into Outer Space, April 22, 1968, O.O.S.A. 2345.

[23] Convention on International Liability for Damage Caused by Space Objects, March 29, 1972, O.O.S.A.

[24] Stephen Hobe, Proceedings, Disseminating and Developing International and National Space Law: The Latin American and Caribbean Perspective, *Proceedings of the UN/Brazil Workshop in Space Law*, ST/SPACE/28, UN Office for Outer Space Affairs (UN Office at Vienna), United Nations 2005, at 4.

sufficiently widespread acceptance, from a sense of legal obligation, even before the act of codification." In Koplow's view, "the treaty became a more-definite, easier-to-cite expression of those rules, but they were promulgated in the first instance by customary international law, not the Outer Space Treaty."[25]

Importantly, if the 1967 Outer Space Treaty is deemed a codification of the customary international law principles contained in the 1963 declaration or recognized in the aftermath of the declaration's adoption, then customary international law may extend the Outer Space Treaty's provisions to the many states that have not ratified it.[26] This has potentially significant consequences since, as of 2011, the Outer Space Treaty had only 101 parties,[27] meaning that nearly half the countries of the world still had not ratified this important instrument.[28] The issue was tested in 1978 when some of the equatorial countries that are not parties to the 1967 Outer Space Treaty tried to question the freedom of stationing satellites in geostationary orbit above their territory. The overwhelming majority of states rejected the position of the equatorial countries on the ground that the rules in the Outer Space Treaty "represent the existing general customary law which shall bind all members of the

---

[25] David A. Koplow, *International Legal Standards and the Weaponization of Outer Space*, SECURITY IN SPACE: THE NEXT GENERATION – CONFERENCE REPORT, MARCH 31–APRIL 1, 2008, UNITED NATIONS INSTITUTE FOR DISARMAMENT REPORT, 2008, at p. 163.

[26] He Qizhi, *The Outer Space Treaty in Perspective*, 25 JOURNAL OF SPACE LAW 93, 97 (1997).

[27] United Nations Office for Outer Space Affairs, Status of International Agreements Relating to Activities in Outer Space, available at: http://www.oosa.unvienna.org/oosa/en/SpaceLaw/treatystatus/index.html (last accessed February 9, 2013). In comparison, the Rescue Agreement has 91 parties, the Liability Convention has 88 parties, the Registration Agreement has 56 parties, and the Moon Agreement has 13 parties. *Id.*

[28] A corollary to the so-called Baxter paradox is that once an international convention is widely recognized as representing customary international law, the pace of new ratifications may slow as there is a diminished benefit for nonparties to ratify the convention. See Richard Baxter, *Treaties and Custom*, 129 RECUEIL DES COURS 36, 64, 73 (1970).

international community independent of formally ratifying or accepting the Treaty."[29]

This is not to say that space law is, or should be, governed only by custom. "Custom, in contrast to treaty, cannot serve as a source of antici- patory creation of legal rights and obligations because it is based on the [past] practice of States."[30] Some of the subsequent outer space conven- tions go beyond the principles enumerated in the 1963 declaration and contain forward-looking provisions that are not yet considered custom- ary international law.

Nor should one conclude that these early customary international law principles form the complete corpus of the customary law governing outer space. The modern practice of states in the exploration and use of outer space continues to generate new customary rules.[31] For example, remote sensing technology did not exist at the time of the 1963 declara- tion or 1967 treaty, but today "there is a consensus among states with respect to the recognition of a right of all States to freely conduct remote sensing programs in outer space" without the prior consent of the sensed states.[32] An area that is receiving contemporary attention is how to regu- late antisatellite weapons, which can create virtual "dead zones" of space debris precluding activities in that region.[33]

While some scholars have referred to the principles enshrined in the 1963 declaration and 1967 treaty as "instant" customary international

---

[29] He Qizhi, *The Outer Space Treaty in Perspective*, 25 JOURNAL OF SPACE LAW 93, 98 (1997); Vladlen S. Vershchetin and Gennady M. Danilenko, *Custom as a Source of International Law of Outer Space*, 13 JOURNAL OF SPACE LAW 22, 32 (1985) (citing the statements of delegates in the Legal Subcommittee of the UN Committee on the Peaceful Uses of Outer Space).

[30] Vladlen S. Vershchetin and Gennady M. Danilenko, *Custom as a Source of International Law of Outer Space*, 13 JOURNAL OF SPACE LAW 22, 23 (1985).

[31] Id.

[32] Vladlen S. Vershchetin and Gennady M. Danilenko, *Custom as a Source of International Law of Outer Space*, 13 JOURNAL OF SPACE LAW 22, 29 (1985).

[33] David Kaplow, *International Legal Standards and the Weaponization of Outer Space*, in SPACE: THE NEXT GENERATION – CONFERENCE REPORT, MARCH 31–APRIL 1, 2008, UNITED NATIONS INSTITUTE FOR DISARMAMENT RESEARCH (2008), at 169.

law,[34] the reality is that the two instruments reflected principles that grew out of the claims and reactions of many states during the course of eighty-three spaceflights from 1957 to 1967. This state practice was not conducted "in a legal vacuum."[35] While ten years is an extremely short period for the formation of customary international law in most fields, the example of space law fits comfortably within the Grotian Moment concept, validating its accelerated formation.

In this regard, the adoption of the 1963 declaration played a particularly significant role in the crystallization of the customary international law that had been forming from state practice in the early years of the space age. While lack of protest can be considered state action in the same way that protest can, the difference is that where states are silent it is harder to deduce their underlying belief (i.e., their *opinio juris*). The 1963 declaration was the first widespread clear indication of *opinio juris* relating to the law of outer space. Thus, Russian space law experts VladienVereschchetin and Gennady Danilenkohave concluded that the "acceleration of the formation of customary principles relating to outer space" was brought about not only by the need to keep pace with technological developments, "but also by the adoption of a number of United Nations General Assembly Resolutions."[36] Like the

---

[34] Bin Cheng, *United Nations Resolutions on Outer Space: "Instant" International Customary Law?* 5 INDIAN JOURNAL OF INTERNATIONAL LAW 23, 35–40 (1965); Farhad Taleie, *The Importance of Custom and the Process of Its Formation in Modern International Law*, 5 JAMES COOK UNIVERSITY LAW REVIEW 27, 38 (1998) ("Clear instances of instant customs are the basic principles governing outer space"); David A. Kaplow, *ASAT-isfaction: Customary International Law and the Regulation of Anti-Satellite Weapons*, 30 MICHIGAN JOURNAL OF INTERNATIONAL LAW 1187, 1232 (2008–9) ("in response to the world community's demand for new global rules in fast-breaking areas, the practices of States in the 1950s regarding satellite over flights provide a leading illustration of the concept of 'instant customary international law'").

[35] Vladlen S. Vershchetin and Gennady M. Danilenko, *Custom as a Source of International Law of Outer Space*, 13 JOURNAL OF SPACE LAW 22, 25 (1985).

[36] Vladlen S. Vershchetin and Gennady M. Danilenko, *Custom as a Source of International Law of Outer Space*, 13 JOURNAL OF SPACE LAW 22, 26 (1985).

1946 *General Assembly Declaration on the Principles of the Nuremberg Charter and Trial*, the 1963 space law declaration had all the attributes of a resolution entitled to great weight as a pronouncement of customary international law: it was labeled a "Declaration of Legal Principles"; it dealt with inherently legal questions; it repeatedly employed the terms "shall" and "will" rather than "should"; it was adopted by a unanimous vote without any reservation; and the principal drafters expressed at the time that it was a codification of customary law.[37] Further, in the years since its adoption, "there has not been any attempt at derogating the Space Law Declaration either as a whole or some of its principles."[38]

The rapid formation of customary international law in this area was in response to new technologies requiring a new international law paradigm. Further, space law was an area where the formulation of new rules by the negotiation and ratification of multilateral conventional could not keep pace with the requirements of international practice. Consequently, in the early years of space law, customary international law, as reflected in the 1963 declaration, played a crucial role and served "as a primary source for the creation of international legal rights and obligations of States."[39] From the traditional view of customary international law formation, the amount of state practice was quite limited, consisting only of the launch of rockets into space by two states and the lack of protest by the states over which these rockets passed. Yet, despite the limited state practice and minimal time, states and scholars have concluded that sometime prior to or shortly after the adoption of the 1963 declaration, the fundamental principles of space law had ripened into customary international law – rendering this an archetypal case of a Grotian Moment.

---

[37] See *supra* Chapter 3, notes 102–8.
[38] Vladimir Kopal, Proceedings, Disseminating and Developing International and National Space Law: The Latin American and Caribbean Perspective, *Proceedings of the UN/Brazil Workshop in Space Law*, ST/SPACE/28, UN Office for Outer Space Affairs (UN Office at Vienna), United Nations, 2005.
[39] Vladlen S. Vershchetin and Gennady M. Danilenko, *Custom as a Source of International Law of Outer Space*, 13 JOURNAL OF SPACE LAW 22, 27 (1985).

7 The Yugoslavia Tribunal's *Tadic* Decision

O N THE EVE OF THE ESTABLISHMENT OF THE INTERNATIONAL
Criminal Tribunal for the Former Yugoslavia in 1993, the
International Committee of the Red Cross "underlined
the fact that according to international humanitarian law as it stands
today, the notion of war crimes is limited to situations of international
armed conflict."[1] Yet, in its first decision, on October 2, 1995, the Appeals
Chamber of the Yugoslavia Tribunal held that the same principles of liability that apply to international armed conflict apply to internal armed
conflicts. Despite dubious provenance, this sweeping decision has been
affirmed by the Rwanda Tribunal and Special Court for Sierra Leone; it
has been codified in the military manuals of several governments; it has
been enshrined in the 1998 Statute of the International Criminal Court;
and it is now recognized as customary international law despite the
dearth of state practice or prolonged period of development. This chapter examines how the occurrence of genocide in Europe for the first time
since the Second World War and the creation of the first international

---

[1] Some Preliminary Remarks by the International Committee of the Red Cross
on the Setting-Up of an International Tribunal for the Prosecution of Persons
Responsible for Serious Violations of International Humanitarian Law Committed
on the Territory of the Former Yugoslavia, DDM/JUR/422b (March 25, 1993), at 2,
reprinted in 2 Virginia Morris and Michael P. Scharf, An Insider's Guide
to the International Criminal Tribunal for the Former Yugoslavia 391–2
(Transnational Publishers, 1995).

criminal tribunal since Nuremberg sowed the seeds for rapid recognition of this expanded area of international criminal liability.

Events Leading to the *Tadic* Decision

Although many states and commentators hoped there would be a permanent war crimes tribunal created in the aftermath of the Nuremberg trial, it would be nearly sixty years before events on the ground and international political currents would align to enable the international community to establish another international war crimes tribunal. Just a few months after the breakup of the Soviet Union, genocide took place in Europe for the first time since Nazi Germany. The location was Bosnia-Herzegovina, which had recently declared its independence from what was left of the former Yugoslavia (Serbia and Montenegro).

Prior to its dissolution in 1991–2, Yugoslavia was not so much an ethnic melting pot as a boiling cauldron of ethnic tension with deep historic roots. The assent of a hard-line Serbian nationalist government in Serbia headed by Slobodan Milosevic prompted Croatia and Slovenia to declare their independence on June 25, 1991, with Bosnia following suit on March 1, 1992. The Bosnian Serbs, under the leadership of their self-styled president, Radovan Karadzic, and military leader, Ratko Mladic, immediately launched attacks against the Croatian and Muslim populations in northeastern and southern Bosnia with the goal of connecting Serb populated regions in northern and western Bosnia to Serbia in the east. Within a few months, the Serbs had expelled, killed, or imprisoned 90 percent of the 1.7 million non-Serbs who once lived in Serbian-held areas of Bosnia.[2]

With the Russian Federation's assumption of the permanent seat and veto of the Soviet Union in the Security Council in December

---

[2] Michael P. Scharf, Balkan Justice: The Story behind the First International War Crimes Trial since Nuremberg 21–8 (Carolina Academic Press, 1997).

1991,[3] the Security Council emerged from the Cold War paralysis of the previous forty years and was experiencing a rare (though short-lived) era of cooperation. The first test for the reinvigorated council was the deepening crisis in the Balkans. The Security Council adopted a series of measures aimed at restoring peace and halting the bloodshed, including imposing economic sanctions on Serbia, establishing a no-fly zone, creating safe areas, authorizing force to ensure the delivery of humanitarian aid, and excluding Serbia from participating in the General Assembly.[4] Finally, on May 25, 1993, the Security Council adopted Resolution 827, establishing "an international tribunal for the sole purpose of prosecuting persons responsible for serious violations of international humanitarian law committed in the territory of the former Yugoslavia since January 1, 1991."[5] Within two years, the tribunal had been set up at the Hague, its eleven judges had been elected by the General Assembly, its chief prosecutor had been selected by the Security Council, and its first trial was ready to begin.

Articles 2 through 5 of the statute appended to Resolution 827, which had been drafted by the UN Office of Legal Affairs and based on proposals submitted by various governments and NGOs, set forth the subject-matter jurisdiction of the tribunal. Article 2 provides that the tribunal has jurisdiction over grave breaches of the four Geneva Conventions of 1949. Article 3, which is the focus of this chapter, confers power on the tribunal to prosecute persons "violating the laws or customs of war," including but not limited to a list of violations culled from the regulations annexed to the 1907 Hague Convention (IV) Respecting the Law and Customs of War on Land. Article 4 provides jurisdiction

---

[3] Michael P. Scharf, *Musical Chairs: The Dissolution of States and Membership in the United Nations*, 28 CORNELL INTERNATIONAL LAW JOURNAL 29, 46–7 (1995).

[4] MICHAEL P. SCHARF, BALKAN JUSTICE, THE STORY BEHIND THE FIRST INTERNATIONAL WAR CRIMES TRIAL SINCE NUREMBERG 33–5 (Carolina Academic Press, 1997).

[5] S.C. Res. 827, U.N. SCOR, 48th Sess., 3217th mtg., U.N. Doc. S/RES/827 (May 25, 1993).

over acts of genocide, and Article 5 covers crimes against humanity. Notably, the Yugoslavia Tribunal's statute did not specify whether the fighting in Yugoslavia constituted international conflict or a civil war (internal armed conflict) – "a question pivotal to the application of the laws of war."[6]

The tribunal's first case, *Prosecutor v. Tadic*, concerned a Bosnian Serb café owner and part-time karate instructor, who lived in the Prijedor district in northwest Bosnia. Dusko Tadic was charged with thirty-one counts of grave breaches of the Geneva Conventions, violations of the laws and customs of war, and crimes against humanity. The charges stemmed from the torture and murder of Muslims at the Serb-run Omarska, Karaterm, and Trnopolje prison camps and the nearby villages of Kozarac, Jaksici, and Sivci during the summer of 1992. In most instances, the indictment assigned three counts to each separate act charged: the first count was charged under Article 2 of the statute, the second count was charged under Article 3, and the third was charged under Article 5.[7]

On June 23, 1995, Tadic's attorneys filed a preliminary motion to dismiss the charges for lack of jurisdiction, arguing in part that the tribunal lacked subject-matter jurisdiction because its statute applies only to crimes committed in connection with an international (as opposed to an internal) armed conflict. On August 10, 1995, the Trial Chamber denied the defense's motion to dismiss, and via interlocutory appeal the Appeals Chamber of the tribunal affirmed the ruling of the Trial Chamber on October 2, 1995.[8]

---

[6] Allison Marston Danner, *When Courts Make Law: How the International Criminal Tribunals Recast the Laws of War*, 49 VANDERBILT LAW REVIEW 1, 23 (2006).

[7] Michael P. Scharf, *Trial and Error: An Assessment of the First Judgment of the Yugoslavia War Crimes Tribunal*, 30 NEW YORK UNIVERSITY JOURNAL OF INTERNATIONAL LAW AND POLITICS 167, 167 (1998).

[8] *Prosecutor v. Tadic*, Appeals Chamber, Decision on the Defense Motion for Interlocutory Appeal on Jurisdiction, Case No. IT-94–1-AR72 (Oct. 2, 1995), reprinted in 35 I.L.M. 32 (1996).

An Analysis of the *Tadic* Decision

In an *amicus* brief filed in *Tadic*, the United States argued that the conflict in Yugoslavia was clearly an international one, and that the members of the Security Council viewed it as such when they established the tribunal.[9] The Appeals Chamber refused to classify the fighting in Bosnia as an international armed conflict, but at the same time it upheld its jurisdiction on the ground that Article 3 of the tribunal's statute applies in both international and internal armed conflict. While recognizing that the article was intended to "reference" the 1907 Hague Convention (IV) Respecting the Laws and Customs of War on Land, which applied only in international armed conflicts, the chamber reasoned that Article 3 was not limited to Hague law because the list of offenses in Article 3 is merely illustrative, not exhaustive.[10] Rather, the Appeals Chamber asserted that Article 3 includes "all violations of international humanitarian law other than the Grave Breaches of the four Geneva Conventions" (which were covered in Article 2 of the Tribunal's Statute).[11] In particular, the Appeals Chamber concluded that Article 3 of its Statute encompasses violations of Hague law, infringements of Geneva law other than grave breaches, and most importantly violations of Common Article 3 of the Geneva Conventions and Additional Protocol II to the Geneva Conventions, which cover certain conduct committed in internal armed conflict.[12] In the view of the Appeals Chamber, Article 3 of the tribunal's

---

[9] Submission of the Government of the United States of America Concerning Certain Arguments Made by Counsel for the Accused in the Case of the Prosecutor of the *Tribunal v. Dusan Tadic*, at 22 (July 17, 1995).

[10] *Prosecutor v. Tadic*, Appeals Chamber, Decision on the Defense Motion for Interlocutory Appeal on Jurisdiction, Case No. IT-94–1-AR72 (Oct. 2, 1995), reprinted in 35 I.L.M. 32 (1996), at para. 87.

[11] *Prosecutor v. Tadic*, Appeals Chamber, Decision on the Defense Motion for Interlocutory Appeal on Jurisdiction, Case No. IT-94–1-AR72 (Oct. 2, 1995), reprinted in 35 I.L.M. 32 (1996), at para. 87.

[12] *Prosecutor v. Tadic*, Appeals Chamber, Decision on the Defense Motion for Interlocutory Appeal on Jurisdiction, Case No. IT-94–1-AR72 (Oct. 2, 1995), reprinted in 35 I.L.M. 32 (1996), at para. 89.

statute "functions as a residual clause designed to ensure that no serious violation of international humanitarian law"[13] (whether in internal or international armed conflict) eludes the tribunal's jurisdiction, thus making "such jurisdiction watertight and inescapable."[14]

One commentator has stated that "the Tribunal's holding that Article 3 extends to civil war is as bold as it is ill-founded."[15] The text of Article 3 empowers the tribunal to prosecute persons for violations of the "laws or customs of war," which the tribunal itself acknowledged was "a term of art used in the past" to make reference to the 1907 Hague Convention, a treaty that applies only to international armed conflicts.[16] Yet the chamber opined that the provision was also intended to incorporate a more modern customary humanitarian law, of which the Hague Convention was only an "important segment."[17]

The Appeals Chamber availed itself of the negotiating record of the tribunal's statute to support its position. However, it disregarded the most important part of that record, namely, the UN secretary-general's report that accompanied the statute, despite the fact that the statute and report were drafted by the UN Office of Legal Affairs, and the Security Council had adopted the statute without revision. The secretary general's report stressed that the tribunal's jurisdiction should be confined to rules of international humanitarian law which are "beyond any doubt

---

[13] *Prosecutor v. Tadic*, Appeals Chamber, Decision on the Defense Motion for Interlocutory Appeal on Jurisdiction, Case No. IT-94-1-AR72 (Oct. 2, 1995), reprinted in 35 I.L.M. 32 (1996), at para. 91.

[14] *Prosecutor v. Tadic*, Appeals Chamber, Decision on the Defense Motion for Interlocutory Appeal on Jurisdiction, Case No. IT-94-1-AR72 (Oct. 2, 1995), reprinted in 35 I.L.M. 32 (1996), at para. 91.

[15] Geoffrey Watson, *The Humanitarian Law of the Yugoslavia War Crimes Tribunal: Jurisdiction in Prosecutor v. Tadic*, 36 VIRGINIA JOURNAL OF INTERNATIONAL LAW 687, 709 (1996).

[16] *Prosecutor v. Tadic*, Appeals Chamber, Decision on the Defense Motion for Interlocutory Appeal on Jurisdiction, Case No. IT-94-1-AR72 (Oct. 2, 1995), reprinted in 35 I.L.M. 32 (1996), at para. 87.

[17] *Prosecutor v. Tadic*, Appeals Chamber, Decision on the Defense Motion for Interlocutory Appeal on Jurisdiction, Case No. IT-94-1-AR72 (Oct. 2, 1995), reprinted in 35 I.L.M. 32 (1996), at para. 87.

part of customary law."[18] Yet, the secretary-general's list of instruments that had "beyond any doubt" become part of customary international law included the Geneva and Hague Conventions, the Genocide Convention, and the Nuremberg Charter, but not Additional Protocol II to the Geneva Conventions.[19]

The Appeals Chamber placed a great deal of emphasis on the interpretive statements made by the Security Council delegations at the time the resolution was adopted. The U.S. delegate, in particular, declared that Article 3 of the draft statute "includes all obligations under humanitarian law agreements in force in the territory of the former Yugoslavia at the time the acts were committed, including Common Article 3 of the 1949 Geneva Conventions, and the 1977 Additional Protocols to those Conventions."[20] It is of note that the United States position was that Common Article 3 and Additional Protocol II should apply, not because they formed part of customary law with individual criminal responsibility, but rather because the parties to the conflict had specifically agreed early on that they would apply these provisions of international humanitarian law.[21] The other two statements that the chamber relied on were far more ambiguous. Thus, the British delegate said that Article 3 is "broad enough to include applicable international conventions," without

---

[18] Report of the Secretary-General Pursuant to Paragraph 2 of Security Council Resolution 808, U.N. SCOR, 48th Sess., 3175th mtg., U.N. Doc. S/RES/808 (1993), reprinted in 32 INTERNATIONAL LEGAL MATERIALS (1993), at para. 34.

[19] Report of the Secretary-General Pursuant to Paragraph 2 of Security Council Resolution 808, U.N. SCOR, 48th Sess., 3175th mtg., U.N. Doc. S/RES/808 (1993), reprinted in 32 INTERNATIONAL LEGAL MATERIALS (1993), at para. 34.

[20] See Provisional Verbatim Record of the 3217th Mtg. of the Security Council., May 25, 1993, at 11, U.N. Doc. S/PV.3217, reprinted in 2 VIRGINIA MORRIS AND MICHAEL P. SCHARF, AN INSIDER'S GUIDE TO THE INTERNATIONAL CRIMINAL TRIBUNAL FOR THE FORMER YUGOSLAVIA 179 (Transnational Publishers, 1995).

[21] See Suggestions Made by the Government of the United States of America, Rules of Procedure and Evidence for the International Tribunal for the Prosecution of Persons Responsible for Serious Violations of International Humanitarian Law Committed in the Former Yugoslavia, IT/14, 17 November 1993, reprinted in 2 VIRGINIA MORRIS AND MICHAEL P. SCHARF, AN INSIDER'S GUIDE TO THE INTERNATIONAL CRIMINAL TRIBUNAL FOR THE FORMER YUGOSLAVIA 516 (Transnational Publishers, 1995).

specifying which conventions were "applicable."[22] And the French delegate said Article 3 covered "all the obligations that flow" from humanitarian conventions in force at the relevant time but did not specify whether France believed obligations under Protocol II did so.[23]

The chamber decision tries to minimize the fact that most of the members of the council took no position on the scope of Article 3. Stressing that "no delegate contested these declarations," the Appeals Chamber concluded that they provided an "authoritative interpretation" of Article 3.[24] But, as Professor Geoffrey Watson, who was present in the Council Chamber when Resolution 827 was adopted, has observed: "The reality is that every State's delegate read a statement prepared or at least vetted in advance by that State's government. No delegate was authorized to jump up and 'object' when it heard the final version of the U.S. or French remarks. Moreover, the declarations ... were made after the delegations had already voted on the resolution."[25]

Meanwhile, the Appeals Chamber conveniently overlooked the fact that an equal number of states expressed qualms about the breadth of the tribunal's subject matter jurisdiction as supported a broad interpretation. The Japanese delegate, for example, suggested that "more extensive legal studies could have been undertaken on various aspects of the Statute, such as the question of the principle of *nullum crimen sine lege*" – a question raised by a broad interpretation of

---

[22] See Provisional Verbatim Record of the 3217th Mtg. of the Security Council., May 25, 1993, at 19, U.N. Doc. S/PV.3217, reprinted in 2 VIRGINIA MORRIS AND MICHAEL P. SCHARF, AN INSIDER'S GUIDE TO THE INTERNATIONAL CRIMINAL TRIBUNAL FOR THE FORMER YUGOSLAVIA 179 (Transnational Publishers, 1995).

[23] See Provisional Verbatim Record of the 3217th Mtg. of the Security Council., May 25, 1993, at 11, U.N. Doc. S/PV.3217, reprinted in 2 VIRGINIA MORRIS AND MICHAEL P. SCHARF, AN INSIDER'S GUIDE TO THE INTERNATIONAL CRIMINAL TRIBUNAL FOR THE FORMER YUGOSLAVIA 179 (Transnational Publishers, 1995).

[24] *Prosecutor v. Tadic*, Appeals Chamber, Decision on the Defense Motion for Interlocutory Appeal on Jurisdiction, Case No. IT-94-1-AR72 (Oct. 2, 1995), reprinted in 35 I.L.M. 32 (1996), at para. 88.

[25] Geoffrey Watson, *The Humanitarian Law of the Yugoslavia War Crimes Tribunal: Jurisdiction in* Prosecutor v. Tadic, 36 VIRGINIA JOURNAL OF INTERNATIONAL LAW 687, 709 (1996).

Article 3.[26] The Spanish delegate noted that the statute could have benefited from improvements, "especially in determining the substantive subject matter and temporal jurisdiction" of the tribunal,[27] and the Brazilian delegate said that many unspecified but important "legal difficulties" were not resolved to his government's satisfaction.[28]

Professor Watson further observes that the state practice relied upon by the Appeals Chamber "is no more compelling than the prepared declarations of a minority of the Security Council."[29] Professor Christopher Greenwood, now a judge on the International Court of Justice, has similarly concluded that "it is also doubtful whether the practice discussed in this part of the [Appeals Chamber] decision really sustains some of the inferences drawn from it."[30]

The Appeals Chamber conceded that traditional international humanitarian law distinguished sharply between international and internal armed conflict, but it asserted with very little evidence of state practice that the distinction has gradually disintegrated as civil strife has become more vicious and large scale.[31] The chamber cited few examples of actual war crimes trials arising out of internal conflict and no examples

---

[26] See Provisional Verbatim Record of the 3217th Mtg. of the Security Council., May 25, 1993, at 22, U.N. Doc. S/PV.3217, reprinted in 2 VIRGINIA MORRIS AND MICHAEL P. SCHARF, AN INSIDER'S GUIDE TO THE INTERNATIONAL CRIMINAL TRIBUNAL FOR THE FORMER YUGOSLAVIA 179 (Transnational Publishers, 1995).

[27] See Provisional Verbatim Record of the 3217th Mtg. of the Security Council., May 25, 1993, at 29, U.N. Doc. S/PV.3217, reprinted in 2 VIRGINIA MORRIS AND MICHAEL P. SCHARF, AN INSIDER'S GUIDE TO THE INTERNATIONAL CRIMINAL TRIBUNAL FOR THE FORMER YUGOSLAVIA 179 (Transnational Publishers, 1995).

[28] See Provisional Verbatim Record of the 3217th Mtg. of the Security Council., May 25, 1993, at 29, U.N. Doc. S/PV.3217, reprinted in 2 VIRGINIA MORRIS AND MICHAEL P. SCHARF, AN INSIDER'S GUIDE TO THE INTERNATIONAL CRIMINAL TRIBUNAL FOR THE FORMER YUGOSLAVIA 179 (Transnational Publishers, 1995).

[29] Geoffrey Watson, *The Humanitarian Law of the Yugoslavia War Crimes Tribunal: Jurisdiction in Prosecutor v. Tadic*, 36 VIRGINIA JOURNAL OF INTERNATIONAL LAW 687, 713 (1996).

[30] Christopher Greenwood, *International Humanitarian Law and the Tadic Case*, 7 EUROPEAN JOURNAL OF INTERNATIONAL LAW 265, 278 (1996).

[31] *Prosecutor v. Tadic*, Appeals Chamber, Decision on the Defense Motion for Interlocutory Appeal on Jurisdiction, Case No. IT-94–1-AR72 (Oct. 2, 1995), reprinted in 35 I.L.M. 32 (1996), at para. 97.

whatsoever of a war crimes trial involving violations of Additional Protocol II. Instead, the tribunal put much emphasis on the fact that the UN General Assembly had twice (in 1968 and in 1970) declared that humanitarian law applies to "all types of armed conflicts."[32] Yet these UN General Assembly resolutions are a questionable source of authority for the chamber's position. The two resolutions predate Additional Protocol II, and while they speak in terms of applying humanitarian law to "all armed conflicts," they do not specifically mention internal armed conflict and they nowhere address the question of individual criminal responsibility for war crimes.[33]

Was the *Tadic* Decision a Grotian Moment?

Notwithstanding the Appeals Chamber's assertion that it was simply "declaring" customary international law, the great weight of authority at the time of the *Tadic* decision viewed war crimes liability as applicable only to international armed conflict. Thus, in its 1993 comments to the United Nations on the establishment of the tribunal, the International Committee of the Red Cross, the organization charged with the application of the laws of war, stated: "according to International Humanitarian Law as it stands today, the notion of war crimes is limited to situations of international armed conflict."[34] A similar view was expressed in the 1993

---

[32] *Prosecutor v. Tadic*, Appeals Chamber, Decision on the Defense Motion for Interlocutory Appeal on Jurisdiction, Case No. IT-94-1-AR72 (Oct. 2, 1995), reprinted in 35 I.L.M. 32 (1996), at paras. 110 and 111.

[33] See *Declaration on Respect for Human Rights in Armed Conflicts*, G.A. Res. 2444, U.N. GAOR, 23d Sess., Supp. No. 18, U.N. Doc. A/7218 (1968), available at http://www1.umn.edu/humanrts/instree/1968c.htm (last accessed February 9, 2013); Basic Principles for the Protection of Civilian Populations in Armed Conflict, G.A. Res. 2675, U.N. GAOR, 25th Sess. Supp. No. 28, U.N. Doc. A/8028 (1970), available at: http://daccess-dds-ny.un.org/doc/RESOLUTION/GEN/NR0/349/40/IMG/NR034940.pdf?OpenElement (last accessed February 9, 2013).

[34] Some Preliminary Remarks by the International Committee of the Red Cross on the Setting-Up of an International Tribunal for the Prosecution of Persons Responsible for Serious Violations of International Humanitarian Law Committed

Report of the UN Commission of Experts on War Crimes in the Former Yugoslavia, which stated: "the content of customary law applicable to internal armed conflict is debatable. As a result, in general, unless the parties to an internal armed conflict agree otherwise, the only offences committed in internal armed conflict for which universal jurisdiction exists are crimes against humanity and genocide, which apply irrespective of the conflict's classification."[35]

When the Security Council established the International Criminal Tribunal for Rwanda in 1994 (a year before the *Tadic* Appeals Chamber decision was issued), the council expressly conferred jurisdiction over individuals accused of violating Common Article 3 and Additional Protocol II. In describing this development, the secretary-general left little doubt that this was a departure from existing customary international law. Thus, the secretary-general reported to the United Nations that

> the Security Council has elected to take a more expansive approach to the choice of the applicable law than the one underlying the statute of the Yugoslav Tribunal, and included within the subject-matter jurisdiction of the Rwanda Tribunal international instruments regardless of whether they were considered part of customary international law or whether they have customarily entailed the individual criminal responsibility of the perpetrator of the crime. Article 4 of the statute, accordingly, includes violations of Additional Protocol II, which, as a whole, has not yet been universally recognized as part of customary international law, and for the first time criminalizes common article 3 of the four Geneva Conventions.[36]

on the Territory of the Former Yugoslavia, DDM/JUR/422b (March 25, 1993), at 2, reprinted in 2 VIRGINIA MORRIS AND MICHAEL P. SCHARF, AN INSIDER'S GUIDE TO THE INTERNATIONAL CRIMINAL TRIBUNAL FOR THE FORMER YUGOSLAVIA 391–2 (Transnational Publishers, 1995).

[35] UN Commission of Experts Established pursuant to Security Council Resolution 780 (1992), Final report, UN Doc. S/1994/674, 27 May 1994, para. 52, available at: http://ess.uwe.ac.uk/comexpert/REPORT_TOC.HTM (last accessed February 9, 2013).

[36] Report of the Secretary General Pursuant to Paragraph 5 of Security Council Resolution 955, 13 February 1995, UN Doc. S/1995/134, at para. 12.

Professor Alison Danner of Vanderbilt University has observed that the ends of great wars are frequently accompanied by a radical transformation of the law of war in their wake.[37] The end of the First World War witnessed the drafting of the 1925 Geneva Protocol banning use of poisonous gas and the 1929 Geneva Conventions to protect wounded soldiers and prisoners of war. The end of the Second World War saw the negotiation of the 1949 Geneva Conventions, granting further protections to soldiers, sailors, prisoners of war, and civilians. But "the hostility to extending the rules to civil wars is manifest in the records from the 1949 and 1974–7 Diplomatic Conferences" that drafted the Geneva Conventions and their Additional Protocols.[38] With its end point the breakup of the Soviet Union in 1991, the Cold War saw its own revolution in the laws of war, marked by the creation of the Yugoslavia Tribunal and the issuance of the *Tadic* Appeals Chamber decision. Professor Danner has called the *Tadic* decision "revolutionary."[39] Professor William Schabas of Middlesex University has written that, with the *Tadic* decision, the Appeals Chamber "stunned international lawyers by issuing a broad and innovative reading of the two war crimes of the ICTY Statute."[40]

Like other Grotian Moments, the Yugoslavia Tribunal was established at a historically unique moment, when the politics of the Security Council had undergone a short-lived makeover due to the dissolution of the Soviet Union. The Appeals Chamber *Tadic* decision, moreover, was issued at a point where "the relevant underlying treaties were old, where underlying conditions had changed, and where there was little prospect

---

[37] Allison Marston Danner, *When Courts Make Law: How the International Criminal Tribunals Recast the Laws of War*, 49 VANDERBILT LAW REVIEW 1, 2 (2006).

[38] Allison Marston Danner, *When Courts Make Law: How the International Criminal Tribunals Recast the Laws of War*, 49 VANDERBILT LAW REVIEW 1, 45 (2006).

[39] Allison Marston Danner, *When Courts Make Law: How the International Criminal Tribunals Recast the Laws of War*, 49 VANDERBILT LAW REVIEW 1, 23 (2006).

[40] WILLIAM SCHABAS, AN INTRODUCTION TO THE INTERNATIONAL CRIMINAL COURT 42 (Cambridge University Press, 2001).

for the treaties' revision."[41] As former president of the Yugoslavia Tribunal Theodor Meron explained shortly after the *Tadic* case, "in many other fields of international law, treaty making is faster than the evolution of customary law. In international humanitarian law, change through the formation of custom might be faster."[42] In justifying its bold judicial action, the Appeals Chamber rhetorically asked: "Why protect civilians from belligerent violence, or ban rape, torture or the wanton destruction of hospitals ... when two sovereign States are engaged in war, and yet refrain from enacting the same bans or providing the same protection when armed violence has erupted 'only' within the territory of a sovereign State?"[43]

Though it would be a stretch to conclude that the *Tadic* decision was in fact a codification of existing customary international law, it did serve as a powerful catalyst for a variety of state actions and statements that rapidly crystallized the new law. Just three years after the Appeals Chamber's decision, the *Tadic* precedent had a powerful effect on the outcome of the Rome Diplomatic Conference to establish an International Criminal Court (ICC). During the negotiations in Rome, the question of whether the ICC's jurisdiction should extend to atrocities committed in civil war was a source of contention. The United States, France, Japan, and the United Kingdom supported the inclusion of civil wars within the jurisdiction of the ICC, while China, India, Indonesia, Pakistan, Russia, and Turkey opposed the application of war crimes to civil wars.[44] The delegates were able to break the deadlock by the unifying force of the

---

[41] Allison Marston Danner, *When Courts Make Law: How the International Criminal Tribunals Recast the Laws of War*, 49 VANDERBILT LAW REVIEW 1, 5 (2006).

[42] Theodor Meron, *The Continuing Role of Custom in the Formation of International Humanitarian Law*, 90 AMERICAN JOURNAL OF INTERNATIONAL LAW 238, 247 (1996).

[43] *Prosecutor v. Tadic*, Appeals Chamber, Decision on the Defense Motion for Interlocutory Appeal on Jurisdiction, Case No. IT-94-1-AR72 (Oct. 2, 1995), reprinted in 35 I.L.M. 32 (1996), at p. 97.

[44] Allison Marston Danner, *When Courts Make Law: How the International Criminal Tribunals Recast the Laws of War*, 49 VANDERBILT LAW REVIEW 1, 45 (2006).

Yugoslavia Tribunal's *Tadic* decision. Thus, declaring that they were following customary international law, the negotiators codified the *Tadic* approach of distinguishing the rules governing international and noninternational conflicts, with a distinct provision in the ICC Statute devoted to each.[45] At the time this book went to press, there were 122 state parties to the ICC Statute,[46] and many of them had enacted domestic statutes enabling their courts to prosecute war crimes in internal as well as international armed conflict.[47] Even nonparties, including China, India, Russia, and the United States, implicitly embraced the *Tadic* decision when they voted in the Security Council on February 26, 2011, to refer the matter of war crimes and crimes against humanity in Libya's civil war to the ICC's jurisdiction.[48]

Subsequently, when the Special Court for Sierra Leone was established in 2002, the drafters followed *Tadic*, giving the hybrid tribunal jurisdiction over war crimes in internal armed conflict.[49] Within a few years of the *Tadic* decision, the Yugoslavia Tribunal, Rwanda Tribunal, and Special Court for Sierra Leone had convicted dozens of defendants for war crimes committed in civil wars. There are no examples of states

---

[45] Rome Statute of the International Criminal Court, Art 8, July 17, 1998, 2187 U.N.T.S. 90 (distinguishing between "international armed conflicts" in paragraph 2(b) and "armed conflict not of an international character" in paragraphs 2(c)–(f)).

[46] For an up-to-date list of ratifications of the ICC Statute, see http://www. coalitionfortheicc.org/?mod=download&doc=4352 (last accessed February 9, 2013).

[47] Amnesty International, UNIVERSAL JURISDICTION: A PRELIMINARY SURVEY OF LEGISLATION AROUND THE WORLD, October 2011, at 1; REPORT OF THE SECRETARY-GENERAL PREPARED ON THE BASIS OF COMMENTS AND OBSERVATIONS OF GOVERNMENTS ON THE SCOPE AND APPLICATION OF THE PRINCIPLE OF UNIVERSAL JURISDICTION, UN Doc. a/65/181, 29 July 2010, at 11, 12.

[48] Security Council Resolution 770, U.N. Doc. SC/10187/Rev.1**, February 26, 2011, available at: http://www.un.org/News/Press/docs/2011/sc10187.doc.htm (last accessed February 9, 2013).

[49] Statute of the Special Court for Sierra Leone, art 3, (16 January 2002), available at: http://www.sc-sl.org/LinkClick.aspx?fileticket=uClnd1MJeEw%3d&tabid=176 (last accessed February 9, 2013).

publicly criticizing the tribunals' jurisprudence regarding culpability for atrocities in internal armed conflict.[50] Professor Danner suggests that is because the developing countries, who long opposed war crimes liability in civil wars, "may not wish to pick a fight with an institution established by the powerful Security Council."[51]

Meanwhile, a growing number of states have incorporated the tribunals' jurisprudence into their military manuals and training materials on the laws of war. The *Manual on the Law of Armed Conflict* issued in 2004 by the United Kingdom, for example, includes references to the case law of the tribunals, including on the definition of armed conflict.[52] The *Tadic* decision was also specifically cited in the handbook for law-of-war training for members of the U.S. Judge Advocate Generals' Corps.[53] The *Tadic* decision has also been cited as persuasive authority by domestic courts, by international organizations, by NGOs, and by scholars.[54] Within a year of the *Tadic* decision, the International Law Commission, noting "that the principle of individual criminal responsibility for violations of the law applicable in internal armed conflicts had been reaffirmed by the International Criminal Tribunal for the former Yugoslavia," codified this legal development in the 1996 Draft Code of Crimes against the Peace and Security of Mankind.[55]

---

[50] Allison Marston Danner, *When Courts Make Law: How the International Criminal Tribunals Recast the Laws of War*, 49 VANDERBILT LAW REVIEW 1, 5 (2006).

[51] Allison Marston Danner, *When Courts Make Law: How the International Criminal Tribunals Recast the Laws of War*, 49 VANDERBILT LAW REVIEW 1, 44 (2006).

[52] U.K. Ministry of Defense, The Manual of the Law of Armed Conflict 29 (2004).

[53] International & Operational Law Department, the Judge Advocate General's Legal Center & School, U.S. Army, Law of War Handbook 82, 144, 209–12 (2004).

[54] Allison Marston Danner, *When Courts Make Law: How the International Criminal Tribunals Recast the Laws of War*, 49 VANDERBILT LAW REVIEW 1, 49 (2006).

[55] Draft Code of Crimes against the Peace and Security of Mankind, art. 20(f) and commentary thereto, *Report of the International Law Commission to the General Assembly*, 51 U.N. GAOR Supp. (No. 10) at 112 and 119, U.N. Doc. A/51/10 (1996), *reprinted in* [1996] 2 YEAR BOOK OF THE INTERNATIONAL LAW COMMISSION, U.N. Doc. A/CN.4/SER.A/1996/Add.1 (Part 2).

Consequences Arising out of This Grotian Moment

One of the principal failings of the codified laws of war had been their inapplicability to internal armed conflicts. The *Tadic* decision effectively transformed the rules negotiated in 1949 and 1977 to make them more relevant to modern conflicts, which frequently involve civil wars rooted in ethnic tension. In essence, with respect to "serious offenses," the *Tadic* decision blurred the line between international and internal armed conflict so that some of the most important rules of customary law applicable to international armed conflict would now apply to civil wars as well. According to the Appeals Chamber, these rules would include "protection of civilians from hostilities, in particular from indiscriminate attacks, protection of civilian objects, in particular cultural property, protection of all those who do not (or no longer) take active part in the hostilities, as well as prohibition of means of warfare proscribed in international armed conflicts and ban of certain methods of conducting hostilities."[56]

As a result of the *Tadic* decision, much of the conduct prohibited by treaties governing international armed conflicts now constitutes prosecutable war crimes when committed in internal armed conflicts. ICJ Judge Christopher Greenwood has concluded that customary international law growing out of the *Tadic* decision "regarding internal armed conflicts is of the greatest importance and is likely to be seen in the future as a major contribution to the development of international humanitarian law."[57] The logical outcome of this development is that war crimes other than grave breaches of the Geneva Conventions, whether committed in international or internal armed conflict, will now be subject to universal jurisdiction, and possibly the requirement of *aut dedere aut judicate* (the

---

[56] *Prosecutor v. Tadic*, Appeals Chamber, Decision on the Defense Motion for Interlocutory Appeal on Jurisdiction, Case No. IT-94–1-AR72, at p. 127 (Oct. 2, 1995), reprinted in 35 I.L.M. 32 (1996).

[57] Christopher Greenwood, *International Humanitarian Law and the Tadic Case*, 7 EUROPEAN JOURNAL OF INTERNATIONAL LAW 265, 279 (1996).

duty to prosecute or extradite) in the same way that grave breaches are.[58] In addition, such war crimes will not be subject to statutes of limitations and may constitute an exception to head of state immunity for former leaders for acts done while in office.[59]

While the jurisprudence of the ad hoc international criminal tribunals has facilitated the accelerated formation of customary international law with respect to other matters such as recognition of recruitment and use of child soldiers as a war crime[60] and of forced marriage as a crime against humanity,[61] none of the other decisions has had the pervasive transformative effect of the *Tadic* decision. This Grotian Moment has even had a significant effect on U.S. policies in its "war on terrorism" – a subject that will be discussed in more detail in Chapter 9. Thus, in the

---

[58] *Cf* Questions Related to the Obligation to Prosecute or Extradite (*Belgium v. Senegal*), July 20, 1012, available at: http://www.icj-cij.org/docket/files/144/17064. pdf (last accessed February 9, 2013) (holding that Senegal has a duty to prosecute or extradite former president of Chad for acts of torture); Interlocutory Decision on the Applicable Law: Terrorism, Conspiracy, Homicide, Perpetration, Cumulative Charging, Special Tribunal for Lebanon Appeals Chamber, Case No. STL-11-01/I (Feb. 16, 2011), paras. 83, 102, available at: http://www.stl-tsl.org/x/file/ TheRegistry/Library/CaseFiles/chambers/20110216_STL-11-01_R176bis_F0010_ AC_Interlocutory_Decision_Filed_EN.pdf (last accessed February 9, 2013) (holding that there is a customary international law duty to prosecute or extradite acts of terrorism).

[59] Jing Guan, *The ICC's Jurisdiction over War Crimes in Internal Armed Conflicts: An Insurmountable Obstacle for China's Accession?* 28 PENNSYLVANIA STATE INTERNATIONAL LAW REVIEW 703, 715 (2010).

[60] *Prosecutor v. Alex Tamba Brima (AFRC Trial Judgment)*, SCSL-04–16-T, Judgment (June 20, 2007) (SCSL, Trial Chamber II); *Prosecutor v. Alex Tamba Brima (AFRC Appeals Judgment)*, SCSL-04–16-A, Judgment (February 22, 2008) (SCSL, Appeals Chamber); *Prosecutor v. Moinina Fofona (CDF Trial Judgment)*, SCSL-04–14-T, Judgment (August 2, 2007) (SCSL, Trial Chamber I); *Prosecutor v. Moinina Fofona (CDF Appeals Judgment)*, SCSL-04–14-A, Judgment (May 28, 2008) (SCSL, Appeals Chamber); *Prosecutor v. Sesay (RUF Trial Judgment)*, SCSL-04–15-T, Judgment (March 2, 2009) (SCSL, Trial Chamber I); *Prosecutor v. Sesay (RUF Appeals Judgment)*, SCSL-04–15-A, Judgment (October 26, 2009) (SCSL, Appeals Chamber); *The Prosecutor v. Thomas Lubanga Dyilo*, ICC-01/04–01/06, Decision on the Confirmation of the Charges January 29, 2007) (ICC, Pre-Trial Chamber I).

[61] Judgment, *Prosecutor v. Brima, Kamara and Kanu*, SCSL, Appeals Chamber, February 22, 2008, para. 195.

2006 landmark case of *Hamdan v. Rumsfeld*, an Al Qaeda detainee held
at Guantanamo Bay argued that the military commission established
by President Bush's executive order did not comply with the minimum
requirements of Common Article 3 of the Geneva Conventions. The
Bush administration responded in part that Common Article 3 applied
only to internal armed conflicts, and that the war against Al Qaeda was
international in scope. In ruling that the military commission was invalid,
the Supreme Court cited the Yugoslavia Tribunal Appeals Chamber
decision in *Tadic* for the proposition that "the character of the conflict is
irrelevant" in deciding whether Common Article 3 applies.[62]

---

[62] *Hamdan v. Rumsfeld*, 126 S.Ct. 2749, 2774 n.63 (2006).

8 The 1999 NATO Intervention

THIS CHAPTER EXAMINES WHETHER THE NATO AIR STRIKES
against Serbia in an effort to prevent ethnic cleansing of
Kosovar Albanians in 1999 resulted in accelerated formation of new rules of customary international law concerning humanitarian intervention. It was significant that the situation was unfolding just
five years after the UN failed to take action to halt genocide in Rwanda.
When Russia and China made clear that they would block the Security
Council from authorizing the use of force against Serbia, NATO pro-
ceeded to commence a seventy-eight-day bombing campaign without
UN approval. The near- universal consensus, however, was that the intervention was justified under the circumstances, leading commentators to
label the situation "unlawful but legitimate."[1] The international reaction
to the 1999 NATO intervention prompted the General Assembly and
Security Council to endorse a new doctrine known as "the responsibility to protect" (R2P), which would authorize humanitarian intervention
in certain limited circumstances in the future. In considering whether
the NATO intervention and adoption of the R2P doctrine constitute a
Grotian Moment, the chapter will explore the evolving meaning of the
R2P doctrine.

---

[1] Independent International Commission on Kosovo, The Kosovo Report: Conflict,
International Response, Lessons Learned (2000).

Historic Status of Humanitarian Intervention

Since the 1648 Peace of Westphalia, state sovereignty has been regarded as the fundamental paradigm of international law. Leading scholars have described the prohibition of the threat or use of force in Article 2(4) of the UN Charter as "the corner-stone of the Charter system."[2] This prohibition goes hand in hand with the nonintervention principle enshrined in Article 2(7) of the UN Charter, which prohibits coercive intervention into the exclusively domestic affairs of a state.[3]

There are only two exceptions to the nonuse of force rule enumerated in the UN Charter. The first covers situations that qualify as self-defense in the face of an armed attack under Article 51 of the charter. The second covers situations where the use of force has been authorized by the Security Council under Article 42 of the charter in response to a threat to the peace, a breach of the peace, or an act of aggression. Article 53(1) further elaborates that "no enforcement action shall be taken under regional arrangements or by regional agencies without the authorization of the Security Council."

In the last twenty years, the Security Council has significantly broadened what it considers to qualify as a threat to the peace. Thus, the council found threats to the peace in situations involving widespread human rights violations and humanitarian atrocities in Southern Rhodesia (1969), South Africa (1977), Somalia (1992), Rwanda (1994), East Timor (1999), Kosovo (1999), and Libya (2011). In 1992, the president of the Security Council acknowledged this conceptual shift, stating that "the mere absence of war and military conflict among States does not itself ensure international peace and security – rather, intrastate

---

[2] JAMES L. BRIERLY, THE LAW OF NATIONS: AN INTRODUCTION TO THE INTERNATIONAL LAW OF PEACE 414 (Oxford University Press, 6th ed. 1963); IAN BROWNLIE, PRINCIPLES OF PUBLIC INTERNATIONAL LAW 732 (Oxford University Press, 7th ed. 2008).

[3] Military and Paramilitary Activities (*Nicaragua v. United States*), 1986 I.C.J. 14, 107–8 (June 27).

humanitarian situations can also become threats to peace and secu-rity."[4] Yet, Security Council action is often thwarted by the threat or use of the veto by its permanent members, and consequently, the coun-cil has failed to authorize humanitarian intervention in situations such as Rwanda in 1994, where 800,000 deaths would likely have been pre-vented had the council acted.

While the Security Council was increasing its ability to respond to atrocities within a state, the United Nations General Assembly adopted a number of instruments designed to limit resort to humanitarian inter-vention outside the framework of the United Nations. These include the *1965 Declaration on the Inadmissibility of Intervention*, which denied legal recognition to intervention "for any reason whatsoever"; the 1970 *Declaration on Principles of International Law Concerning Friendly Relations and Cooperation*, which confirmed that "no State or group of States has the right to intervene ... in the internal or external affairs of any other State"; and the 1987 *Declaration on the Enhancement of the Effectiveness of the Principle of Refraining from the Threat or Use of Force in International Relations*, which stated that "no consideration of whatever nature may be invoked to warrant resorting to the threat or use of force in violation of the Charter."[5]

The 1999 NATO Intervention

Chapter 7 introduced the reader to the conflagration that engulfed Bosnia in 1991–2. The Kosovo crisis six years later emerged out of the same historic backdrop of ethnic tensions. Kosovo was a Serbian province

---

[4] Mehrdad Payandeh, *With Great Power Comes Great Responsibility? The Concept of the Responsibility to Protect within the Process of International Lawmaking*, 35 YALE JOURNAL OF INTERNATIONAL LAW 470, 495 (2010) (quoting Note by the President of the Security Council, U.N. Doc. S/23500 [Jan. 31, 1992]).

[5] Nicholas J. Wheeler, *Reflections on the Legality and Legitimacy of NATO's Intervention in Kosovo*, in THE KOSOVO TRAGEDY: THE HUMAN RIGHTS DIMENSIONS 149 (Ken Booth, ed., Psychology Press, 2001).

where the population was 90 percent ethnic Albanian Muslims and 10 percent Serbian Eastern Orthodox.[6] In 1998, purportedly in response to the threat posed by Kosovar insurgents, Serb military and security forces launched a series of attacks that appeared intended to ethnically cleanse the region.

In Resolution 1199 of March 31, 1998, the UN Security Council determined that the situation in Kosovo constituted a threat to the peace and, acting under Chapter VII of the UN Charter, called upon the parties to comply with certain provisional measures for quelling the conflict.[7] The preamble of the resolution referred to the "recent intense fighting in Kosovo" and "in particular the excessive and indiscriminate use of force by Serbian security forces and the Yugoslav Army which had resulted in numerous civilian casualties and, according to the Secretary-General, the displacement of over 230,000 persons from their homes."

Resolution 1203 of October 24, 1998, repeated that the Kosovo situation constituted a threat to the peace; insisted upon the cessation of hostilities, withdrawal of certain forces, and the commitment of the parties to seek a political resolution; and authorized an OSCE Kosovo Verification Mission and a NATO Air Verification Mission to monitor compliance with the provisional measures required under Resolution 1199.[8] But the Security Council resolutions did not authorize the use of force, and Russia made it clear that it would veto any attempt to do so.

Nevertheless, after peace negotiations broke down in March 1999, NATO decided to launch a series of aerial attacks against military and strategic targets in Serbia with the aim to persuade the Serbian government, headed by Slobodan Milosevic, to comply with United Nations Security Council Resolutions 1199 and 1203. After the massacres of Kosovars in Drenica, Gornje Obrinje, and Racak, the NATO states

---

[6] Noel Cox, *Developments in the Laws of War: NATO Attacks on Yugoslavia and the Use of Force to Achieve Humanitarian Objectives*, (2002) NEW ZEALAND ARMED FORCES LAW REVIEW 13–24 (2002).

[7] S.C. Res. 1160, para. 8 (March 31, 1998).

[8] S.C. Res. 1203, paras. 1–3 (October 24, 1998).

had reached the conclusion that unless action was taken, a humanitarian catastrophe would unfold, potentially eclipsing that of Bosnia.[9] The bombing campaign, called "Operation Allied Force," involved 912 aircraft, which flew a total of 37,225 bombing missions.[10] A significant feature of the Kosovo operation was the purity of the actors' motives – "there were no strategic or material interests of NATO nations in Kosovo."[11]

In explaining its decision to issue an activation order to use NATO force in the Kosovo crisis, the North Atlantic Council stated, "The unrestrained assault by Yugoslav military, police and paramilitary forces, under the direction of President Milosevic, on Kosovar civilians has created a massive humanitarian catastrophe, which also threatens to destabilize the surrounding region. … These extreme and criminally irresponsible policies, which cannot be defended on any grounds, have made necessary and justify the military action by NATO."[12]

In the early days of the bombing campaign, British Prime Minister Tony Blair explained the humanitarian justification for the action. "This is not a battle for NATO; this is not a battle for territory; this is a battle for humanity. This is a just cause, it is a rightful cause."[13] When pressed in parliament for the legal rationale for the NATO bombing campaign, Blair's secretary for defense, George Robertson, provided the following elucidation: "Our legal justification rests upon the accepted principle that force may be used in extreme circumstances to avert a humanitarian

---

[9] Steven Haines, *The Influence of Operation Allied Force on the Development of the Jus Ad Bellum*, 85 INTERNATIONAL AFFAIRS 477, 480 (2009).

[10] Patrick T. Egan, *The Kosovo Intervention and Collective Self-Defense*, 8 INTERNATIONAL PEACEKEEPING 39, 40 (2001).

[11] Fernando R. Teson, *Kosovo: A Powerful Precedent for the Doctrine of Humanitarian Intervention*, 2 AMSTERDAM LAW FORUM 119 (2009).

[12] *NATO, The Situation in and around Kosovo: Statement Issued at the Extraordinary Ministerial Meeting of the North Atlantic Council Held at NATO Headquarters, Brussels, on 12th April 1999*, Press Release M-NAC-1(99)51, Brussels, April 12, 1999.

[13] Dino Kritsiotis, *The Kosovo Crisis and NATO's Application of Armed Force against the Federal Republic of Yugoslavia* 49 THE INTERNATIONAL AND COMPARATIVE LAW QUARTERLY 330, 341 (2000).

catastrophe. Those circumstances clearly existed in Kosovo. The use of force in such circumstances can be justified as an exceptional measure in support of purposes laid down by the Security Council, but without the Council's express authorization, when that is the only means to avert an immediate and overwhelming humanitarian catastrophe."[14]

Similar statements were issued by the Canadian and Dutch ambassadors. Thus, the Canadian ambassador claimed that "humanitarian considerations underpin our action. We cannot simply stand by while innocents are murdered, an entire population is displaced, and villages are burned."[15] The Dutch ambassador acknowledged that his government would always prefer to base action on a specific Security Council resolution when taking up arms to defend human rights, but if "due to one or two permanent members' rigid interpretation of the concept of domestic jurisdiction such a resolution is not attainable, we cannot sit back and simply let the humanitarian catastrophe occur." Rather, he concluded, "we will act on the legal basis we have available, and what we have available in this case is more than adequate."[16]

Later, when Serbia attempted to bring a case against the NATO states before the International Court of Justice,[17] the United States listed the following factors in defense of Operation Allied Force:

- the humanitarian catastrophe that has engulfed the people of Kosovo as a brutal and unlawful campaign of ethnic cleansing has forced

---

[14] Dino Kritsiotis, *The Kosovo Crisis and NATO's Application of Armed Force against the Federal Republic of Yugoslavia* 49 THE INTERNATIONAL AND COMPARATIVE LAW QUARTERLY 330, 342 (2000) (quoting UK Parliamentary Debate, 25 March 1999).

[15] Nicholas J. Wheeler, *Reflections on the Legality and Legitimacy of NATO's Intervention in Kosovo,* in THE KOSOVO TRAGEDY: THE HUMAN RIGHTS DIMENSIONS 153 (Ken Booth, ed., Psychology Press, 2001).

[16] Nicholas J. Wheeler, *Reflections on the Legality and Legitimacy of NATO's Intervention in Kosovo,* in THE KOSOVO TRAGEDY: THE HUMAN RIGHTS DIMENSIONS 153 (Ken Booth, ed., Psychology Press, 2001).

[17] The Court later concluded that it lacked jurisdiction over the case brought by Serbia.

many hundreds of thousands to flee their homes and has severely endangered their lives and well-being;

- the acute threat of the actions of the Federal Republic of Yugoslavia [Serbia] to the security of neighboring States, including the threat posed by extremely heavy flows of refugees and armed incursions into their territories;
- the serious violation of international humanitarian law and human rights obligations by forces under the control of the Federal Republic of Yugoslavia [Serbia], including widespread murder, disappearances, rape, theft and destruction of property; and finally
- the resolutions of the Security Council, which have determined that the actions of the Federal Republic of Yugoslavia [Serbia] constitute a threat to peace and security in the region and, pursuant to Chapter VII of the Charter, demanded a halt to such actions.[18]

Belgium was even more explicit in its defense before the International Court of Justice, claiming that the NATO action was necessary "to rescue a people in peril, in deep distress." Belgium then went on to characterize the application of force as "an armed humanitarian intervention, compatible with Article 2(4) of the Charter, which covers only intervention against the territorial integrity or political independence of a State."[19] Similarly, Germany told the Court that the NATO action had been undertaken "as a last resort in order to put a stop to the massive human rights violations perpetrated by the Federal Republic of Yugoslavia [Serbia] in Kosovo and to protect the population of Kosovo from the unfolding humanitarian catastrophe."[20] Professor Bruno Simma, who was soon thereafter elected to be a judge of the International Court of Justice, commented that the German government "called a spade a

[18] CR 99/24, Verbatim Record of May 11, 1999), available at http://www.icj-cij.org/ icjwww/idocket/iybe/iybeframe.htm (last accessed February 9, 2013).

[19] CR 99/15, Verbatim Record of May 10, 1999, available at http://www.icj-cij.org/ icjwww/idocket/iybe/iybeframe.htm (last accessed February 9, 2013).

[20] CR 99/18, Verbatim Record of May 10, 1999, available at http://www.icj-cij.org/ icjwww/idocket/iybe/iybeframe.htm (last accessed February 9, 2013).

spade and spoke of the NATO threat as an instance of 'humanitarian intervention.'"[21]

On March 25, Russia sponsored a draft resolution in the Security Council that sought to condemn the NATO action as an unlawful act in violation of the UN Charter.[22] According to the Russian Delegation, the vote was to be a choice between law and lawlessness.[23] The Independent International Commission on Kosovo, chaired by the former chief prosecutor of the International Criminal Tribunal for the Former Yugoslavia, Richard Goldstone, would later conclude that the 1999 NATO intervention was "illegal but legitimate."[24] But during the Security Council debate the NATO states did not take the position that the air strikes were illegal but morally justified. Rather, they argued that their action had the backing of international law.[25] In the end, the proposed resolution was defeated by twelve votes to three, with only China and Namibia joining Russia in support of the measure.[26] Voting in opposition were the five NATO members on the Security Council (the United Kingdom, Canada, France, the Netherlands, and the United States), joined by Argentina, Bahrain, Gabon, the Gambia, Malaysia, and Slovenia.[27] The sizable rejection of the draft resolution indicated that there was a broad base

---

[21] Bruno Simma, *NATO, the UN and the Use of Force: Legal Aspects*, 10 EUROPEAN JOURNAL OF INTERNATIONAL LAW 1, 12–13 (1999).

[22] UN Doc. S/1999/328 (March 25, 1999).

[23] Dino Kritsiotis, *The Kosovo Crisis and NATO's Application of Armed Force against the Federal Republic of Yugoslavia* 49 THE INTERNATIONAL AND COMPARATIVE LAW QUARTERLY 330, 347 (2000).

[24] Independent International Commission on Kosovo, The Kosovo Report: Conflict, International Response, Lessons Learned (2000).

[25] Nicholas J. Wheeler, *Reflections on the Legality and Legitimacy of NATO's Intervention in Kosovo*, in THE KOSOVO TRAGEDY: THE HUMAN RIGHTS DIMENSIONS 154 (Ken Booth, ed., Psychology Press, 2001).

[26] Dino Kritsiotis, *The Kosovo Crisis and NATO's Application of Armed Force against the Federal Republic of Yugoslavia* 49 THE INTERNATIONAL AND COMPARATIVE LAW QUARTERLY 330, 342 (2000).

[27] Dino Kritsiotis, *The Kosovo Crisis and NATO's Application of Armed Force against the Federal Republic of Yugoslavia* 49 THE INTERNATIONAL AND COMPARATIVE LAW QUARTERLY 330, 342 (2000).

of support for the NATO action. Outside the council, NATO's intervention was endorsed by the European Union, the Organization of Islamic States, and the Organization of American States.[28] Moreover, key states in the area, including Romania, Slovenia, and Bulgaria, granted NATO access to their airspace for Operation Allied Force, transforming their support into action.[29] Other than Russia, China, India, and Iraq, there was virtually no public protest of the NATO action across the globe.[30]

After seventy-eight days, the NATO bombing campaign ultimately succeeded in driving Milosevic back to the negotiating table, where he signed an agreement providing autonomy for Kosovo under the temporary administration of the United Nations and protection of NATO forces. Subsequently, the Security Council adopted Resolution 1244 of June 10, 1999, which some have interpreted as providing a sort of after-the-fact ratification of Operation Allied Force. The resolution put in place the foundations for the international civil and security presence in Kosovo that accompanied the end of hostilities.[31]

Development of the Responsibility to Protect Doctrine

In the aftermath of the 1999 NATO bombing campaign, the issue of humanitarian intervention emerged as an important aspect of Secretary-General Kofi Annan's reform agenda at the United Nations. When Annan delivered his annual report to the UN General Assembly

[28] Nicholas J. Wheeler, *Reflections on the Legality and Legitimacy of NATO's Intervention in Kosovo*, in THE KOSOVO TRAGEDY: THE HUMAN RIGHTS DIMENSIONS 158 (Ken Booth, ed., Psychology Press, 2001).

[29] Dino Kritsiotis, *The Kosovo Crisis and NATO's Application of Armed Force against the Federal Republic of Yugoslavia* 49 THE INTERNATIONAL AND COMPARATIVE LAW QUARTERLY 330, 346 (2000).

[30] Antonio Cassese, *Ex Injuriaius Oritur: Are We Moving towards Legitimatization of Forcible Humanitarian Countermeasures in the World Community?* 10 EUROPEAN JOURNAL OF INTERNATIONAL LAW 23, 28 (1999).

[31] Dino Kritsiotis, *The Kosovo Crisis and NATO's Application of Armed Force against the Federal Republic of Yugoslavia* 49 THE INTERNATIONAL AND COMPARATIVE LAW QUARTERLY 330, 348 (2000).

later that year, he presented in stark terms the dilemma facing the international community with respect to the idea of unauthorized humanitarian intervention: "To those for whom the greatest threat to the future of international order is the use of force in the absence of a Security Council mandate, one might ask – not in the context of Kosovo – but in the context of Rwanda: If, in those dark days and hours leading up to the genocide, a coalition of States had been prepared to act in defense of the Tutsi population, but did not receive prompt Council authorization, should such a coalition have stood aside and allowed the horror to unfold?"[32] In his *Millennium Report* to the General Assembly in 2000, Annan posed a similar question: "If humanitarian intervention is, indeed an unacceptable assault on sovereignty, how should we respond to a Rwanda, to a Srebrenica – to gross and systematic violations of human rights that offend every precept of our common humanity?"[33]

Rising to the challenge posed by the secretary-general's appeal, the government of Canada established the International Commission on Intervention and State Sovereignty (ICISS), which in December 2001 submitted its report to Secretary-General Annan. The ICISS report, entitled *The Responsibility to Protect*,[34] contained two important innovations. The first was its suggestion that the debate be shifted from focusing on the right to intervene to the responsibility to protect victims of serious human rights violations, a concept that comprises prevention, reaction, and postconflict support.[35] The second was its assertion that sovereignty implies a responsibility of the state to protect its citizens from human rights violations, and when the state is unable or unwilling

---

[32] UN Doc. SG/SM/7136-GA/9596, 20 September 1999.

[33] The Secretary-General, *Report of the Secretary-General, We the Peoples: The Role of the United Nations in the Twenty-First Century*, paras. 215–19, U.N. Doc. A/54/2000 (March 27, 2000).

[34] INTERNATIONAL COMMISSION ON INTERVENTION AND STATE SOVEREIGNTY: THE RESPONSIBILITY TO PROTECT (2001).

[35] INTERNATIONAL COMMISSION ON INTERVENTION AND STATE SOVEREIGNTY: THE RESPONSIBILITY TO PROTECT, paras. 2.28–2.29. (2001).

to fulfill its sovereign responsibility, "it becomes the responsibility of the international community to act in its place."[36]

Drawing from principles of "just war theory,"[37] the ICISS report sets forth criteria for deciding when military humanitarian intervention is warranted. According to the ICISS, such action should only be employed in extreme cases of large-scale loss of life or ethnic cleansing and where (1) the action is motivated by the "right intention"; (2) the action is a "last resort"; (3) the action is proportional to the threat; and (4) the action carries with it a reasonable chance of ending the suffering.[38]

On the most important question of who can authorize humanitarian intervention, the ICISS report emphasizes the primary role of the Security Council. However, should the Security Council fail to react (as when it is paralyzed by a permanent member's veto), the report states that action by the General Assembly under the Uniting for Peace Resolution[39] is a possible alternative that would "provide a high degree of legitimacy for an intervention."[40]

The report also mentions the possibility of action by regional organizations, while pointing out that the UN Charter requires that they act

---

[36] INTERNATIONAL COMMISSION ON INTERVENTION AND STATE SOVEREIGNTY: THE RESPONSIBILITY TO PROTECT, para. 2.29 (2001).

[37] Luke Glanville, *The Responsibility to Protect beyond Borders*, Human Rights Law Review 1, 197 (2012).

[38] INTERNATIONAL COMMISSION ON INTERVENTION AND STATE SOVEREIGNTY: THE RESPONSIBILITY TO PROTECT, paras. 4.19, 4.32, 4.43 (2001).

[39] Uniting for Peace, G.A. Res. 377 (V), U.N. Doc. A/1775 (November 3, 1950).

[40] INTERNATIONAL COMMISSION ON INTERVENTION AND STATE SOVEREIGNTY: THE RESPONSIBILITY TO PROTECT, paras. 6.29–6.30 (2001). Adopted in 1950, the Uniting for Peace Resolution provides: "That if the Security Council, because of lack of unanimity of the permanent members, fails to exercise its primary responsibility for the maintenance of international peace and security in any case where there appears to be a threat to the peace, breach of the peace or act of aggression, the General Assembly shall consider the matter immediately with a view to making appropriate recommendations to Members for collective measures, including in the case of a breach of the peace or act of aggression the use of armed force when necessary, to maintain or restore international peace and security." *See* Uniting for Peace, G.A. Res. 377(V), U.N. Doc. A/1775 (November 3, 1950).

with authorization of the Security Council.[41] Following the reference to the Security Council, however, the ICISS report refers to cases in which regional organizations have carried out an intervention and only subsequently sought the approval of the Security Council, concluding that "there may be certain leeway for future action in this regard."[42]

As to whether individual states or regional organizations can ever legally act without Security Council authorization, the report is intentionally ambiguous. While observing the lack of a global consensus on the issue, the report avoids deeming such interventions illegal.[43] Further, the report points out that there will be damage to the international order if the Security Council is bypassed but also emphasizes that there will be "damage to that order if human beings are slaughtered while the Security Council stands by."[44] The ICISS finds it intolerable that "one veto can override the rest of humanity on matters of grave humanitarian concern."[45] Thus, the ICISS urges the permanent members of the Security Council to refrain from using the veto in cases of genocide and large-scale human rights abuses and cautions that coalitions might take action if the council fails to live up to its responsibility.[46]

Was the International Reaction to the NATO Intervention a Grotian Moment?

In the 1986 *Nicaragua* case, the International Court of Justice observed that "reliance by a State on a novel right or an unprecedented exception

---

[41] INTERNATIONAL COMMISSION ON INTERVENTION AND STATE SOVEREIGNTY: THE RESPONSIBILITY TO PROTECT, paras. 6.31–6.35 (2001).

[42] INTERNATIONAL COMMISSION ON INTERVENTION AND STATE SOVEREIGNTY: THE RESPONSIBILITY TO PROTECT, paras. 6.35, 6.5 (2001).

[43] INTERNATIONAL COMMISSION ON INTERVENTION AND STATE SOVEREIGNTY: THE RESPONSIBILITY TO PROTECT, paras. 6.36–6.37 (2001).

[44] INTERNATIONAL COMMISSION ON INTERVENTION AND STATE SOVEREIGNTY: THE RESPONSIBILITY TO PROTECT, para. 6.37 (2001).

[45] INTERNATIONAL COMMISSION ON INTERVENTION AND STATE SOVEREIGNTY: THE RESPONSIBILITY TO PROTECT, paras. 6.13, 6.20 (2001).

[46] INTERNATIONAL COMMISSION ON INTERVENTION AND STATE SOVEREIGNTY: THE RESPONSIBILITY TO PROTECT, paras. 6.39, 256 (2001).

to the principle [of non-intervention] might, if shared in principle by other States, tend toward a modification of customary international law."[47] Prior to the 1999 NATO bombing campaign, there had been several cases when foreign intervention was employed to halt widespread atrocities without Security Council approval. Hence, India stopped the slaughter in East Pakistan in 1971, Tanzania ended Idi Amin's mass killing in Uganda in 1978, and Vietnam's intervention put an end to Pol Pot's killing fields in Cambodia in 1979.[48] But unlike the 1999 Kosovo intervention, in these three cases self-defense, rather than humanitarian concern, was the primary justification asserted.[49] The fact that the intervening states relied on self-defense, rather than asserting a right to humanitarian intervention, undermined arguments that the law had changed. Moreover, in the cases of India and Vietnam, only a Soviet veto prevented the Security Council from condemning the actions as violations of international law.[50]

A fourth case of pre-1999 humanitarian intervention is worth mentioning. After the end of the first Gulf War, in 1991 the United Kingdom and United States unilaterally imposed and enforced no-fly zones over the northern and southern thirds of Iraq in order to protect the Kurds and Marsh Arabs from attack. Before the British House of Commons on February 26, 2001, the secretary of state for defense, Geoff Hoon, explained: "The legal justification for the patrolling of the no-fly zones does not rest on Security Council Resolution 688. That has not been

---

[47] Case Concerning Military and Paramilitary Activities in and against Nicaragua (1986) I.C.J. Reports 14, 109 (para. 207).

[48] Nicholas J. Wheeler, *Reflections on the Legality and Legitimacy of NATO's Intervention in Kosovo*, in THE KOSOVO TRAGEDY: THE HUMAN RIGHTS DIMENSIONS 150 (Ken Booth, ed., Psychology Press, 2001).

[49] Simon Chesterman, *No More Rwandas No More Kosovos: Intervention and Prevention*, in VELASO AND DANIEL ORTEGA NIETO (EDS.), THE PROTECTION OF HUMAN RIGHTS: A CHALLENGE IN THE 21st CENTURY 175–200 (El Colegio de Mexico, 2007).

[50] Simon Chesterman, *No More Rwandas No More Kosovos: Intervention and Prevention*, in VELASO AND DANIEL ORTEGA NIETO (EDS.), THE PROTECTION OF HUMAN RIGHTS: A CHALLENGE IN THE 21st CENTURY 175–200 (El Colegio de Mexico, 2007).

the government's position. In terms of humanitarian justification, we are entitled to patrol the no-fly zones to prevent a grave humanitarian crisis. That is the legal justification in international law."[51] Very few states, however, supported the position of the United Kingdom and United States with respect to legality of the Iraqi no-fly zones. Three permanent members of the Security Council – Russia, China, and France – repeatedly protested the legality of the UK and U.S. action.[52] And opposition within and outside the Council steadily mounted as the no-fly zone proved to be a permanent fixture, ending only after the 2003 U.S. and UK invasion of Iraq.

In contrast to these situations, in the case of the 1999 NATO intervention in Serbia, a major application of armed force had taken place for humanitarian purposes without Security Council authorization but with widespread support by the international community. According to one scholar, the NATO intervention was "a case that expanded, rather than breached, the law, similar to the Truman proclamation about the Continental Shelf."[53] Others have described the NATO intervention as "a watershed event" and "an important transition point in the shift from one international order to the next."[54] Moreover, the NATO intervention led to the ICISS's articulation of the Responsibility to Protect doctrine, a concept that has been described as the "most dramatic normative development of our time"[55] and a "revolution in consciousness in international affairs."[56]

---

[51] HC Deb February 26, 2001 vol 363 cc 620–34.

[52] Christine Grey, *From Unity to Polarization: International Law and the Use of Force against Iraq*, 13 EUROPEAN JOURNAL OF INTERNATIONAL LAW 1, 10 (2002).

[53] Fernando R. Teson, *Kosovo: A Powerful Precedent for the Doctrine of Humanitarian Intervention*, 2 AMSTERDAM LAW FORUM 119 (2009).

[54] Heiko Borchert and Mary N. Hampton, *The Lessons of Kosovo: Boon or Bust for Transatlantic Security?* ORBIS 369 (2002).

[55] Ramesh Thakur and Thomas G. Weis, *R2P: From Idea to Norm – and Action?* 1 GLOBAL RESPONSIBILITY TO PROTECT 22 (2009).

[56] Jeremy Sarkin, *Is the Responsibility to Protect an Accepted Norm of International Law in the post-Libya Era?* 1 CRONINGEN JOURNAL OF INTERNATIONAL LAW 11, 16 (2012).

The rapid acceptance of the R2P doctrine within a few short years of the NATO intervention renders this development a potential candidate for recognition as a Grotian Moment. The 2001 ICISS report characterized the responsibility to protect as "an emerging principle of customary international law,"[57] and the 2005 High-level Panel Report described it as an "emerging norm,"[58] an assessment shared by the secretary-general.[59] The R2P Doctrine was then unanimously endorsed at the 2005 World Summit by the heads of state and government of every UN member state, and later by the United Nations Security Council. On the basis of these developments, Professor Ved Nanda of Denver University School of Law argues that a government can no longer "hide behind the shield of sovereignty, claiming non-intervention by other States in its internal affairs, if it fails to protect the people under its jurisdiction from massive violations of human rights."[60] Yet, two roadblocks prevented humanitarian intervention outside the framework of the United Nations from actually ripening into a norm of customary international law.

The first impediment was the ambiguity of the initial manifestation of *opinio juris* that accompanied the acts of the NATO states. The participating NATO states were not comfortable with the idea that the bombing campaign would create a new rule of customary international law justifying a broad notion of unilateral humanitarian intervention. Thus, in July 1999, U.S. Secretary of State Madeleine Albright stressed that the air strikes were a "unique situation *sui generis* in the region of the

---

[57] INTERNATIONAL COMMISSION ON INTERVENTION AND STATE SOVEREIGNTY: THE RESPONSIBILITY TO PROTECT, paras. 2.24, 6.17 (2001).

[58] Report of the High-Level Panel on Threats, Challenges and Change: A More Secure World: Our Shared Responsibility, U.N. Doc. A/59/565 (December 2, 2004), para. 203.

[59] *United Nations Secretary-General, in Larger Freedom: Towards Development, Security and Human Rights for All – Report of the Secretary-General*, U.N. GAOR, 59th Sess., UN Doc. a/59/2005 (2005), at para. 135.

[60] Ved Nanda, *The Protection of Human Rights under International Law: Will the U.N. Human Rights Council and the Emerging New Norm "Responsibility to Protect" Make a Difference?* 35 DENVER JOURNAL OF INTERNATIONAL LAW & POLICY 353, 373 (2007).

Balkans," concluding that it was important "not to overdraw the various lessons that come out of it."[61] UK Prime Minister Tony Blair, who had earlier suggested that humanitarian interventions might become more common,[62] subsequently retreated from that position, emphasizing the exceptional nature of the Kosovo operation.[63]

The reason for the reluctance of the United States and United Kingdom to acknowledge a precedent that could ripen into customary international law was explained by Michael Matheson, the acting legal adviser of the U.S. Department of State at the time of the intervention, in the following terms:

> About six months before the actual conflict, at the time when NATO was considering giving an order to threaten the use of force, the political community of NATO got together and had a discussion about what the basis of such threat of force would be. At the end of the discussion, it was clear that there was no common agreement on what might be the justification. There were some NATO members who were prepared to base it on a new doctrine of humanitarian intervention; but most members of the NATO Council were reluctant to adopt a relatively open-ended new doctrine. So at the end of that week, the NATO political community said, here is a list of all of the important reasons why it is necessary for us to threaten the use of force. And at the bottom, it said that under these unique circumstances, we think such actions would be legitimate. There was deliberate evasion of making a "legal" assertion.
>
> And this same process occurred in the U.S. Government. There were some who wanted to articulate that humanitarian intervention in now the basis for U.S. action. There was another theory from the Department of Defense, which wanted to adopt sort of an expanded idea of self-defense based on the general interest of the United States

---

[61] U.S. Secretary of State Madeleine Albright, Press Conference with Russian Foreign Minister Igor Ivanov, Singapore, July 26, 1999, available at: http://secretary.state. gov./www/statements/1999/990726b.html (last accessed February 9, 2013).

[62] Colin Brown, *Blair's Vision of Global Police*, INDEPENDENT, April 23, 1999.

[63] UK Parliamentary Debates, Commons, April 26, 1999, co 30 (Prime Minister Blair).

in the region; but on reflection, nobody was really prepared to throw all the eggs into either of those baskets. So we ended up with a formulation similar to that of NATO, where we listed all of the reasons why we were taking action and, in the end, mumbled something about its being justifiable and legitimate but not a precedent. So in a sense, it was something less than a definitive legal rationale – although it probably was taken by large parts of the public community as something like that.[64]

When the principal state actors assert that their actions are sui generis and not intended to constitute precedent, this does not create a favorable climate for the cultivation of a new rule of customary international law.[65]

Nevertheless, by providing a legal veneer to the 1999 NATO intervention, the 2001 ICISS report seemed to represent a large step forward in the process of crystallizing a modern right of humanitarian intervention outside the UN framework. Thus, Antonio Cassese, who served as president of the International Criminal Tribunal for the Former Yugoslavia and later as president of the Special Tribunal for Lebanon, argued that "NATO's action may support an emerging custom allowing the use of forcible countermeasures to impede a state from committing large-scale atrocities within its own territory, in circumstances where the Security Council is incapable of responding to the crisis."[66] But the formation of the new customary rule hit a second obstruction when the 2004 High-Level Panel Report, which was endorsed by the U.N. secretary-general, and the 2005 World Summit Outcome Document, which was endorsed by the

---

[64] MICHAEL P. SCHARF AND PAUL R. WILLIAMS, SHAPING FOREIGN POLICY IN TIMES OF CRISIS: THE ROLE OF INTERNATIONAL LAW AND THE STATE DEPARTMENT LEGAL ADVISER 124–5 (Cambridge University Press, 2010) (quoting remarks by Michael Matheson).

[65] Bruno Simma, *NATO, the UN and the Use of Force: Legal Aspects*, 10 EUROPEAN JOURNAL OF INTERNATIONAL LAW 1 (1999).

[66] Antonio Cassese, *Ex Iniuria Ius Oritur: Are We Moving towards International Legitimization of Forcible Humanitarian Countermeasures in the World Community?* 10 EUROPEAN JOURNAL OF INTERNATIONAL LAW 23 (1999).

General Assembly and Security Council, were written to reflect a much
narrower conception in which humanitarian intervention is only lawful
when authorized by the Security Council.

The ICISS report was the subject of unfortunate timing. Shortly after
the report was issued, in March 2003, the United States and a "coalition
of the willing" invaded Iraq without Security Council authorization in
part to prevent Iraq from deploying weapons of mass destruction and in
part to respond to Saddam Hussein's historic record of atrocities against
Iraq's Kurdish and Shi'ite populations.[67] The action was controversial
and widely unpopular across the globe. By November 2003, the worry
over the "lack of agreement amongst Member States on the proper role
of the United Nations in providing collective security" prompted the UN
secretary-general to create the High-Level Panel on Threats, Challenges
and Change.[68]

In the High-Level Panel's report, published in December 2004, the
panel specifically endorsed "the emerging norm that there is a collective international responsibility to protect, exercisable by the Security
Council authorizing military intervention as a last resort," and urged the
permanent members to refrain from using the veto in cases of genocide
and large-scale human rights abuses.[69] But, while the High-Level Panel
supported the conceptual change in the understanding of sovereignty
as responsibility, responsibility that is shared by the state and the international community, the panel's characterization of the R2P doctrine
was much more restrictive than that of the ICISS. Influenced by the
widespread criticism of the March 2003 invasion of Iraq, the High-Level

[67] Ved Nanda, *The Protection of Human Rights under International Law: Will the U.N. Human Rights Council and the Emerging New Norm "Responsibility to Protect" Make a Difference?* 35 DENVER JOURNAL OF INTERNATIONAL LAW & POLICY 353, 371–2 (2007).

[68] Report of the High-Level Panel on Threats, Challenges and Change: A More Secure World: Our Shared Responsibility, U.N. Doc. A/59/565 (December 2, 2004).

[69] Report of the High-Level Panel on Threats, Challenges and Change: A More Secure World: Our Shared Responsibility, U.N. Doc. A/59/565 (December 2, 2004), paras. 203, 256.

Panel, departing from the approach of the ICISS report, focused exclusively on action taken by the Security Council and did not mention the possibility of authorization by the General Assembly or actions by states or regional organizations outside the UN framework.

A year later, the secretary-general returned to the R2P concept in his 2005 report, *In Larger Freedom*. Like the High-level Panel's, the secretary-general's 2005 report focused only on the Security Council and did not discuss the possibility of humanitarian interventions without authorization of the council. In the secretary-general's words, "The task is not to find alternatives to the Security Council as a source of authority but to make it work better."[70]

Up through 2005, the Responsibility to Protect had been considered only by the secretary-general and specialized commissions. The R2P doctrine received its first endorsement by states at the September 2005 World Summit, attended by the world's heads of state and government at the United Nations. While unanimously endorsing the general concept, the World Summit Outcome Document reflected an even more restrictive approach than the High-level Panel report. The heads of state and government vaguely affirm that they are prepared to act in a timely manner and on the basis of a case-by-case evaluation. Yet, "they neither recognize specific responsibilities of the Security Council, nor mention the possibility of unilateral or collective action with the authorization of the General Assembly or outside the U.N. framework."[71]

A year later, the Responsibility to Protect made its first appearance in a Security Council resolution when the council referred to the relevant paragraphs of the World Summit Outcome Document and explicitly reaffirmed the responsibility to protect with regard to the protection

[70] *United Nations Secretary-General, Report of the Secretary-General, in Larger Freedom: Toward Development, Security and Human Rights for All*, U.N. Doc. a/59/2005 (March 21, 2005), at para. 126.

[71] Mehrdad Payandeh, *With Great Power Comes Great Responsibility? The Concept of the Responsibility to Protect within the Process of International Lawmaking*, 35 YALE JOURNAL OF INTERNATIONAL LAW 469, 476, (2010).

of civilians in armed conflict.[72] Later that year, the Security Council acknowledged the concept with regard to the situation in Darfur.[73] In 2011, the council again referenced Responsibility to Protect in the context of Security Council authorization for force in Libya.[74]

In 2009, ten years after the NATO intervention, the secretary-general issued a report entitled "Implementing the Responsibility to Protect."[75] The report suggests a three-pillar approach: first is the state's responsibility to protect its population from serious crimes, second is the international community's commitment to support the state in complying with its obligations under the first pillar, and third is the timely and decisive response by the international community should a state not live up to its responsibility to protect.[76] The General Assembly scheduled a formal debate on the secretary-general's 2009 report.

In anticipation of the General Assembly's debate, the president of the General Assembly circulated a concept note in which he emphasized that the 2005 Summit Document does not entail any "legally binding commitment" but that it is for the General Assembly to develop and elaborate a legal basis for the R2P concept.[77] In the ensuing General Assembly debate, ninety-four speakers representing 180 states submitted statements (some speakers spoke on behalf of regional groups). Unfortunately, nothing close to a consensus on the content of the R2P doctrine emerged. Significantly, a number of states voiced serious concerns about "the concept's potential for abuse as a pretext for unilateral

---

[72] S.C. Res. 1674, para. 4, U.N. Doc. S/RES/1674 (April 28, 2006).

[73] S.C. Res. 1706, preamble, U.N. Doc. S/RES/1706 (August 31, 2006).

[74] S.C. Res. 1973, preamble, U.N. Doc. S/RES/1973 (March 17, 2011).

[75] *The Secretary-General, Report of the Secretary-General, Implementing the Responsibility to Protect*, U.N. Doc. A/63/677 (January 12, 2009).

[76] *The Secretary-General, Report of the Secretary-General, Implementing the Responsibility to Protect*, U.N. Doc. A/63/677 (January 12, 2009), paras. 13–27, 28–48, 49–66.

[77] Letter and Concept Note from Office of the President, U.N. General Assembly, to Permanent Missions and Permanent Observer Missions to the United Nations (July 17, 2009), available at: http://www.un.org/ga/president/63/letters/ResponsibilitytoProtect170709.pdf (last accessed February 9, 2013).

intervention and equated the responsibility to protect with humanitarian intervention."[78] Ultimately, the General Assembly adopted a resolution that reaffirmed the principles and purposes of the UN Charter as well as the commitment to the responsibility to protect in the World Summit Outcome Document in its preamble. In its operative paragraphs, the resolution merely "takes note" of the secretary-general's report and decides to continue its consideration of the topic in the future.[79] It is telling that the initial proposed text ("takes note with appreciation" of the secretary-general's report) did not garner sufficient support, and, like the ICISS's original conception of the R2P doctrine, it had to be watered down for adoption. Since 2009, the General Assembly has not held another formal debate on the topic, but rather has held "informal interactive dialogues" about implementing the Responsibility to Protect.

These developments signify that the R2P doctrine has been morphed into a conceptual framework for discourse, which may be quite politically useful but is without legal implications. The prohibition of the use of force in the absence of Security Council authorization has been left intact, leading the Rapporteur of the UN Working Group on Enforced or Involuntary Disappearances to comment that "the last few years has shown that the political context within which the doctrine has to operate has severely limited its operation."[80] These developments prompted former U.S. Secretary of State Madeline Albright to decry in 2008 that "the notion of national sovereignty as sacred is [once again] gaining ground."[81]

[78] Mehrdad Payandeh, *With Great Power Comes Great Responsibility? The Concept of the Responsibility to Protect within the Process of International Lawmaking*, 35 YALE JOURNAL OF INTERNATIONAL LAW 469, 479 (2010).

[79] G.A. Res. 63/308, U.N. Doc. A/RES/63/308 (October 7, 2009).

[80] Jeremy Sarkin, *Is the Responsibility to Protect an Accepted Norm of International Law in the Post-Libya Era?* 1 CRONINGEN JOURNAL OF INTERNATIONAL LAW 11, 13 (2012).

[81] Madeline Albright, *The End of Intervention*, NEW YORK TIMES, June 11, 2008.

The issue of whether Responsibility to Protect is now inextricably coupled to Security Council authorization was tested in 2008, when Russia cited the R2P doctrine to justify its use of force to protect threatened Russian populations in the neighboring country of Georgia that year.[82] Perceiving the military action as a land grab, the United States, European Union, and many other countries protested the Russian invasion of the South Ossetia and Abkhazia provinces of Georgia.[83] As Nancy Soderberg, former U.S. ambassador to the United Nations, has explained, "The Georgia case was really an abuse of power by Russia under an abuse of the Responsibility to Protect Doctrine, and it was not authorized by the U.N. and was resoundingly condemned by the international community."[84] In a *Los Angeles Times* Op Ed, Gareth Evans, one of the principal authors of the ICISS report, argued that the Russian action was clearly invalid because Russia failed to obtain authorization from the Security Council.[85] As Evans explained,

> The 2005 General Assembly position was very clear that, when any country seeks to apply forceful means to address an R2P situation, *it must do so through the Security Council.* The Russia-Georgia case highlights the risks of states, whether individually or in a coalition, interpreting global norms unilaterally. The sense of moral outrage at reports of civilians being killed and ethnically cleansed can have the unintended effect of clouding judgment as to the best response, which is another reason to channel action collectively through the United Nations. That other major countries may have

---

[82] Brian Barbour and Brian Gorlick, *Embracing the "Responsibility to Protect": A Repertoire of Measures Including Asylum for Potential Victims*, 20 INTERNATIONAL JOURNAL OF REFUGEE LAW 533, 559 (2008).

[83] RONALD D. ASMUS, A LITTLE WAR THAT SHOOK THE WORLD: GEORGIA, RUSSIA, AND THE FUTURE OF THE WEST (Palgrave Macmillan, 2010).

[84] National Public Radio, Talk of the Nation, February 6, 2012, transcript available at www.npr.org/2012/02/06/146474734/the-worlds-responsibility-to-protect (last accessed February 9, 2013).

[85] Gareth Evans, *Russia and the Responsibility to Protect*, Los Angeles Times, August 31, 2008, available at: http://www.gevans.org/opeds/oped93.html (last accessed February 9, 2013).

been indifferent to this constraint in the past doesn't justify Russian actions in Georgia.[86]

While the ~~Russian invocation of the R2P doctrine for its invasion of Georgia constituted a setback for the idea that humanitarian intervention~~ can be lawful outside the UN framework, developments at a diplomatic conference in Africa two years later have kept the idea alive. Meeting in Kampala, Uganda, in June 2010, the 119 parties to the International Criminal Court Statute (along with the United States, Russia, China, and several other nonparties) decided by consensus to add the crime of aggression to the Court's jurisdiction. During the negotiations, several delegations wanted to exempt incidents of humanitarian intervention from the jurisdiction of the ICC. To that end, these delegations sought language that would limit prosecutions to "flagrant" violations of the UN Charter, wars of aggression, unlawful uses of force, or acts of aggression geared toward occupying or annexing territory. A second group of delegations wanted no qualifier at all, on the theory that every use of force not authorized by the Security Council or taken in self-defense should be potentially subject to prosecution.[87] The term "manifest" emerged as an acceptable qualifier that bridged the gap between the two groups. As bolstered by an understanding proposed by the United States,[88] the term was meant to serve a "double function," referring both to the character (the degree of clarity or ambiguity surrounding the illegality of the act of aggression) and the scale or gravity of the act.[89] The negotiating record

---

[86] Gareth Evans, *Russia and the Responsibility to Protect*, Los Angeles Times, August 31, 2008, available at: http://www.gevans.org/opeds/oped93.html (emphasis added) (last accessed February 9, 2013).

[87] Beth Van Schaack, *Negotiating at the Interface of Power and Law: The Crime of Aggression*, 49 COLUMBIA JOURNAL OF TRANSNATIONAL LAW n. 46 (2011).

[88] Resolution RC/Res.6, Annex III, para. 7, June 28, 2010: "It is understood that in establishing whether an act of aggression constitutes a manifest violation of the Charter of the United Nations, the three components of character, gravity and scale must be sufficient to justify a 'manifest' determination. No one component can be significant enough to satisfy the manifest standard by itself."

[89] Claus Kress and Leonie von Holtendorff, *The Kampala Compromise on the Crime of Aggression*, 8 J. INT'L CRIM. JUSTICE 1179, 1193 b, 55 (2010).

indicates that the purpose of the qualifier was in part to exempt cases of military humanitarian intervention such as the 1999 NATO action in Kosovo.[90] The implicit agreement of the state parties to the ICC Statute to exempt cases of true humanitarian intervention from the definition of the crime of aggression subject to prosecution by the Court suggests that the right to resort to such force might still ripen into customary international law in the future.

The ongoing crisis in Syria might provide the opportunity for it to do so. According to a February 2012 report commissioned by the United Nations Human Rights Council, Syrian leader Basher al-Assad's security forces committed "widespread, systematic, and gross human rights violations" by indiscriminately using heavy weapons, including tanks, artillery, and helicopter gunships, against civilian anti-government protestors.[91] At the time this book went to press, the situation in Syria was worsening by the day, with more than sixty thousand civilian casualties and counting.[92] Russia and China twice "double vetoed" Security Council resolutions condemning the Syrian government for these actions and calling for regime change.[93] As the violence escalates, the

---

[90] Robert Heinsch, *The Crime of Aggression after Kampala: Success or Burden for the Future*, 2 GOETINGEN JOURNAL OF INTERNATIONAL LAW 713, 730 (2010). When proposing the "manifest" understanding, the head of the US Delegation at Kampala, State Department Legal Adviser Harold Hongju Koh, told the Review Conference, "If Article 8bis were to be adopted as a definition, understandings would need to make clear that those who undertake efforts to prevent war crimes, crimes against humanity or genocide – the very crimes that the Rome Statute is designed to deter – do not commit 'manifest' violations of the U.N. Charter within the meaning of Article 8 bis." Statement of Harold Koh, Review Conference of the International Criminal Court, Kampala, Uganda, June 4, 2010.

[91] Independent International Commission of Inquiry, *Report of the Independent International Commission of Inquiry on the Syrian Arab Republic*, paras. 2, 39–46, U.N. Doc. A/HRC/19/69 (February 22, 2012).

[92] Jennifer M. Freedman, *Syria Death Toll Climbs past 40,000 Mark*, BLOOMBERG NEWS, November 23, 2012; Joe Sterling and Salma Abdelaziz, *U.N.'s Syria Death Toll Jumps Dramatically to 60,000-plus*, CNN, January 3, 2013.

[93] Jeremy Sarkin, *Is the Responsibility to Protect an Accepted Norm of International Law in the post-Libya Era?* 1 CRONINGEN JOURNAL OF INTERNATIONAL LAW 11, 24 (2012).

moral pressure to use force (for example, to establish no-fly zones and safe areas) outside the framework of the United Nations will increase. Yet, Syria presents complications on a scale far beyond that of Libya, whose regime was toppled by revolutionaries in six months with support of Security Council–authorized air strikes. Unlike in Libya, there presently exists no widely supported, well-organized Syrian opposition; the opposition does not control significant areas in Syria; the government of Syria has dangerous allies including the government of Iran and the Islamic groups Hamas and Hezbollah; and regional organizations have not called for military intervention.[94]

Whatever ultimately happens in Syria, it is clear that the 1999 NATO intervention did not fulfill its potential to represent a Grotian Moment. The NATO action and response of the international community did not immediately effect a change in international law in such a way as to render unilateral humanitarian intervention a lawful exception to Article 2(4) of the UN Charter. In the thirteen years since Kosovo the doctrine has yet to be employed by the international community in a situation where Security Council approval for the use of force is absent. Nevertheless, the 1999 intervention did give rise to the Responsibility to Protect doctrine, which may mean more in the future than it does at present.

---

[94] Jason Dominguez Meyer, *From Paralysis in Rwanda to Boldness in Libya: Has the International Community Taken "Responsibility to Protect" from Abstract Principle to Concrete Norm under International Law?* 34 HOUSTON JOURNAL OF INTERNATIONAL LAW 87, 105–6 (2011).

9 The Response to 9/11

THIS CHAPTER EXAMINES WHETHER THE SYSTEMATIC AL
Qaeda terrorist attacks against the World Trade Center
and Pentagon on September 11, 2001, and the international
community's political and tactical reactions to those attacks have generated a Grotian Moment, leading to new rules of customary international
law concerning use of force against nonstate actors. The International
Court of Justice had previously opined in the 1986 *Nicaragua* case that
victim states could not resort to force in response to attacks by nonstate actors unless those actors were effectively controlled by the territorial state.[1] A few days after the September 11 attacks, however, the UN
Security Council adopted Resolution 1368, which was widely viewed
as confirming the right to use force in self-defense against al Qaeda in
Afghanistan, and there was little international protest when the United
States invaded Afghanistan shortly thereafter. With the subsequent
deployment of unmanned drones to hunt down al Qaeda terrorists in
Afghanistan, Pakistan, Yemen, and Somalia, the response to 9/11 is not
just about the radical change in the terrorist threat but also in the technology used to combat them. Invoking the term "constitutional moment"
to describe these developments, Professor Ian Johnstone of the Fletcher
School of Law and Diplomacy concludes that "in contrast to where the

---

[1] Military and Paramilitary Activities in and against Nicaragua (*Nicaragua v. United States*) (merits), para. 195, 1986 I.C.J. 14, 103–104 (June 26).

law stood in 1986 ... it is a fair inference today that self-defense may be invoked against non-state actors."[2] This chapter examines the validity of Professor Johnstone's supposition.

Use of Force against Nonstate Actors prior to 9/11

The inherent right to use force in self-defense under international law is codified in Article 51 of the UN Charter. The charter contains an important limit to that right, permitting use of force in self-defense only "if an armed attack occurs."[3] The UN Charter does not define "armed attack," but the International Court of Justice in the *Nicaragua* case held that only the "most grave forms of the use of force" constitute an armed attack.[4] According to the ICJ, to qualify as an armed attack triggering the right of self-defense, the assault must reach a certain significant scale of violence above "mere frontier incidents."[5] However, the ICJ has also suggested that a string of small-scale attacks can in aggregate constitute an armed attack.[6] Assuming that the attack threshold is reached either by a particularly severe terrorist attack or by a series of attacks, two questions arise: first, whether the armed attack must be attributable to the state against whom the force will be used; and second, whether targeting terrorists before they launch a new attack is lawful.

---

[2] Ian Johnstone, *The Plea of "Necessity" in International Legal Discourse: Humanitarian Intervention and Counter-terrorism*, 43 Columbia Journal of Transnational Law 337, 370 (2005).

[3] UN Charter, Art. 51.

[4] Military and Paramilitary Activities in and against Nicaragua (*Nicaragua v. United States*) (merits), para. 195, 1986 ICJ 14, 103–4 (June 26).

[5] Military and Paramilitary Activities in and against Nicaragua (*Nicaragua v. United States*) (merits), para. 195, 1986 ICJ 14, 93 (June 26).

[6] Military and Paramilitary Activities in and against Nicaragua (*Nicaragua v. United States*) (merits), paras. 119–20, 1986 ICJ 14, 93 (June 26); Armed Activities on the Territory of the Congo (*Democratic Republic of the Congo v. Uganda*) 2005 ICJ 168 (December 19) ("even if this series of deplorable attacks could be regarded as cumulative in character, they still remained non-attributable to the DRC").

State Attribution

The International Court of Justice has repeatedly held that unless the acts of nonstate actors are attributable to the territorial state, use of force against nonstate actors in that state is unlawful. This is because when a rebel group or terrorist organization is physically located within the territory of another state that is not in effective control of its operations, the right of self-defense collides with two other fundamental principles of international law, the sovereign equality of states and the renunciation of force in international relations.[7] The rationale behind the attribution requirement is that a state cannot be held responsible for the acts of all whose activities originate in its territory. "If it were otherwise, Colombia, for example, might be liable for the acts of international drug traffickers working from Colombia, or Russia might be held responsible for the international activities of the Russian Mafia."[8] Thus, under the ICJ's holdings in *Nicaragua*,[9] *Oil Platforms*,[10] the *Wall* advisory opinion,[11] and the *Congo* case,[12] to use force against a terrorist organization whose conduct is not imputable to the territorial state would itself constitute an unlawful armed attack, warranting justified use of force in response by the territorial state.

Under the International Court of Justice's jurisprudence, attribution requires that the territorial state have "effective control" of the nonstate actors. This standard originated in the *Nicaragua* case, where the Court was presented with the question of whether the actions of

---

[7] UN Charter, Arts. 2(1) and 2(4).

[8] Greg Travalio and John Altenburg, *Terrorism, State Responsibility, and the Use of Military Force*, 4 CHICAGO JOURNAL OF INTERNATIONAL LAW 97 (2003).

[9] Military and Paramilitary Activities in and against Nicaragua (*Nicaragua v. United States*) (merits), para. 195, 1986 ICJ 14, 195 (June 26).

[10] Oil Platforms (*Iran v. United States*) 2003 ICJ 161, 195 (November 6).

[11] The Construction of a Wall in the Occupied Palestinian Territory, Advisory Opinion, 2003 ICJ 136, 139 (July 9).

[12] Armed Activities on the Territory of the Congo (*Democratic Republic of the Congo v. Uganda*) 2005 ICJ 168 (December 19).

Nicaragua in supporting rebels in El Salvador through the provision of weapons was sufficient to justify military action by the United States in collective self-defense with El Salvador. The Court stated that sending "armed bands" into the territory of another state would be sufficient to constitute an armed attack, but "the supply of arms and other support to such bands cannot be equated with an armed attack."[13] In the same case, the ICJ found that the acts of the U.S.-assisted Nicaraguan rebel group called the "Contras" could not be attributed to the United States because there was no clear evidence that the United States had "exercised such a degree of control in all fields as to justify treating the Contras as acting on its behalf."[14] It is important to note here that the *Nicaragua* attribution requirement was not designed to answer the question of whether an attack by an independent nonstate actor could trigger the right of self-defense against that nonstate actor, but rather the question of whether an attack by the nonstate actor could be considered an armed attack by the state that sent the armed groups and therefore justify force in self-defense against that state.

Anticipatory Self-Defense under Customary International Law

Anticipatory self-defense is the use of force to stop an attack that has not actually commenced but is reasonably believed to be imminent. The concept recognizes that "no State can be expected to await an initial attack which, in the present state of armaments, may well destroy the State's capacity for further resistance and so jeopardize its very existence."[15] Anticipatory self-defense has its modern customary international law origins in the *Caroline* incident.

---

[13] Military and Paramilitary Activities in and against Nicaragua (*Nicaragua v. United States*) (merits), paras. 119–20, 1986 ICJ 14, 126–7 (June 26).

[14] Military and Paramilitary Activities in and against Nicaragua (*Nicaragua v. United States*) (merits), paras. 119–20, 1986 ICJ 14, 62 (June 26).

[15] D. W. BOWETT, SELF-DEFENSE IN INTERNATIONAL Law 191 (1958).

During the *Caroline* incident of 1837, Canada (then part of the United Kingdom) faced an armed insurrection mounted from U.S. territory led by nonstate actors. The United Kingdom responded to the armed insurrection by attacking the insurgent's supply ship, the *Caroline*, while it was docked on the U.S. side of the Niagara River. In an exchange of diplomatic notes between the United States secretary of state, Daniel Webster, and the British foreign minister, Lord Ashburton, the two sides agreed that a state would be justified in using force against nonstate actors in another state where the "necessity for self defense" was "instant, overwhelming, leaving no choice of means, and no moment for deliberation."[16] While courts and commentators often substitute the term "imminent" for the longer formulation, the *Caroline* definition is widely recognized as reflecting customary international law. Some states and commentators, however, have argued that anticipatory self-defense is not lawful under the UN Charter.

Three separate incidents involving attacks by Israel, purportedly in anticipatory self-defense, illuminate the contours of customary international law related to anticipatory self-defense prior to September 11.[17] The first was the Israeli attack that kicked off the June 1967 (Six Day) War. Although Israel was the first to strike, a number of factors taken together convinced most of the international community that an armed attack on Israel was imminent, and therefore that its anticipatory actions were lawful in self-defense. Those factors included the peremptory expulsion of the UN peacekeeping force from the Sinai; the unprecedented massing of Egyptian forces along the Israeli border; the closure of the Straits of Tiran, effectively blockading Israel's only southern access to the high

---

[16] Letter from Daniel Webster, U.S. Secretary of State, to Mr. Fox (April 24, 1841), reprinted in 29 British and Foreign State Papers 1129, 1138 (James Rigway & Sons 1857).

[17] Several other countries, including the United States, invoked self-defense to justify military operations during the decades leading up to the 9/11 attacks, but these three incidents provide a particularly useful basis for discussion of the state of the law prior to 2001.

seas; the bellicose statements of the Egyptian president; and the sudden alliances of Jordanian and Iraqi forces under Egyptian control.[18] In the aftermath of the Israeli anticipatory attack, draft resolutions condemning Israel in the Security Council and General Assembly were defeated by wide margins,[19] and the contention that Israel's actions were lawful under the circumstances was not widely challenged at the time.[20]

The second incident occurred in June 1981, when Israel launched air strikes against the Iraqi Osiraq nuclear installation a few days before it was to become operational. Despite Israel's claim that the attack was a justifiable act of anticipatory self-defense because the reactor would provide Iraq the ability to develop nuclear weapons that would be used against Israel, the UN Security Council unanimously adopted a resolution strongly condemning the Israeli action as a "clear violation of the Charter of the United Nations and the norms of international conduct" and calling on Israel to refrain from launching similar attacks against Iraq's nuclear facilities in the future.[21] The UN General Assembly followed the Security Council a few months later by voting 109 to 2 for adoption of Resolution 36/27, which condemned Israel for the "premeditated and unprecedented act of aggression," and demanded that Israel pay prompt and adequate compensation for the damage and loss of life it had caused.[22] The international condemnation was led by France, which stated that the reactor it had provided to Iraq was solely for scientific research. The UK likewise stated that the Osiraq reactor was not capable of producing weapons-grade material, while the International Atomic Energy Agency confirmed that inspections had revealed no

---

[18] *See* MICHAEL WALZER, JUST AND UNJUST Wars 82–3 (Basic Books, 1977).

[19] UN SCOR, 22nd Sess., 135th mtg., at 5, UN GAOR, 5th Emergency Special Session, 154th mtg., at 15–17.

[20] Ohio State University Law Professor John Quigley has written a new book comprehensively challenging the factual predicate for Israel's anticipatory attack. *See* JOHN QUIGLEY, THE SIX DAY WAR AND ISRAELI SELF-DEFENSE (Cambridge University Press, 2012).

[21] UNSC Res. 487, 36 UN SCOR, 2288th mtg., UN Doc. S/RES/487 (1981).

[22] UN G.A. Res. 36/27 (XXXVI), UN Doc.A/RES/36/27 (1981).

noncompliance with the safeguards agreement.[23] The problem, therefore, with Israel's invocation of anticipatory self-defense in this case was that Israel could not convince the international community that an attack was imminent.

The third incident occurred in October 1985, when Israel launched air strikes against the headquarters of the Palestine Liberation Organization (PLO) in Tunisia in response to a series of PLO terrorist attacks against Israeli citizens. In arguing that it had acted lawfully, Israel told the Security Council, "it cannot be overlooked or overstated, that the PLO has in Tunisia an extraterritorial base from which they conduct their terrorist operations. We have struck only at this base and at no other facility, buildings or area. But apart from this, a country cannot claim the protection of sovereignty when it knowingly offers a piece of its territory for terrorist activity against other nations, and that is precisely what happened here."[24] Despite evidence of the PLO's continuing threat to Israel, the Security Council condemned the Israeli action by a vote of 14–0, with the United States abstaining.[25] Reflecting the sentiment of several delegations, the East German Delegation stressed that Israel's attack was not simply against the PLO but "also against the sovereignty and territorial integrity of an Arab State, the Republic of Tunisia," which was not involved in the attacks.[26] Consistent with the *Nicaragua* case, the international response to the Israeli 1985 air strike in Tunisia affirmed that, absent state attribution for terrorist acts, use of force could not be lawfully employed against a state that harbors a terrorist group.

---

[23] SHAI FELDMAN, NUCLEAR WEAPONS AND ARMS CONTROL IN THE MIDDLE EAST 110 (MIT Press, 1996).

[24] Provisional Verbatim Record of the 2615th Meeting of the Security Council, UN Doc. S/PV. 2615 (October 4, 1985), available at: http://unispal.un.org/UNISPAL.NSF/0/1BD0C735449FE9980525658B005E624E.

[25] S.C. Res. 573 (1985), October 4, 1985.

[26] Provisional Verbatim Record of the 2615th Meeting of the Security Council, UN Doc. S/PV. 2615 (October 4, 1985), available at: http://unispal.un.org/UNISPAL.NSF/0/1BD0C735449FE9980525658B005E624E.

Did 9/11 Alter the Paradigm?

When the rules governing use of force in self-defense were promulgated, most international conflicts were conducted by states utilizing large movements of military personnel and munitions.[27] In the past, nonstate actors (pirates, guerrillas, drug traffickers, and terrorists) appeared less threatening to state security than the well-funded, well-organized, and potent armed forces of an enemy state. To the extent that terrorists were a concern, it was because they were financed by state supporters, such as Iraq, Syria, Libya, Iran, Cuba, and North Korea.[28] The terrorist attacks of September 11, 2001, changed that perception by starkly illustrating that small groups of nonstate actors, acting from failed States without direct government support, can exploit relatively inexpensive and commercially available technology to conduct very destructive attacks over great distance.[29]

A Different Kind of Threat

In August 1996, Osama bin Laden, the multimillionaire leader of a then-little-known group called al Qaeda, issued a statement entitled

---

[27] At the time of the adoption of the UN Charter, there had been only a handful of instances in which states pursued ongoing military operations against nonstate actors in the territory of other states. A survey of such actions would include the American military expedition into Mexico in 1916, which was provoked by attacks on American territory by the armed bands of Francisco (Poncho) Villa; the American military attack on pirates using Spanish-held Amelia Island off the Florida coast as a base of operations in 1817; and the 1838 *Caroline* incident, in which Britain attacked a steamer in order to prevent an attack by nonstate actors on Canada. See Roy S. Schondorf, *Extra-State Armed Conflicts: Is There a Need for a New Legal Regime?* 37 NEW YORK UNIVERSITY JOURNAL OF INTERNATIONAL LAW & POLICY 1, 2 n.6 (2004).

[28] See list of state supporters of terrorism, maintained by the U.S. Department of State, available at: http://www.state.gov/j/ct/list/c14151.htm (last accessed February 9, 2013).

[29] Olumide K. Obayemi, *Legal Standards Governing Pre-Emptive Strikes and Forcible Measures of Anticipatory Self-Defense under the U.N. Charter and General International Law*, 12 ANNUAL SURVEY OF INTERNATIONAL & COMPARATIVE LAW 19, 23–4 (2006).

"Ladenese Epistle: Declaration of War," in which he called for all
Muslims to make holy war (jihad) against American forces in Saudi
Arabia, and specifically advocated the use of terrorism with the goal of
"great losses induced on the enemy side (that would shake and destroy
its foundations and infrastructures)."[30] In February 1998, bin Laden followed the Declaration of War by issuing a religious edict (fatwa) to all
Muslims, declaring that "to kill the Americans and their allies – civilians and military – is an individual duty for every Muslim who can do it
in any country in which it is possible to do it."[31] The fatwa further called
on "every Muslim who believes in God and wishes to be rewarded to
comply with God's order to kill the Americans and plunder their money
wherever and whenever they find it."[32]

Subsequent events proved that bin Laden's al Qaeda was not a mere
group of "crackpots," making grandiose proclamations of war, but a
well-funded, well-organized, and deadly new terrorist organization
with franchise cells across the globe.[33] The targets of al Qaeda attacks
have included the U.S. embassies in Kenya and Tanzania in 1998, the
U.S.S. *Cole* in Yemen in 2000, and the simultaneous attack on the World
Trade Center and Pentagon on September 11, 2001.[34] The death toll
from September 11 was more than three thousand, which is higher than
that of the American casualties in the War of 1812, the U.S.-Mexican

---

[30] Osama bin Laden, Ladenese Epistle: Declaration of War (August 24, 1996),
quoted in Davis Brown, *Use of Force against Terrorism after September 11th: State
Responsibility, Self-Defense and Other Responses*, 11 CARDOZO JOURNAL OF
INTERNATIONAL & COMPARATIVE LAW 1, 25 (2003).

[31] Osama bin Laden et al., Jihad against Jews and Crusaders: World Islamic Front
Statement (February 23, 1998), *quoted in* Davis Brown, *Use of Force against Terrorism
after September 11th: State Responsibility, Self-Defense and Other Responses*, 11
CARDOZO JOURNAL OF INTERNATIONAL & COMPARATIVE LAW 1, 26 (2003).

[32] *Id.*

[33] Joshua Bennett, *Exploring the Legal and Moral Bases for Conducting Targeted
Strikes outside of the Defined Combat Zone*, 26 NOTRE DAME JOURNAL OF LAW,
ETHICS PUBLIC POLICY 549, 551 (2012).

[34] Davis Brown, *Use of Force against Terrorism after September 11th: State Responsibility,
Self-Defense and Other Responses*, 11 CARDOZO JOURNAL OF INTERNATIONAL &
COMPARATIVE LAW 1, 26–7 (2003).

War, or the Japanese attack on Pearl Harbor in 1941.[35] In addition to the loss of life, the damage to the American economy has been appraised at more than $650 billion.[36] Al Qaeda attacks since 9/11 have included the November 2003 truck bombings in Istanbul, which injured 700 and killed 74 people; the March 2004 train bombings in Madrid, which injured 1,800 and killed 191 people; and the July 2005 train and bus bombings in London, which injured 700 and killed 56 people.[37]

The 9/11 attacks forced states to reevaluate the long-standing notion that only a state has the capacity to commit an armed attack against another state giving rise to the right to respond with force in self-defense. Post 9/11, terrorist threats issue from stateless entities that possess many of the attributes of a state – wealth, willing forces, training, organization, and potential access to weapons of mass destruction. If such a nonstate actor commits a series of attacks against a state, and the acts are of suffi-cient scale and effect to amount to an armed attack, then arguably force in self-defense should be permitted against the nonstate actor that pres-ents a continuing threat where the host state has manifested an inability or unwillingness to respond effectively to the threat.

The International Response to 9/11

The day after the 9/11 attack, the United States informed the UN Security Council that it had been the victim of an armed attack and declared its intent to respond under Article 51 of the UN Charter.[38] The

---

[35] Davis Brown, *Use of Force against Terrorism after September 11th: State Responsibility, Self-Defense and Other Responses*, 11 CARDOZO JOURNAL OF INTERNATIONAL & COMPARATIVE LAW 1, 27 (2003).

[36] Norman G. Printer, Jr., *The Use of Force against Non-State Actors under International Law: An Analysis of the U.S. Predator Strike in Yemen*, 8 UNIVERSITY OF CALIFORNIA LOS ANGELES JOURNAL OF INTERNATIONAL LAW & FOREIGN AFFAIRS 331, 353 (2003).

[37] Paul Carlsten, Al Qaeda Attacks in Europe since September 11, THE TELEGRAPH, March 21, 2012.

[38] Statement of Ambassador James B. Cunningham, U.S. Deputy Representative to the United Nations, Transcript of the 4370th meeting of the Security Council, at 3, U.N. Doc. S/PV.4370 (September 12, 2001).

North Atlantic Treaty Organization (NATO) for the first time in its history invoked Article 5 of the North Atlantic Treaty, which treats an armed attack on one member as an armed attack on all of them.[39] The Organization of American States (OAS) took a similar stance in OAS Resolution 797. Invoking the 1947 Inter-American Treaty of Reciprocal Assistance, which provides that in the event of an armed attack on an American state the parties agree that "each one of [them] undertakes to assist in meeting the attack in the exercise of the inherent right of individual or collective self-defense,"[40] the OAS called upon "the government of the member States and all other governments to use all necessary means at their disposal to pursue, capture, and punish those responsible for the attacks, and to prevent additional attacks."[41] Meanwhile the United States and Australia jointly invoked the collective defense article of the ANZUS Treaty, which provides for the parties collectively to "resist armed attack" and "act to meet the common danger."[42] In addition, the Japanese government took the position that the September 11 attack was an attack on the United States and soon thereafter enacted legislation to enable Japan to deploy its forces in support of U.S. operations against al Qaeda.[43]

Consistent with these developments, the Security Council adopted Resolution 1368, which condemned the 9/11 attacks and "recognized the

---

[39] NATO Press Release 124, September 12, 2001, cited in Davis Brown, *Use of Force against Terrorism after September 11th: State Responsibility, Self-Defense and Other Responses*, 11 CARDOZO JOURNAL OF INTERNATIONAL & COMPARATIVE LAW 1, 28 (2003).

[40] Inter-American Treaty for Reciprocal Assistance, Sept. 2, 1947, 21 U.N.T.S. 77.

[41] OEA/SER.G CP/RES. 797 (1293/01, Sept. 19, 2001).

[42] Security Treaty between Australia, New Zealand and the United States of America, Arts. II and IV, Sept. 1, 1951, 131 U.N.T.S. 83, 86.

[43] Davis Brown, *Use of Force against Terrorism after September 11th: State Responsibility, Self-Defense and Other Responses*, 11 CARDOZO JOURNAL OF INTERNATIONAL & COMPARATIVE LAW 1, 29 (2003) (citing Government of Japan, Ministerial Meeting Concerning Measures against Terrorism and Press Conference of the Prime Minister, Wednesday, September 19, 2001; Government of Japan, Basic Plan Regarding Response Measures Based on the Anti-Terrorism Special Measures Law, Cabinet Decision of Nov. 16, 2001).

inherent right of individual or collective self-defense in accordance with the Charter."[44] This action was not a Chapter VII authorization to use force, but rather a confirmation that the United States could invoke its right to respond with force under Article 51 of the UN Charter, despite the fact that al Qaeda was a nonstate actor. Consistent with that right, on October 7, 2001, the United States informed the council that it had launched Operation Enduring Freedom.[45] Air strikes were directed at camps allegedly belonging to al Qaeda and other Taliban military targets throughout Afghanistan. There was no international protest or condemnation of these actions[46]; rather through word and actions, a long list of states expressed support for the operation.[47]

Had al Qaeda been a state, its attacks (both in the aggregate and some of the most spectacular individual attacks) would have passed the "scale and effect" test of the *Nicaragua* case. But as al Qaeda was a nonstate actor based in Afghanistan, under the *Nicaragua* precedent, use of force against al Qaeda in Afghanistan would only be permissible if Afghanistan had "effective control" of the terrorist organization.

Some commentators argue that Afghanistan met the *Nicaragua* test of effective control because Afghanistan's Taliban regime and al Qaeda were in effect partners. Yet, the facts do not establish that al Qaeda acted as an agent or instrumentality of the Afghan state, but rather that al Qaeda pursued an independent agenda and acted autonomously within

---

[44] S.C. Res. 1368 (2001), 3rd preambular paragraph.

[45] Letter, dated October 7, 2001, from the Permanent Representative of the United States of America, to the United Nations addressed to the President of the Security Council, UN SCOR, 56th session at 1, UN Doc. S?2001/946 (2001).

[46] Rebecca Kahan, *Building a Protective Wall around Terrorists – How the International Court of Justice's Ruling in the Legal Consequences of the Construction of a Wall in the Occupied Palestinian Territory Made the World Safer for Terrorists and More Dangerous for Member States of the United Nations*, 28 FORDHAM INTERNATIONAL LAW JOURNAL 827, 842–3 (2005).

[47] Benjamin Langille, *It's Instant Custom: How the Bush Doctrine Became Law after the Terrorist Attacks of September 11, 2001*, 26 BOSTON COLLEGE INTERNATIONAL & COMPARATIVE LAW REVIEW 145, 146, 155 (2003).

Afghanistan.[48] Neither did the Taliban government of Afghanistan endorse the September 11 attack. Rather, Taliban officials denied that bin Laden had anything to do with the attack, asserting that "bin Laden lacked the capability to pull off large-scale attacks" and proclaiming their confidence that a U.S. investigation would find him innocent.[49]

On the other hand, the Taliban government knowingly harbored al Qaeda, providing its members a place of refuge and allowing the organization to use Afghanistan as a base from which to plan, sponsor, and launch international terrorist operations. The Taliban government repeatedly ignored the Security Council's demands to close down the terrorist training facilities in Afghanistan and extradite bin Laden, thereby enabling al Qaeda to represent a continuing threat to the United States.

The Bush Doctrine: Attacks against States Harboring Terrorist Groups

A week after the terrorist attacks of 9/11, the United States announced the "Bush Doctrine" when President George Bush declared: "Our war on terror begins with al-Qaeda, but it does not end there. It will not end until every terrorist group of global reach has been found, stopped and defeated. Either you are with us or you are with the terrorists."[50] The most important aspect of the doctrine was encapsulated in Bush's statement that "we will make no distinction between the terrorists who

---

[48] ALEX STRICK VAN LINSCHOTEN AND FELIX KUEHN, AN ENEMY WE CREATED: THE MYTH OF THE TALIBAN–AL QAEDA MERGER IN AFGHANISTAN 1990–2010 (C. Hurst & Co., 2012).

[49] Facts On File World News Digest, September 11, 2001, at 697A1, quoted in Davis Brown, *Use of Force against Terrorism after September 11th: State Responsibility, Self-Defense and Other Responses*, 11 CARDOZO JOURNAL OF INTERNATIONAL & COMPARATIVE LAW 1, 11 (2003).

[50] See President George Bush's seminal speech on September 20, 2001, to the joint session of Congress, quoted in Olumide K. Obayemi, *Legal Standards Governing Pre-Emptive Strikes and Forcible Measures of Anticipatory Self-Defense under the U.N. Charter and General International Law*, 12 ANNUAL SURVEY OF INTERNATIONAL & COMPARATIVE LAW 19 (2006).

committed these acts and those who harbor them."[51] In a speech before a joint session of Congress on September 20, 2001, President Bush said, "from this day forward, any nation that continues to harbor or support terrorism will be regarded by the United States as a hostile regime."[52]

In the words of White House spokesman Ari Fleisher, the Bush Doctrine represented "a dramatic change in American policy."[53] Yet, in a five-day debate in the United Nations General Assembly, where state after state condemned the 9/11 attacks, not one objection was voiced to the newly announced U.S. policy.[54]

Although it represented a clear departure from the *Nicaragua* case, the Bush Doctrine was rooted in historic provenance. The general affirmative obligation that every state not knowingly allow "its territory to be used for acts contrary to the rights of other States" was first articulated by the International Court of Justice in the 1949 *Corfu Channel* case. There, the ICJ held Albania liable for damage to British warships that struck mines in Albanian territorial waters.[55] Although Great Britain could not prove that Albania had laid the mines or had engaged another state to do so, the ICJ found that Albania must have known of the existence of the mines because Albania was known to have jealously guarded its side of the Corfu Strait, and this was enough to establish Albania's liability.

---

[51] George W. Bush, Address to the Nation on the Terrorist Attacks, September 11, 2001, quoted in Davis Brown, *Use of Force against Terrorism after September 11th: State Responsibility, Self-Defense and Other Responses*, 11 CARDOZO JOURNAL OF INTERNATIONAL & COMPARATIVE LAW 1, 17 (2003).

[52] Address to a Joint Session of Congress and the American People, September 20, 2001, *quoted in* Greg Travalio and John Altenburg, *Terrorism, State Responsibility, and the Use of Military Force*, 4 CHICAGO JOURNAL OF INTERNATIONAL LAW 98, 108 (2003).

[53] Statement of Ari Fleisher, September 21, 2001, *quoted in* Greg Travalio and John Altenburg, *Terrorism, State Responsibility, and the Use of Military Force*, 4 CHICAGO JOURNAL OF INTERNATIONAL LAW 98, 108 (2003).

[54] Greg Travalio and John Altenburg, *Terrorism, State Responsibility, and the Use of Military Force*, 4 CHICAGO JOURNAL OF INTERNATIONAL LAW 98, 109 (2003).

[55] The Corfu Channel (merits), 1949 ICJ 4 (April 9).

This principle is analogous to the rules relating to neutrality adopted in the Hague Convention (V) some one hundred years ago.[56] According to the Hague Convention, "neutral powers" may not permit belligerents to move troops, munitions, or supplies across their territory; nor may they allow their territory to be used to form "corps of combatants" nor "recruiting agencies."[57] Should the neutral state prove unwilling or unable to uphold these proscriptions, the other belligerent state is justified in attacking the enemy forces in the territory of the neutral state.[58]

The application of this concept to terrorism was confirmed by Security Council Resolution 1373, adopted shortly after September 11, 2001.[59] In reaffirming the right of self-defense in the context of the September 11 attacks while asserting that states are prohibited from allowing their territory from being used as a safe haven for terrorist groups, the resolution signifies that allowing known terrorists to operate freely in their territory triggers the right to self-defense against the nonstate actors located within the host state's territory.

Summing up the current state of international law, UN Special Rapporteur Philip Alston has stated: "A targeted killing conducted by one State in the territory of a second State does not violate the second State's sovereignty [where] the first, targeting State has a right under international law to use force in self-defense under Article 51 of the U.N. Charter, [and] the second State is unwilling or unable to stop armed attacks against the first State launched from its territory."[60]

---

[56] Hague Convention (V) Respecting the Rights and Duties of Neutral Powers and Persons in Case of War on Land, 36 Stat 2310 (1907).

[57] Id. at arts.2, 4. 5.

[58] Ashley S. Deeks, *Unwilling or Unable: Toward a Normative Framework for Extraterritorial Self-Defense*, 52 Virginia Journal of International Law 483, 497–501 (2012).

[59] S.C. Res. 1373, UN Doc. S/RES/1373 (Sept. 28, 2001).

[60] Philip Alston, Special Rapporteur on Extrajudicial, Summary or Arbitrary Executions, *Study on Targeted Killings*, para. 29, Human Rights Council, UN Doc. a/HRC/14/24/Add.6 (May 28, 2010).

The fact that the "unwilling or unable" test has its roots in the customary law of neutrality anchors the test's legitimacy as applied to use of force in self-defense against nonstate actors present in a foreign country.[61]

The extent of permissible military action used to combat terrorists in a country unwilling or unable to control them depends on the level of support provided by the harboring state. Consistent with the Hague Convention (V) discussed earlier, with its precept of proportionality, "if a State does nothing but allow terrorists to operate from its territory, providing no meaningful support, the extent of the permissible military force is only that which is necessary to deal with the terrorist threat itself. Neither the military of the harboring State nor its infrastructure is a permissible target."[62] In such case, there is a distinction between using force in a state versus against the state.[63] A swift, high-precision strike against terrorists or their training facilities in the territorial state (a so-called in and out operation) represents a reasonably limited interference with the territorial integrity or political independence of the territorial state under these circumstances.[64] The use of force against the nonstate actor taken in self-defense is a lawful use of force, and the territorial state cannot therefore mount a forcible resistance in the name of its own self-defense.[65] If, on the other hand, the territorial state is implicated in

---

[61] Ashley S. Deeks, *Unwilling or Unable: Toward a Normative Framework for Extraterritorial Self-Defense*, 52 VIRGINIA JOURNAL OF INTERNATIONAL LAW 483, 497 (2012).

[62] Greg Travalio and John Altenburg, *Terrorism, State Responsibility, and the Use of Military Force*, 4 CHICAGO JOURNAL OF INTERNATIONAL LAW 98, 112 (2003).

[63] NOAM LUBELL, EXTRATERRITORIAL USE OF FORCE AGAINST NON-STATE ACTORS 36 (Oxford University Press, 2010).

[64] In 1976, Israel conducted a raid on the Ugandan airport in Entebbe to rescue Israeli hostages held by Palestinian hijackers. The hijackers were killed. At the UN Security Council meeting, the Israeli representative argued that the operation was not against the territorial integrity or political independence of Uganda. See Security Council Official Records, 31st Year, 1939th Meeting, July 9, 1976, UN Doc. S/PV.1939 (1976).

[65] NOAM LUBELL, EXTRATERRITORIAL USE OF FORCE AGAINST NON-STATE ACTORS 41 (Oxford University Press, 2010).

the terrorist attack, than the victim state may have the right to use force against the territorial state and its agents, in addition to using it against the nonstate actor.[66]

Preventive Self-Defense

A more controversial aspect of the Bush Doctrine was its assertion of an expanded right of anticipatory self-defense against terrorist threats. In the National Security Strategy issued in the aftermath of 9/11, President Bush explained:

> For centuries, international law recognized that nations need not suffer an attack before they can lawfully take action to defend themselves against forces that present an imminent danger of attack. Legal scholars and international jurists often conditioned the legitimacy of preemption on the existence of an imminent threat – most often a visible mobilization of armies, navies, and air forces preparing to attack. We must adapt the concept of imminent threat to the capabilities and objectives of today's adversaries. Rogue States and terrorists do not seek to attack us using conventional means.... Instead, they rely on acts of terror and, potentially, the use of weapons of mass destructions – weapons that can easily be concealed, delivered covertly and used without warning. The United States has long maintained the option of preemptive actions to counter a sufficient threat to our national security. The greater the threat, the greater is the risk of inaction – and the more compelling the case for taking anticipatory action to defend ourselves, even if the uncertainty remains as to the time and place of the enemy's attack. To forestall or prevent such hostile acts by our adversaries, the United States will, if necessary, act preemptively. The United States will not use force in all cases to preempt emerging threats, nor should nations use preemption as a pretext for aggression. Yet in an age where the enemies of civilization openly and actively seek

---

[66] NOAM LUBELL, EXTRATERRITORIAL USE OF FORCE AGAINST NON-STATE ACTORS 40 (Oxford University Press, 2010).

the world's most destructive technologies, the United States cannot remain idle while dangers gather.[67]

As depicted in the National Security Strategy, the Bush Doctrine did not just advocate anticipatory self-defense – striking an enemy as it prepares an attack – but also "preventive self-defense" – striking an enemy even in the absence of specific evidence of an imminent attack. To that end, the Bush administration implemented a policy of targeted killing of key al Qaeda figures in Afghanistan, Pakistan, Iraq, Yemen, Somalia, and elsewhere.

This expansion of the anticipatory self-defense concept was seen as warranted by the unique attributes of the continuing threat posed by the al Qaeda terrorist organization.[68] Al Qaeda and its affiliates are well funded with access to deadly means, potentially including chemical, bio-logical, and nuclear weapons. They attack without warning, target civil-ians indiscriminately, and employ suicide missions on a regular basis. They had committed a series of prior attacks against the United States and publicly announced an intention to continue to attack in the future. Arguably under these circumstances, it is reasonable to deem an attack by such organizations as "continuing" or "always imminent" for pur-poses of the *Caroline* standard.[69]

In implementing the Bush Doctrine, the United States began to employ newly developed technology in the form of unmanned Predator drones equipped with laser-guided Hellfire missiles controlled by

---

[67] National Security Council, the National Security Strategy of the United States of America 15 (2002), available at: http://www.whitehouse.gov/nsc/nss.pdf (last accessed February 9, 2013).

[68] The National Defense Strategy of the United States of America, U.S. Department of Defense, March 2005, p. 9.

[69] Greg Travalio and John Altenburg, *Terrorism, State Responsibility, and the Use of Military Force*, 4 CHICAGO JOURNAL OF INTERNATIONAL LAW 98, 112 (2003). *Contra* Philip Alston, Special Rapporteur on Extrajudicial, Summary or Arbitrary Executions, *Study on Targeted Killings*, para. 45, Human Rights Council, UN Doc. a/HRC/14/24/Add.6 (May 28, 2010) (characterizing preventive self-defense as "deeply contested and lack[ing] support under international law").

operators located thousands of miles away. Predator drones eliminate the risk to U.S. pilots. They are capable of remaining in the air ten times longer and cost about one-twentieth as much as combat aircraft.[70] Because they are slow and vulnerable to signal jamming, the drones are not perceived to be a serious threat to an advanced military, but they are ideal for use against nonstate actors in failed or struggling states.[71] The first drone strike outside Afghanistan occurred in 2002 in Yemen, killing alleged al Qaeda leader Ali Aaed Senyan al-Harithi and four other men.[72]

When it took office, the Obama administration embraced the Bush Doctrine and greatly expanded the drone targeted killing program. According to President Obama's CIA director, Leon Panetta, because of their precision and effectiveness, drones have become "the only game in town in terms of confronting or trying to disrupt the al Qaeda leadership."[73]

The Obama administration's State Department legal adviser, Harold Koh, delivered a major policy speech at the Annual Meeting of the American Society of International Law on March 25, 2010, in which he provided the legal justification for the administration's use of drones to fight terrorist groups around the world. Koh began by stressing that the attacks of 9/11 triggered the U.S. right of self-defense against al Qaeda and other terrorist organizations. Echoing the Bush administration's characterization of a "global war" against al

---

[70] Michael W. Lewis, *Drones and Boundaries of the Battlefield*, 47 TEXAS INTERNATIONAL LAW JOURNAL 293, 296 (2012).

[71] Michael W. Lewis, *Drones and Boundaries of the Battlefield*, 47 TEXAS INTERNATIONAL LAW JOURNAL 293, 298 (2012).

[72] Molly McNab and Megan Matthews, *Clarifying the Law Relating to Unmanned Drones and the Use of Force: The Relationships between Human Rights, Self-Defense, Armed Conflict, and International Humanitarian Law*, 39 DENVER JOURNAL OF INTERNATIONAL LAW & POLICY 661, 673 (2011).

[73] See Andrew C. Orr, *Unmanned, Unprecedented, and Unresolved: The Status of American Drone Strikes in Pakistan under International Law*, 44 CORNELL INTERNATIONAL LAW JOURNAL 729, 735 (2011) (quoting LA TIMES story).

Qaeda,[74] Koh asserted "as a matter of international law, the United States is in an armed conflict with al-Qaeda, as well as the Taliban and associated forces, in response to the horrific 9/11 attacks, and may use force consistent with its inherent right to self-defense under international law."[75] Some commentators have argued that the armed conflict with al Qaeda must be limited to territory on which the threshold of violence for an armed conflict is currently occurring, which at the time of this writing would consist of Afghanistan and parts of Pakistan.[76] Koh's broader formulation recognizes that the limited approach would effectively create sanctuaries for terrorist organizations in failed and weak states such as Yemen, Somalia, Libya, and Sudan.

Next, Koh argued that the right to use force in self-defense against al Qaeda was continuous in light of the continuous threat presented: "As recent events have shown, al-Qaeda has not abandoned its intent to attack the United States, and indeed continues to attack us. Thus, in this ongoing armed conflict, the United States has the authority under international law, and the responsibility to its citizens, to use force, including lethal force, to defend itself, including by targeting persons such as high-level al-Qaeda leaders who are planning attacks."[77] But then Koh walked back somewhat from the conception of preventive war enshrined in the Bush Doctrine, saying: "Of course, whether a particular individual will be targeted in a particular location will depend upon considerations specific to each case, including those related to the imminence of the threat, the sovereignty of the other States involved,

---

[74] Harold Hongju Koh, Remarks, Annual Meeting of the American Society of International Law, March 25, 2010, available at: http://www.state.gov/s/l/releases/remarks/139119.htm (last accessed February 9, 2013).

[75] Harold Hongju Koh, Remarks, Annual Meeting of the American Society of International Law, March 25, 2010, available at: http://www.state.gov/s/l/releases/remarks/139119.htm (last accessed February 9, 2013).

[76] Michael W. Lewis, *Drones and Boundaries of the Battlefield*, 47 TEXAS INTERNATIONAL LAW JOURNAL 293, 298 (2012).

[77] Harold Hongju Koh, Remarks, Annual Meeting of the American Society of International Law, March 25, 2010, available at: http://www.state.gov/s/l/releases/remarks/139119.htm (last accessed February 9, 2013).

and the willingness and ability of those States to suppress the threat the target poses."[78]

Two years later, U.S. Attorney General Eric Holder provided further details about the Obama administration's criteria for authorizing a targeted killing. According to Holder, authorization would require three findings: "First, the U.S. government has determined, after a thorough and careful review, that the individual poses an imminent threat of violent attack against the United States; second, capture is not feasible; and third, the operation would be conducted in a manner consistent with applicable law of war principles."[79]

Until now, we have been examining principles related to *jus ad bellum* (the lawfulness of the resort to force). Attorney General Holder's statement reminds us that a forcible response to terrorists must also comply with the fundamental rules of *jus in bello* (the lawfulness of the means employed and target selected). In his speech before the American Society of International Law, Harold Koh described the applicable *jus in bello* principles as

> first, the principle of distinction, which requires that attacks be limited to military objectives and that civilians or civilian objects shall not be the object of the attack; and second, the principle of proportionality, which prohibits attacks that may be expected to cause incidental loss of civilian life, injury to civilians, damage to civilian objects, or a combination thereof, that would be excessive in relation to the concrete and direct military advantage anticipated.[80]

[78] Harold Hongju Koh, Remarks, Annual Meeting of the American Society of International Law, March 25, 2010, available at: http://www.state.gov/s/l/releases/remarks/139119.htm (last accessed February 9, 2013).

[79] Contemporary Practice of the United States Relating to International law, Attorney General Discusses Targeting of U.S. Persons, 106 AMERICAN JOURNAL OF INTERNATIONAL LAW 673, 675 (2012). In February 2013, the U.S. Department of Justice released an undated White Paper setting forth a legal framework for targeted killings outside areas of active hostilities, available at: http://msnbcmedia.msn.com/i/msnbc/sections/news/020413_DOJ_White_Paper.pdf.

[80] Harold Hongju Koh, Remarks, Annual Meeting of the American Society of International Law, March 25, 2010, available at: http://www.state.gov/s/l/releases/remarks/139119.htm (last accessed February 9, 2013).

Koh's description assumes that the high-level members of al Qaeda themselves are lawful targets. Since they are not part of a military, the laws of war would treat al Qaeda members presumptively as civilians who are immune from targeting unless they either "directly participate in the hostilities" or take on a "continuous combat function" within the group.[81] In May 29, 2009, the International Committee of the Red Cross published a study entitled "Interpretive Guidance on the Notion of Direct Participation in Hostilities under International Humanitarian Law," whose aim was in part to define when targeted killings of members of terrorist groups would be consistent with international humanitarian law.[82] The "Interpretive Guidance" report states that "individuals whose continuous function involves the preparation, execution, or command of acts or operations amounting to direct participation in hostilities assume a continuous combat function."[83] The targeted killings to date appear to involve al Qaeda figures who would meet this description.

Meanwhile, there has been little protest as other states have begun to cite the U.S. response to al Qaeda to justify their own acts against terrorist groups operating from neighboring states. Examples include the following:

- The April 2002 killing by Russian armed forces of "Chechen rebel warlord" Omar Ibn al Khattab.[84]

[81] Michael W. Lewis, *Drones and Boundaries of the Battlefield*, 47 TEXAS INTERNATIONAL LAW JOURNAL 293, 298 (2012).

[82] Kenneth Watkin, *Opportunity Lost: Organized Armed Groups and the ICRC "Direct Participation in Hostilities" Interpretive Guidance*, 42 NEW YORK UNIVERSITY JOURNAL OF INTERNATIONAL LAW AND POLITICS 641 (2010).

[83] Nils Melzer, *Interpretive Guidance on the Notion of Direct Participation in Hostilities under International Humanitarian Law*, 90 INTERNATIONAL REVIEW OF THE RED CROSS 991, 1007 (2009).

[84] Philip Alston, Special Rapporteur on Extrajudicial, Summary or Arbitrary Executions, *Study on Targeted Killings*, para. 7, Human Rights Council, UN Doc. a/HRC/14/24/Add.6 (May 28, 2010).

- The February 2008 offensive by Turkish forces against PKK bases in northern Iraq[85]
- The March 2008 air strike by Colombia against a FARC terrorist camp just inside Ecuador's border, killing the FARC's second in command, Raul Reyes[86]
- The December 2009 use of force by Ethiopian armed forces against the "Islamic Courts terrorist group," which had been conducting a series of cross-border attacks from Somalia[87]
- The May 2011 mission by U.S. Navy Seals to kill Osama bin Laden at his secret compound in northern Pakistan[88]
- The September 2011 Predator drone attack by the United States that killed U.S. national Anwar al-Awlaki in Yemen[89]
- The October 2011 Kenyan incursion into Somalia in response to cross-border attacks by the al Shabaab terrorist group[90]

---

[85] Theresa Reinold, *State Weakness, Irregular Warfare, and the Right to Self-Defense Post-9/11*, 105 AMERICAN JOURNAL OF INTERNATIONAL LAW 244, 269 (2011).

[86] Ashley S. Deeks, *Unwilling or Unable: Toward a Normative Framework for Extraterritorial Self-Defense*, 52 VIRGINIA JOURNAL OF INTERNATIONAL LAW 483, 534 (2012). Unlike the other incidents listed previously, in this case the OAS called the Colombian incursion "a violation of the sovereignty and territorial integrity of Ecuador" and declared that "the right of each State to protect itself ... does not authorize it to commit unjust acts against another State." Theresa Reinold, *State Weakness, Irregular Warfare, and the Right to Self-Defense Post-9/11*, 105 AMERICAN JOURNAL OF INTERNATIONAL LAW 244, 274 (2011).

[87] Awol K. Allo, *Ethiopia's Armed Intervention in Somalia: The Legality of Self-Defense in Response to the Threat of Terrorism*, 39 DENVER JOURNAL OF INTERNATIONAL LAW & POLICY 139 (2010).

[88] Jordan J. Paust, *Permissible Self-Defense Targeting and the Death of Bin Laden*, 39 DENVER JOURNAL OF INTERNATIONAL LAW & POLICY 569, 579–80 (2011).

[89] Jordan J. Paust, *Propriety of Self-Defense Targeting of Members of Al Qaeda and Applicable Principles of Distinction and Proportionality*, 18 INTERNATIONAL LAW STUDENTS ASSOCIATION JOURNAL OF INTERNATIONAL & COMPARATIVE LAW 565, 574 (2012).

[90] International Crisis Group, *The Kenyan Military Intervention in Somalia*, Africa Report No. 184 – February 15, 2012.

A Grotian Moment That Is Still One Case Away

Scholars have opined that "the attack of September 11th and the American response represent a new paradigm in the international law relating to the use of force."[91] This was manifested in the statements of the United States, NATO, the OAS, and other states that 9/11 constituted an armed attack by al Qaeda that warranted force in self-defense; Security Council Resolutions 1368 and 1373 confirming the right to use self-defense in the context of the 9/11 attacks; the international community's positive reaction to the U.S. invasion of Afghanistan to dismantle al Qaeda and topple its Taliban supporters; and finally the UN special rapporteur's conclusion that force in self-defense could be used against terrorist groups operating in the territory of states unwilling or unable to control them. The reaction to 9/11 thus broke with the conception of Article 51 as a state-centered norm.

Moreover, in the aftermath of the 9/11 attack and response, the international community embraced the concept of anticipatory self-defense in the context of use of force against terrorists, confirming that the *Caroline* doctrine survived the UN Charter's limitations on resort to self-defense. Thus, the UN High-Level Panel concluded in its 2004 report that "a threatened State, according to long established international law, can take military action as long as the threatened attack is imminent, no other means would deflect it and the action is proportionate."[92]

What is more, the protracted quest of the international community to arrive at a consensus definition of terrorism received a substantial boost in 2011 when the Appeals Chamber of the Security Council–created Special Tribunal for Lebanon (STL)[93] concluded that "although it is held by many

---

[91] Davis Brown, *Use of Force against Terrorism after September 11th: State Responsibility, Self-Defense and Other Responses*, 11 CARDOZO JOURNAL OF INTERNATIONAL & COMPARATIVE LAW 1, 2 (2003).

[92] The High-Level Panel, *Report of the High-Level Panel on Threats, Challenges and Change*, 188, UN Doc. a/59/565 (December 2, 2004).

[93] The Special Tribunal for Lebanon (STL), established in 2007 by the United Nations Security Council to prosecute those responsible for the 2005 bombings that killed

scholars and other legal experts that no widely accepted definition of terrorism has evolved in the world society because of the marked difference of views on some issues, closer scrutiny reveals that in fact such a definition has gradually emerged."[94] On the basis of its extensive review of state practice and indicators of *opinio juris*, the Appeals Chamber declared that the customary international law definition of terrorism consists of

> the following three key elements: (i) the perpetration of a criminal act (such as murder, kidnapping, hostage-taking, arson, and so on), or threatening such an act; (ii) the intent to spread fear among the population (which would generally entail the creation of public danger) or directly or indirectly coerce a national or international authority to take some action, or to refrain from taking it; (iii) when the act involves a transnational element.[95]

The STL's definition of terrorism, together with the listing of terrorist groups and individuals by the Security Council's sanctions committee,[96] removed one of the greatest obstacles to use of force against terrorists, namely, the argument that "one man's terrorist was another man's freedom fighter."

One commentator has asserted that "the Bush Doctrine, first proclaimed by the U.S. in response to the terrorist attacks of September 11,

---

former Lebanese Prime Minister Rafiq Hariri and twenty-two others, is the world's first international court with jurisdiction over the crime of terrorism. *See* Statute of the Special Tribunal for Lebanon, *appended to* S.C. Res. 1757, UN Doc. S/RES/1757 (May 30, 2007).

[94] Interlocutory Decision on the Applicable Law: Terrorism, Conspiracy, Homicide, Perpetration, Cumulative Charging, Special Tribunal for Lebanon Appeals Chamber, Case No. STL-11-01/I (Feb. 16, 2011), paras. 83, 102, available at: http://www.stl-tsl.org/x/file/TheRegistry/Library/CaseFiles/chambers/20110216_STL-11-01_R176bis_F0010_AC_Interlocutory_Decision_Filed_EN.pdf [Interlocutory Decision] (last accessed February 9, 2013).

[95] *Id.* at para. 85.

[96] The UN Security Council adopted Resolution 1267 on October 15, 1999, under chapter VII of the UN Charter, authorizing the Security Council's Sanctions Committee to establish a list of sanctioned individuals, groups, and/or entities that were found to be associated with Al Qaeda and the Taliban. S.C. Res. 1267, UN Doc S/Res/1267 (October 15, 1999).

2011, became an instant custom during the days and weeks following the attacks."[97] Yet, 9/11 is better characterized as a Grotian Moment that is still at least one case away from fruition. The problem is that the Bush administration's assertion that there is no difference between terrorists and states that harbor them, and its assertion of a right to preventive self-defense against such states, was unnecessarily broad and lacking nuance. A state may, for example, harbor a few terrorists or serve as the organization's headquarters. The terrorists may be poorly armed or possess weapons of mass destruction. The state may provide the terrorists funding, passports, training, and intelligence or may simply be acquiescing to their presence. The Bush Doctrine provides no guidance on how these different scenarios should be treated. Concern that the imprecision of the Bush Doctrine would lead to assertions by other states to justify aggression in the name of self-defense prompted pushback that took the form of two post-911 cases decided by the International Court of Justice.

In its 2004 *Wall* advisory opinion, the ICJ rejected the Israeli claim to self-defense on the reasoning that self-defense under Article 51 is not available to Israel against nonstate actors operating on territories under the control of Israel.[98] In its 2005 *Armed Activities on the Territory of the Congo* case, the ICJ required the responsibility of the Congo for the attacks of Ugandan rebels operating from the Congolese territory in order to find Uganda's right to self-defense lawful.[99] These cases signaled

---

[97] Benjamin Langille, *It's Instant Custom: How the Bush Doctrine Became Law after the Terrorist Attacks of September 11, 2001*, 26 BOSTON COLLEGE INTERNATIONAL & COMPARATIVE LAW REVIEW 145, 154 (2003).

[98] Legal Consequences of the Construction of a Wall in the Occupied Palestinian Territory, Advisory Opinion, 2004 I.C.J. 136, 194 (July 9).

[99] Armed Activities on the Territory of the Congo (*Democratic Republic of the Congo v. Uganda*), 2005 ICJ 168 (holding that Uganda could not rely on self-defense to justify its military operation in the Congo because (1) Uganda did not immediately report to the Security Council after its use of force, as required by Article 51; (2) Uganda's actions were vastly disproportionate to the threat; and (3) there was no evidence from which to impute the attacks against Ugandan villages by rebel groups operating out of the Congo to the government of Congo).

the ICJ's "determination to counter a more permissive reading of Article 51" brought on by the international community's reaction to 9/11.[100]

Scholars and certain members of the International Court of Justice have been highly critical of the ICJ's continued insistence since 9/11 that self-defense is only available in cases where the attack by nonstate actors can be attributed to the territorial state. Scholars point out that the ICJ holdings are inconsistent with the wellspring of the customary law on self-defense, the *Caroline* case, which confirmed that anticipatory force in self-defense was lawful against nonstate actors whose conduct was not attributable to a state.[101] Writing separately in the *Wall* case, Judge Higgins said, "there is, with respect, nothing in the text of Article 51 that thus stipulates that self-defense is available only when an armed attack is made by a State."[102] Similarly, writing separately in the *Congo* case, Judge Koojimans noted that in the era of al Qaeda, it is "unreasonable to deny the attacked State the right to self-defense merely because there is no attacker State."[103] Judge Simma similarly concluded in his separate opinion in the *Congo* case that "Security Council resolutions 1368 (2001) and 1373 (2001) cannot but be read as affirmations of the view that large-scale attacks by non-State actors can qualify as 'armed attacks' within the meaning of Article 51."[104]

While the International Court of Justice's *Wall* and *Congo* decisions may have put brakes on the rapidly crystallizing customary international law emerging from 9/11, their long-term impact on the development of

---

[100] Theresa Reinold, *State Weakness, Irregular Warfare, and the Right to Self-Defense Post-9/11*, 105 AMERICAN JOURNAL OF INTERNATIONAL LAW 244, 261 (2011).

[101] See R. Y. Jennings, *The Caroline and McLeod Cases*, 32 AMERICAN JOURNAL OF INTERNATIONAL LAW 82, 82–9 (1938) (quoting 61 Parliamentary Papers (1843)).

[102] Legal Consequences of the Construction of a Wall in the Occupied Palestinian Territory, Advisory Opinion, 2004 ICJ 136 (July 9) (Separate opinion of Judge Higgins).

[103] Armed Activities on the Territory of the Congo (*Democratic Republic of the Congo v. Uganda*), 2005 ICJ 168 (Separate Opinion of Judge Koojimans), para. 28.

[104] Armed Activities on the Territory of the Congo (*Democratic Republic of the Congo v. Uganda*), 45 I.L.M. 271, 308–9, Dec. 19, 2005 (*Democratic Republic of the Congo v. Uganda*) (separate opinion of Judge Simma), para. 11.

the law of self-defense against terrorists will likely be negligible. This is because the situations in the *Wall* and *Congo* cases are quite distinguishable from that of a state using force against terrorists operating in a foreign state. In the *Wall case*, the ICJ stressed that the right to self-defense under Article 51 of the UN Charter only applied to attacks emanating from another state and did not apply to attacks originating within the Occupied Territories, because the area was controlled by Israel.[105] In *Congo*, as in *Nicaragua*, the use of force was not limited to attacking the terrorist group itself, but involved widespread attacks throughout the territorial state.

This case study indicates how international courts are both capable of catalyzing and setting back the formation of customary international law during a potential Grotian Moment. In light of these conflicting currents, there may not yet be an established norm of customary international law allowing states to use anticipatory self-defense against nonstate actors regardless of attribution, but the law is visibly moving in this direction.

---

[105] Legal Consequences of the Construction of a Wall in the Occupied Palestinian Territory, Advisory Opinion, 2004 ICJ 136, 139 (July 9).

10 Conclusion

BY TRADITION, JURISTS, STATESMEN, AND SCHOLARS HAVE looked exclusively to two factors – (1) widespread state practice and (2) manifestations of a conviction that the practice is required by international law – to divine whether an emergent rule has attained customary international law status. This book has examined the largely overlooked role of a third factor – a context of fundamental change – that can serve as an accelerating agent, enabling customary international law to form much more rapidly and with less state practice than is normally the case.

Historically, crystallization of new rules of customary international law was viewed as a protracted process that took decades, if not centuries, to complete. Indeed, the term "crystallization" is often employed by the International Court of Justice and scholars to equate formation of customary rules with the slow growth of crystalline minerals. While working on this book, I was invited to tour the headquarters of the Kyocera Corporation in Kyoto, Japan, which is headed by the patron of Case Western Reserve University's Inamori Ethics Prize. Among the products Kyocera manufactures are recrystallized gemstones. Just as Kyocera is able to create precious gemstones in a short time under intense heat and pressure, so too can a context of fundamental change intensify and accelerate the formation of customary international law.

Named in honor of Hugo Grotius, whose masterpiece *De Jure Belli ac Pacis* helped marshal in the modern system of international law,

"Grotian Moments" are transformative developments that generate the unique conditions for accelerated formation of customary international law. In these circumstances, General Assembly resolutions and judgments of international tribunals often play a heightened role in confirming the newly emergent rule, thus adding a gloss to the Kirgis "sliding scale theory"[1] discussed in Chapter 2.

While there were dozens of possible candidates ranging from the invention of nuclear weapons to the creation of the Internet, with the guidance of ICJ Judge Chris Greenwood I settled on six case studies since World War II that seemed at first glance to fit the profile of a Grotian Moment. As summarized next, the first four case studies examined in the book turned out to be clear-cut instances of Grotian Moments. Each represented a radical legal development. In each, the development was ushered in by the urgency of dealing with fundamental change. In some cases the change was the advent of new technology, as with offshore drilling (Chapter 5) and outer space flight (Chapter 6). In others it was in the form of pervasive moral outrage regarding shocking revelations of crimes against humanity, as preceded the establishment of the Nuremberg Tribunal (Chapter 4) and the creation of the Yugoslavia Tribunal (Chapter 7). And each was followed by widespread and/or authoritative recognition of the existence of a new rule of customary international law, despite the short duration and dearth of underlying state practice.

As described in Chapter 4, the establishment of the Nuremberg Tribunal in 1945 was a novel response to the Holocaust, the gravest atrocity in the history of humankind. Although the Nuremberg Charter was signed by fewer than two dozen states and the Nuremberg Tribunal and Control Council Law Number 10 trials consisted of only a dozen separate cases tried by a handful of courts over a period of just three years, the International Court of Justice, European Court of Human

---

[1] Frederic. L. Kirgis, Jr., *Custom on a Sliding Scale*, 81 AMERICAN JOURNAL OF INTERNATIONAL LAW 146, 149 (1987).

Rights, several international criminal tribunals, and a number of domestic courts have cited the 1946 General Assembly resolution affirming the principles of the Nuremberg Charter and judgments as an authoritative declaration of customary international law. The Nuremberg Tribunal claimed that it was applying existing law, but its revolutionary charter provisions and holdings literally launched the new field of international criminal law. Among its contributions, Nuremberg extended the concept of universal jurisdiction – up to then applied only to piracy – to war crimes, crimes against humanity, and arguably the crime of aggression, and it developed a unique form of liability, JCE, especially tailored for international criminal prosecutions.

Chapter 5 recounts the story of President Harry Truman's 1945 proclamation that the resources on the continental shelf off the coast of the United States belonged to the United States. This represented a major departure from the existing customary international law of the sea under which the areas seward of the narrow territorial sea were open to exploitation by any state. The proclamation was driven by technological developments enabling exploitation of offshore oil and gas supplies and the intense postwar demand for such resources for a rebuilding world. Though the United States recognized that it was acting as a custom pioneer, it was careful to couch its justification in legal terms that would render the action easier to accept and replicate by other states. Despite the far-reaching change it represented, the Truman Proclamation was met with no protest; rather, within five years, half of the world's coastal states had made similar claims to the resources of their continental shelves, leading commentators to declare that the continental shelf concept had become virtually instant customary international law. By 1969, the International Court of Justice had confirmed that the Truman declaration quickly generated customary international law binding on states that had not ratified the 1958 Law of the Sea Convention on the Continental Shelf.

As Chapter 6 details, the 1960s saw great leaps in rocket technology, led by the Soviet Union and the United States, inaugurating the era of space flight. Rather than treat outer space like the high seas, the international community embraced a unique set of rules to govern this new area as codified in the General Assembly *Declaration on the Principles of Outer Space*, which was unanimously approved in 1963. Though the amount of state practice was limited to a few dozen space flights launched by two states and the lack of protest by the states over which these rockets passed, states and scholars have concluded that the 1963 declaration represented an authoritative statement of customary international law that rapidly formed in response to new technologies requiring a new international law paradigm.

As we saw in Chapter 7, the establishment of the Yugoslavia Tribunal was made possible because of a unique constellation of events at the end of the Cold War, which included the breakup of the Soviet Union, Russia's assumption of the Soviet seat in the Security Council, and the occurrence of genocide in Europe for the first time since Nazi Germany. In its inaugural case, the Appeals Chamber of the Yugoslavia Tribunal rendered a revolutionary decision that for the first time held that individuals could be held criminally liable for violations of Common Article 3 and Additional Protocol II of the Geneva Conventions for war crimes committed in internal conflict. Like the Nuremberg Tribunal, the Yugoslavia Tribunal purported to be applying existing law, though its decision was in fact unprecedented and closed a gaping hole in the coverage of international humanitarian law. The decision was soon thereafter affirmed by the Rwanda Tribunal and Special Court for Sierra Leone, and it was codified in the 1998 Statute of the International Criminal Court, which has been ratified by 122 states.

These case studies suggest that the Grotian Moment concept has several practical applications. It can explain the rapid formation of customary rules in times of fundamental change, thereby imbuing those rules with greater authority. It can counsel governments when to seek the path of a UN General Assembly resolution as a means of facilitating the formation of customary international law, and how to craft such a resolution to ensure that it is viewed as a capstone in the formation of such customary rules. It can in apt circumstances strengthen the case for litigants arguing the existence of a new customary international rule. And it can furnish international courts the confidence to recognize new rules of customary international law in appropriate cases despite a relative paucity and short duration of state practice.

At the same time, one must approach the Grotian Moment concept with caution. Chapter 1 warns that during times of international flux, it may be easy to identify a turning point that is not really there. Thus it is with the fifth and sixth case studies, which also manifested many of the attributes of a Grotian Moment, but in each careful examination revealed that an essential ingredient was lacking to bring the crystallization of customary international law to realization.

As Chapter 8 details, in contrast to earlier cases of unilateral humanitarian intervention that had been met with widespread condemnation, the NATO air strikes against Serbia to protect Kosovar Albanians from ethnic cleansing in 1999 engendered widespread support by the international community. In its formulation of the Responsibility to Protect Doctrine two years later, the report of the International Commission on Intervention and State Sovereignty (ICISS) provided a novel legal veneer for unilateral humanitarian intervention that seemed poised to develop quickly into customary international law. But the principal states behind the NATO intervention retreated from the position that their acts were a lawful exercise of unilateral humanitarian intervention, emphasizing instead the exceptional nature of the military operation. These statements effectively slowed momentum for the ripening of a new rule of customary international law. Then, while the United Nations was considering steps to endorse the ICISS report and Responsibility to Protect Doctrine, the United States launched a controversial invasion of Iraq in 2003, citing humanitarian concerns as one of the justifications for its action. Rather than endorsing unilateral humanitarian intervention, the UN General Assembly and Security Council produced a formulation that instead reaffirmed the importance of Security Council authorization before states or regional organizations can take such action. While the Responsibility to Protect concept has influenced the international debate related to responding to various crises, ultimately it did not represent a fundamental change in the law of intervention.

Finally, Chapter 9 examines the response to the terrorist attacks of September 11, 2001. Prior to the 9/11 attacks, international law required attribution to the territorial state before a victim state could launch an extraterritorial attack in self-defense against nonstate actors present there. That requirement appeared to be fundamentally altered when the international community widely approved the United States military action against al Qaeda in Afghanistan as lawful force in self-defense. Al Qaeda was generally viewed as representing a new kind of threat, in which a nonstate actor possessed many of the attributes of a state – independent wealth, willing forces with global reach, sophisticated training and organization using newly developed communications technology, and potential access to weapons of mass destruction. Moreover, the tactics of al Qaeda were to attack without warning, target civilians indiscriminately, and employ suicide missions on a regular basis. In response, the so-called Bush Doctrine was devised to permit states to target key al Qaeda figures and destroy al Qaeda bases in weak or failed states that had proven unwilling or unable to prevent al Qaeda from operating in their territory. But lacking nuance, the broadly articulated Bush Doctrine provoked pushback from the International Court of Justice, which, in the 2004 *Wall* and 2005 *Congo* cases, reaffirmed that state attribution remained a prerequisite for using force in self-defense against non-state actors. In light of the widespread criticism of these holdings, including from some of the ICJ's most respected members, this judicial action is unlikely to be the final word, but in the short term it has weakened the capacity for the law of 9/11 to blossom into a Grotian Moment.

Taken together, the six case studies provide several valuable insights about the nature and function of the Grotian Moment concept. In all six case studies, the (potential) Grotian Moment began with a custom pioneer – a state (or international tribunal) willing to initiate a new practice contrary to existing customary international law in order to create a new rule of customary international law. However, none of these pioneers took the position that they were breaking new ground. Rather, they followed an approach that can be likened to putting new wine in old bottles, characterizing their innovations as consistent with existing law, though in fact they were fermenting a new vintage.

Moreover, the case studies indicate that in addition to responding to technological, economic, or societal change, Grotian Moments are in part made possible by geopolitical realignment, often following war. Thus, the affirmation of the Nuremberg Principles and the development of the continental shelf concept occurred in the immediate aftermath of the conclusion of World War II. Similarly, the establishment of the Yugoslavia Tribunal and issuance of the *Tadic* decision on the application of war crimes to internal armed conflicts occurred during a unique period following the end of the Cold War and collapse of the Soviet Union. The international community's response to the attacks of 9/11 appeared to represent a geopolitical realignment in the common cause against terrorism, but subsequent actions by the United States (such as the mistreatment of terrorist detainees at Guantanamo Bay and CIA black sites) fractured the growing consensus about when, where, and how to employ force against nonstate actors.

Further, in the cases of Nuremberg, the continental shelf, and space law, the Grotian Moments led to rapid formation of fundamental principles of customary international law though definitional ambiguities (e.g., with respect to the precise meaning of aggression, continental shelf, and outer space) continued to be worked out and evolve in subsequent years. This indicates that the rapidly formed customary international law resulting from a Grotian Moment does not have to be fleshed out fully or rigidly fashioned in order to represent a radical change in the law.

Significantly, several of the case studies attest to the important role that General Assembly resolutions can play as an essential ingredient in bringing a Grotian Moment to fruition. The 1946 *Affirmation of the Principles of International Law Recognized by the Charter of the Nuremberg Tribunal* and the 1963 *Declaration of Legal Principles Governing the Activities of States in the Exploration and Use of Outer Space* are examples of General Assembly resolutions that had a significant impact on the formation and codification of customary international law. The form, content, and context of these resolutions enhanced their role as midwife to the birth of customary rules despite the limited state practice on which the resolutions were based. Conversely, the case study of the 1999 NATO intervention demonstrated how General Assembly and Security Council resolutions can derail a potential Grotian Moment from reaching its destination.

Similarly, the case studies of space law and the *Tadic* decision demonstrated how negotiation of a multilateral treaty can culminate a Grotian Moment. The 1967 space treaty rechristened the rules of customary international law that were codified in the 1963 General Assembly declaration. The negotiation of the 1998 Rome Statute of the International Criminal Court confirmed the customary international law status of the application of war crimes to international armed conflict, which was articulated just three years earlier by the Yugoslavia Tribunal. Because they represented customary rules, the provisions of these treaties on space law and war crimes liability were deemed applicable to nonparties and parties alike.

Likewise, in some of the case studies, the decisions of international tribunals supplied the authoritative gloss that completed the Grotian Moment by confirming the existence of the new rule of customary law. The ICJ *North Sea Continental Shelf* case, for example, confirmed the customary law status of the Truman Proclamation. In contrast, the ICJ's *Wall* and *Congo* cases set back the crystallization of the law of self-defense against terrorist groups whose conduct is not attributable to the state that harbors them. Thus, like General Assembly resolutions, international court decisions take on a heightened significance in the process of norm creation during a potential Grotian Moment.

The final two case studies indicate how a quickly ripening norm can be set back by state practice or articulations that constitute a perceived abuse of the norm. Thus, the U.S. invasion of Iraq in 2003 and the Russian invasion of Georgia in 2008 renewed concerns that a doctrine permitting unilateral humanitarian intervention would be readily prone to abuse, thereby derailing the momentum that had been gaining behind the R2P concept as legal justification for humanitarian action outside the UN framework. Similarly, perceptions that the Bush Doctrine was overbroad and easily subject to abuse slowed momentum for a change in the law of self-defense against nonstate actors.

Interestingly, the case studies did not prove Professor Bederman's supposition that it is more difficult for a new rule to replace a long established rule than for a new rule to arise in a previously unregulated realm.[2] Although Bederman's thesis could be easily applied to the rapid crystallization of space law or the Nuremberg Principles, in the cases of the continental shelf and the application of war crimes to internal armed conflict, well-settled rules were quickly replaced during those Grotian Moments.

Finally, while some scholars have characterized one or more of these cases as "virtual instant custom," the Grotian Moment concept is to be distinguished from the controversial notion of instant custom. Grotian Moments represent instances of rapid, as opposed to instantaneous, formation of customary international law. In addition to General Assembly resolutions and international court decisions, Grotian Moments require some underpinning of state practice, whereas advocates of the concept of instant custom argue that customary law can form in the absence of state practice. The necessary state practice during a Grotian Moment can precede the General Assembly resolution consistent with Professor McDougle's "claim and response" approach,[3] or it can follow the resolution as envisioned in Professor D'Amato's "articulation and act"

---

[2] David J. Bederman, *Acquiescence, Objection and the Death of Customary International Law* 21 DUKE JOURNAL OF COMPARATIVE AND INTERNATIONAL LAW 31, 38 (2010).

[3] M. S. McDougal and N. A. Schlei, *The Hydrogen Bomb Tests in Perspective: Lawful Measures for Security*, 64 YALE LAW JOURNAL 648 (1955).

approach,[4] but in none of the case studies did state votes on the resolutions themselves provide the only foundation of state practice.

Despite the distinction between so-called instant custom and the phenomenon of Grotian Moments, some states and commentators may not welcome the articulation of a concept that rationalizes rapid formation of customary international law. For some, international law is best created exclusively through treaties, as to which states can opt out by nonaction, simply by declining to ratify the instrument. So long as customary norms take many decades to ripen into law, customary international law does not seem threatening. But it is another matter if customary law can form within just a few years and is deemed binding on states that have not affirmatively manifested their persistent objection. In such case, they may fear a concept of law formation that appears more revolutionary than evolutionary.

Yet, such fears are misplaced. This book does not advocate a new approach, but rather provides doctrinal grounding for, and historical analysis of, a phenomenon that has existed since at least World War II. The case studies substantiate international recognition that customary international law must have the capacity in unique circumstances to respond to rapidly evolving developments by producing rules in a timely and adequate manner. They also demonstrate that not every momentous technological, geo-political, or societal change results in accelerated formation of customary international law – for like recrystallized gem stones, true Grotian Moments are both precious and relatively rare.

* * *

---

[4] ANTHONY A. D'AMATO, CONCEPT OF CUSTOM IN INTERNATIONAL LAW 88 (1971).

Index

221